THE CENTER FOR WOMEN AND FAMILIES

Thank you for purchasing *Crumbs in the Keyboard*!

    The contributors to *Crumbs in the Keyboard* are donating 100% of their royalties from the sale of this book to The Center for Women and Families in Louisville, Kentucky. Echelon Press is matching those monies dollar for dollar.
    By purchasing *Crumbs*, you have helped in the fight against domestic violence.
    The Center For Women and Families exists to serve and advocate for women and families affected by domestic violence, sexual assault, and economic hardship. The Center has been serving the Louisville area since 1912 and is now a private non-profit agency serving fourteen counties in Kentucky and Indiana. The Center services include 24-hour crisis intervention, individual and group counseling, hospital advocacy, legal advocacy, and services and community outreach and education. The Domestic Violence Program also provides emergency and transitional shelter to women who are victims and their children. Finally, the Center provides programs to help people achieve economic independence.

www.thecenteronline.org

Center for Women and Families (main number)
(502) 581-7200

Center For Women and Domestic Violence Program
(502) 581-7222

Crumbs in the Keyboard

Stories From Courageous Women Who Juggle Life & Writing

Benefiting

THE CENTER FOR WOMEN AND FAMILIES

Edited By Pamela Johnson & Sheryl Hames Torres

Permissions and copyright information for the articles included in this book:

In Memory of Nancy Richards-Akers. ©2002 Laura Mills-Alcott.

The Writer's Journey. ©2002 Kimberly Cox.

Burnt Pumpkins. ©2002 Jacqueline Elliot.

Tending To My Garden. ©2002 Janice Stayton.

The Labyrinth. Reprinted with permission. ©2000 Patricia Crossley.

Passing On The Pen and Paper. ©2002 Cheri Lee Funk.

(Continued on page 274)

P.O. Box 1084, Crowley, TX 76036

Copyright © 2002 by Pamela Johnson and Sheryl Hames Torres

All rights reserved. No part of this book may be used or reproduced in any form without permission, except as provided by the U.S. Copyright Law. For information, please address Echelon Press™, P.O. Box 1084, Crowley, TX 76036.

ISBN 1-59080-096-6

Cover illustration © Ariana Overton
Interior illustrations © Nancy Lepri

Printed and bound in the United States of America.

Contents

Acknowledgements 9
Pamela Johnson

Why the Crumbs Project? 11
Sheryl Hames Torres

In Memory of Nancy Richard-Akers 13
Laura Mills-Alcott

The Past 15
Author Unknown

The Writer's Journey 17
The Writer's Journey *Kim Cox*
Burnt Pumpkins *Jacqueline Elliot*
Tending To My Garden *Janice Stayton*
The Labyrinth *Pat Crossley*
Passing On The Pen and Paper *Cheri Lee Funk*
What did I do—So I Can Do It Again? *Robin D. Owens*
Top 10 Things Not to Say To An Editor *Lisa Craig*
Mama's Five Myths About Writing *Denise Weeks*
Writing As An Explorer *Gerry Benninger*
When the Writing Gets Tough *Barbara Baldwin*
Walk With Me in the Rain *Barbara Baldwin*
We're All In This Together *Cherie Claire*
Lynne's Book *Diana Lee Johnson*

Mama Told Me There'd Be Days Like This 49
Pinwheels and Hats *Holly Fuhrman*
Sushi Break *Elaine Hopper*
There Are No Shortcuts *Sheryl Hames Torres*
Out of the Mouths of Babes *Julie Pitzel*
My Mom Writes Books! *Elizabeth Delisi*

Crumbs in the Keyboard

Peace Between The Lines *Marilyn Griffith*
Everything Has Its Season *Lisa Marie Long*
Grand Theft Manuscript *Carrie Weaver*
Day-to-Day Determination *Jennifer Turner*
Spaces of Time *Jacqueline Elliot*
Steps to Writing Time *Robin Bayne*
To My Children *Tabatha Yeatts*
The Mom Story *Rebecca Vineyard*
I Owe My Career To Burger King *Laurie Schnebly Campbell*
Oh The Noise! *Margaret Marr*
Hot Sex and Cold Dinners *Carol Zachary*
My Mother Writes What? *Janet Miller*
A Day in the Life of a Writing Mom *Lori Zecca*
When and How *Jessica Ann Bimberg*
Creative Moms Have No Down Time *Cherie Claire*
Shadow Stretches *Amy B. Crawshaw*
The Juggling Act *Shirley Kawa-Jump*
Stealing Minutes *Cathy McDavid*
A Two-Page Day *Maureen McMahon*
There Resides In Me *Stacey L. King*
The Napkin *Pamela G. Smith*

Sometimes It Takes Grit 107
No! I'm NOT Just Housewife! *Lisa Marie Long*
Life is Good *Sharon Porpiglia*
You Don't "Work" *Nancy Lepri*
Still learning After All These Years *Kimberly Cox*
Rise and Shine *Laurie White*
So You Think You Want to Be a Romance Writer? *Pamela Arden*
Broken Promises *Pamela Gayle Smith*
Road Warrior *Trudy Doolittle*
Writing With Pain, Fatigue, and a Fuzzy Brain *M. Kathleen Crouch*
What Goes Around Comes Around *Barbara Donlon Bradley*
A New Perspective on Rejection *Lisa Craig*
Write to Survive, Survive to Write *Robin D. Owens*
A Career Based on Two Words *Pamela Johnson*

Crumbs in the Keyboard

Playing Tag With The Muse 137
The Other Woman *Leslie Burbank*
The Muse *Joni Seabolt*
Never Plan a Day of Writing *Pat Snellgrove*
A Writer's Moon *Barbara Baldwin*
The Muse As a Puppy *Linda Voss*
The Blair Writing Project *Lori A. McDonald*
Soap Bubble Rhetoric *Barbara Baldwin*
Dreams *Janet Lane*
Caller ID and the Neurotic Writer *Laurie Schnebly Campbell*
Where Do You Get All Those Crazy Ideas? *Denise Weeks*
Another Point of View *Candace Sams*
The "Muse"-ings of an Author's Cat *Vurlee Toomey*

Inspiration When We Weren't Looking 167
It Never Occurred To Me *Ariana Overton*
Dreams vs. Reality *Su Kopil*
Spun Yarn *Terri Hartley*
One Moment In Time *Laurie Alice Eakes*
The Value of Human Life *Karen Syed*
I Found My Lights *Rae Shapiro*
The Nature of the Beast *Kathryn Smith*
Subtle Delights *Kate Walsh*
The Round Peg *Diana Lee Johnson*
The Call of the Novel *Cate Rowan*
Writer's Block *Cheri Lee Funk*
After the Crumbs *Christine McClimans*
Journey Through Darkness *Anna Seley*
Belief—The Ultimate Muse *Kathleen Long*
Inspiration = Sugar + Spice +Dreams *Diana Rowe Martinez*
Perfect Love *Pamela Thibodeaux*
Butterfly *Teresa T. Saldana*

Wisdom From the Trenches 209
Uphill Climb: My Quest for Publication *Sally Painter*
Break a Pencil *Lori Soard*
Synchronicity *Su Kopil*

Crumbs in the Keyboard

How to Deal With Rejection *Elizabeth Delisi*
Balance and Control *Janice Stayton*
Chili Again *Joyce Tres*
Daily Resolution: A Writer's Affirmation *Gerry Benninger*
"Feeeel" Your Way To Success! *Marjorie Daniels*
The Path *Gwen Kirchner*
You Can Make Your Dreams Come True *Joyce Lavene*
Living the Dream *Joanie MacNeil*
The Right Answer *Nancy Lynn*
Sticks and Stones *Marcia Kacperski*
Let Your Imagination Fly *Sue Fineman*
To Everything There Is A Season *Pat Crossley*
What Makes a Writer? *Lisa Craig*
Keeping the Faith *Helen Polaski*
Cleaning The Toilet and TV Interviews T*ammie Clark Gibbs*
Following The Artist's Way *Robin D. Owens*
Coffee In My Keyboard: Dealing With Rejection *Laurie Alice Eakes*
James Said *Christine McClimans*
Stranded With A Few Of My Best Friends *Lisa Craig*
By His Grace *Terri Hartley*

Resources 257
Afterword 259
Contributors 260
Permissions (continued)..273

Crumbs in the Keyboard

Acknowledgements

One thing I have learned on this un-chartered journey I call writing is that all you need to do is send out a call for help to writers and fifty emails will appear in your computer mailbox. It is not arrogance that brings out the spirit of camaraderie among authors. It is the knowledge that at one point, on some level, they have been where you are, and want to give back. Authors, the vast majority of published and 'in-waiting', are a very unique and giving group of individuals. Never has this been more evident to me than while working on this book.

I am humbled to have met and worked with so many wonderfully gifted authors on this project. Some names you will recognize, others you may or may not one day recognize, but all have contributed a special piece of their heart and soul to this project and that is what makes this compilation so wonderfully rich in content.

I'd like to thank my co-editor and friend, Sher Hames Torres for sharing this dream with me. If there is evidence of pure southern tenacity laced with bone-dry humor-it's Sher, and that has kept us climbing at times when the hills got pretty steep.

I have many blessings for which to be thankful for (and truly *most* days that includes my family!) In truth, it is the unconditional support and comedic wit of my family that has helped me push through this project.

Special thanks to Karen and Stacey at Echelon Press, to Ariana for sharing her gift of cover art, to Nancy for her perfect illustrations, and to Su Kopil for her support of this project from the beginning. Thanks to Fern Michaels for her guidance and support of this project--you'll never know how much it is appreciated.

Most of all--sincere thanks to each author in this book. I do not pretend to completely understand the journey that some of these women have taken thus far, but their stories encourage me, they empower me, and they challenge me, both as an author and as a human being.

I trust they will do they same for you.

Pamela Johnson
Co-Editor, The Crumbs Project

Crumbs in the Keyboard

Crumbs in the Keyboard

Why The Crumbs Project?

Every morning, I wake up to something different. "Just ten more minutes," or "not oatmeal again," or "Mama, he's hidden my shoe again!" or "catch the dog! She's run off with my pants!" Sometimes it's a warm, wiggly body crawling in bed with us, vying for covers and his/her portion of our bed. Or a large, warm arm draped over my body against the cold and nightmares. Bliss.

I go to bed every night after snuggly hugs and sloppy kisses, after the bad dream spray has been dolled out and hidden under pillows, lunches made, our earthly belongings protected by locking up the dog (our rug in training who thinks dog houses are figments of someone's warped imagination) in the laundry room, and prayers.

The quiet time between kiddie bedtime and parental bedtime belongs to my husband and me. Unwind time. Regroup time. More often than not, a good portion of that time is spent with me on my computer working, him on his playing games, but we meet in the middle for hugs and kisses, an offered soda or snack, a snippet of conversation or two. Then after our downtime, we cuddle all night. Bliss.

This is still my life after more than twenty years with this man. I feel loved. I feel safe. I feel protected. I feel honored and lucky. I feel supported in every way.

My husband and I have weathered adversity. We survived body-destroying infertility therapy and the anguish when we were told we'd have no kids. We survived moving to a new state and starting over from scratch. We survived feasts and famines. And we survived the shock from not one, but two miracle pregnancies.

Not once in all the years I've known him, despite my husband's fiery Spanish/Cajun blood, have I ever feared for my safety, or for the safety of my children. We both have tempers, but have never once taken them out on each other. We've used outlets to stream any negative energy and fatigue into positive results, my writing and needlework for me, his "trash modeling," and art for him.

Our kids have inherited our quick tempers and borderline hyperactive

Crumbs in the Keyboard

natures, but learned at an early age that while anger is natural, lashing out isn't. They have never seen us lash out, and God willing, never will.

Not every child can say that.

Not every woman feels the security I do. Statistics tell us that in this country alone, 27 million women will experience violence in their marriage every year and 18 million of those women are repeatedly abused. Ninety to ninety-five percent of all abuse cases go unreported to the police, and a good portion of that number is due to the rising percentage of men who are physically abused and are too embarrassed to admit that the little woman gave him the bruises and scars.

The Crumbs Project is our version of a telethon donation. Our little tribute for the faceless, hidden victims, those men and women and children who hide in embarrassment, and fear for their lives if they "tell." Only they don't have telethons for domestic abuse.

When Pam came to me with this idea and offered me a way to do my part, I considered myself lucky. We've worked together tirelessly to see it to fruition. We don't kid ourselves that we're going to be able to cure the problem with our little book. Crumbs won't even be a Band-Aid for the problem, but it is a show of concern, of caring, of attention, of awareness. We're merely the quarter dropped in the boot on the corner. But, if we can offer a giggle, a smile, a line or two to catch your attention and make you think. If we can issue a wake up call and offer even a second of hope to the person who's huddling in the corner trying not to attract an angry abuser's attention, well then, it's a start.

I wish you all love, gentleness, safety and security. I wish for you all what I have…bliss.

God bless you all and keep you safe.

Sheryl Hames Torres
Co-Editor, The Crumbs Project

Crumbs in the Keyboard

In Memory of Nancy Richards-Akers
Laura Mills Alcott

I met romance author Nancy Richards-Akers in July 1997, at the RWA convention in Orlando. Our friendship continued after the convention, and over the course of the next two years, we chatted often.

Nancy was a writer whose work I truly admired, but more than her writing, I admired the person she was inside. She had a wicked sense of humor, she went out of her way to help other writers, but most of all, she had a beautiful spirit.

On June 2, 1999, Nancy emailed me to ask a favor. She was going through a bitter divorce from a highly abusive husband, and it had taken its toll on her - emotionally, mentally and physically. Jeremy Akers, an attorney, was angry that Nancy had left him, and he knew how to exact his revenge; he retained the house, the money, and the children.

But like a Phoenix, Nancy was determined to rise from the ashes, start over and rebuild her life.

The first thing she wanted to focus on was her career. For quite some time she'd been unable to concentrate on her writing, but now she was determined to get back in the swing, and get the new book completed. We also discussed ways to promote her books.

The second favor she asked was that I help her promote the lovely designer handbags she created. The impending divorce had devastated her financially, and the designer handbags would be an additional source of income to help her reach her goals a little quicker.

I scheduled Nancy as the featured guest for The Romance Club Author Chat the following Wednesday. In the meantime, I was working on some promotional ideas for her books and designer handbags.

In the wee hours of the morning of June 6, 1999, as I was creating a web page for Nancy's handbags, author Sally Painter sent me an Instant Message, asking if I had heard about Nancy Richards-Akers. I told Sally that Nancy and I had been talking over the last few days, but that I thought things were turning around for her. This is when Sally told me that Nancy had been murdered.

Crumbs in the Keyboard

I was stunned, didn't believe it. Nancy was a romance writer, determined to have her happy ending. She deserved her happy ending!

The Washington Post online had already gotten a news blurb out on the incident. In horror I read how her husband, in front of her two young children, had shot Nancy twice in the back of the head. It was her eleven-year-old son who called 911. Later that night, the husband took his own life in a Washington D. C. park before officers could reach him.

Nancy's death rocked the romance community. It was the third murder of a romance author by a husband in three years.

Nancy Richards-Akers didn't get her happily ever after. But it doesn't have to be the same for other women.

Statistics show domestic violence is all too common an occurrence in our society. But there are people out there who can help.

No woman deserves to be abused, and no man has a right to abuse her.

If you are a victim of domestic violence, or know someone who is, get help now. Do not wait another day, because tomorrow may be too late. Your telephone directory should have your local women's shelter and crisis hotline listed, and in the back of this book you'll find other abuse hotline numbers.

This book is dedicated to the memory of Nancy Richards-Akers, and other women like her, who have endured the nightmare of abuse. Let us keep her memory alive, and do our part to stop the abuse.

Crumbs in the Keyboard

The Past
Author Unknown

She came tonight as I sat alone.
The girl I used to be.
And she gazed at me with her earnest eye
And questioned reproachfully:
Have you forgotten the many plans
And hopes I had for you?
The great career, the splendid fame,
All the wonderful things to do?
Where is the mansion of stately height
With all its gardens rare?
The silken robes that I dreamed for you
And the jewels in your hair?
And as she spoke, I was very sad
For I wanted her pleased with me.
This slender girl from the shadowy past
The girl that I used to be.
So gently rising, I took her hand
And guided her up the stairs
Where peacefully sleeping, my babies lay
Innocent, sweet, and fair.
And I told her that these are my only gems,
And precious they are to me;
That silken robes is my motherhood
Of costly simplicity.
And my mansion of stately height is love,
And the only career I know
Is serving each day in these sheltered walls
For the dear ones who come and go.
And as I spoke to my shadowy guest,

Crumbs in the Keyboard

She smiled through her tears at me.
And I saw the woman that I am now
Pleased the girl I used to be.

The Writer's Journey

Crumbs in the Keyboard

The Writer's Journey
Kim Cox

Writers love to write, but when and how did they get started? I've read many author bios and the answers usually differ. Some say they knew they wanted to write from the time they held their first crayon, while others didn't know until much later in life. It may have taken a change in a writer's life to bring them to the point of putting pen to paper.

My answer is the latter. I was almost thirty before the thought of writing ever entered my mind. I wasn't even that much of a reader until my late teens/early twenties. During my early years of school, I believe I found one book I liked in the library. I remember it was about a girl and a horse, but it wasn't *Black Beauty*. I can't even remember the title, but it was something like Tigg.

In high school, we were graded every day on a story the English teacher picked from our literary books the day before. We were to read the story for homework and be quizzed the next morning. I don't believe I read one of those stories, but usually passed all the quizzes she gave us. You see, before the bell rang for that class to begin, I would talk to some of my classmates, and they would tell me what the story was about.

After graduation, I began to read historical romances and loved them, though I skipped over pages and pages of description about a room, a portrait or a dress. And I still don't care for a lot of description in the books I read.

About the only other things I read were confessional magazines. I still love them because regardless of what the titles suggest, these magazines are full of stories about everyday people with everyday struggles to overcome.

Then I found Mary Higgins Clark, Sidney Shelton, VC Andrews and yes, Danielle Steel. I read everything of theirs I could get my hands on. I still read Mary Higgins Clark and Sidney Shelton every chance I get. In my eyes, they are the king and queen of suspense.

So, how did I get started writing? Lee, my husband, and I had been married almost a year when he had to go to work out of state. I worked as a night desk clerk at a local motel, but soon had to quit. We only had one vehicle, and Lee took that with him. He set up a ride for me, but one day, without notice, she just stopped coming to get me. Thinking back, I really don't blame her. It wasn't on her way to anywhere, and she had to drag her small child out in the cold to take me. I took a cab a couple of times, but that cost almost a day's pay. It wasn't worth it.

So then I was home alone all the time, and lonely. I started thinking about my life growing up and decided to write my memoirs. Maybe I would make a book out of them some day. I wrote by hand and filled three spiral notebooks. A year later, I bought a typewriter and then a word processor and went about typing the memoirs. After about three typed chapters, I bought a *Writer's Market* and studied how to submit to publishers. Many of them only wanted a synopsis and the first three chapters. Deciding where to submit wasn't easy, but I narrowed it down and started sending it out. I got one form rejection after another. The adult publishers said it wasn't right for their market, submit to a young adult publisher. The young adult publishers said it wasn't right for them because it gave out the wrong message to teenagers.

It's still buried in a box in the bottom of a closet.

After subscribing to *Writer's Digest Magazine*, I signed up for their short story writing course and not only enjoyed it, but I learned a lot. I changed my pregnant teenager novel to a short story. It was rejected also. It still sent out the wrong message to teenagers. A couple of years ago, I saw a story about date rape, and it gave me the idea to change the slant a bit, and turn the story into fiction. I submitted it to the "Trues" (confessional magazines--*True Story, True Romance, True Confessions,* etc.)

True Romance liked the story but liked someone else's who had included the date rape drug, *Roofies* better. This was about the time all the news on the use of *Roofies* came out. You have to remember, in writing, whether you get published or not has a lot to do with timing. So I read up on date rape and the drugs these criminals used. No, I didn't include the drug in my story, but I did write a totally different story with it. The editor of *True Romance* has it on hold until the violence isn't so harsh on readers still raw from recent events. Timing.

I also took a short story and novel writing course through NRI, who also offered a computer, with big floppies, no hard drive, just a word processing disk. I started a book I still haven't finished. I wrote a mystery short story for a contest. No, it didn't final and I never sold it. There was too much story, covering too large of a span of time to be a short story. It was, however, a quick

Crumbs in the Keyboard

write. I was writing on my first book when another novel contest came up. I ditched the first one because I thought it would be faster to write a book from my mystery short story. So I did that and submitted the book to a contest. Again, no it didn't final, and it didn't sell, at least, not right away. During these times, I only wrote in long and short intervals (and still do sometimes). It took my mother dying of cancer to make me realize I needed to get serious if I ever planned to sell my book to a publisher.

I bought a new computer, and I read about the Internet and online services, trying to choose the best avenue for my new career. I picked the one that offered the most for writers. I found workshops and message boards full of other authors and aspiring authors. I found a place I fit in and love it. Soon, I found a critique group, which turned me around and made all the difference. RWA had never been heard of in my small town, and I'm not sure they know about it now.

Online, I learned about the romantic suspense category and changed my mystery to just that. Many years, titles, rejections and rewrites later, I sold this book to RFI West, and it will be released February 2002.

Probably the most important things to remember if you want to write and want what you write to be published is to study your craft, be consistent in your writing (write on a schedule and try to write every day), and most of all, stay determined. Never give up.

Burnt Pumpkins
Jacqueline Elliott

The children and I bought a tube of pumpkin-faced cookie dough,
they asked me to bake them,
I had to get in touch with my muse so.
I heard loud cacophony come from the living room,
Jesse pounded nails in the wall to hang the maple leaf festoon.
I inhaled deeply before reading him the riot act.
And saw Jayline in the mirror behind him,
signaling the end of their pact.
They cried out in ringing lyrical glee,
as I asked if they wanted a pumpkin shaped cookie.
I turned on the oven and sliced them just right,
went back to the keyboard to finish writing for the night.
My immortal hero just crossed the brick and mortar bridge,
when I heard from the kitchen someone open the fridge.
Wafting through the air came a hardy smell,
the pumpkins were so burnt even a vampire could tell.
I cried out in horror, they were the color of dark Koi,
the children let out a cry of joy!

Crumbs in the Keyboard

Tending To My Garden
Janice Stayton

Many years ago, young and stubborn in my authorship, I use to think my written words were to stand as is, and not to change one dotted "I." It kept me in darkness and from my full potential as an author, until.

Somewhere along the way, I realized critique partners are the gardeners who tend to my precious garden. An author is like a garden that is in season year around. She needs daily water, sunshine and care. Without it the weeds, those sneaky well-rooted habits strive to overpower our beautiful creation, our story. Critique partners help me to hoe, water, to spray poison directly on those bad writing habits, the weeds. Their color and beauty in the garden (the details of the story) flourish, highlighted, as though under a microscope. Accepting wise advice, I, you, we, allow our manuscript to become a work of art, a sellable product. Off to the editor it goes.

If critique partners do it write, RIGHT, they offer suggestions of growth. If we know why they offer, it takes seed and sprouts at an accelerating speed. On the next first write of the next draft, miraculously the words we think and write are better, even profound.

The possibilities are endless to each of us. We only need to keep our minds open to learn and receive from others, then sort through the suggestions, picking and choosing ones that will improve the work, putting aside others to ponder another time. Simple example, instead of using, "looked" all the time, we now use a verb that will fit the sentence. "Gazed, glanced, glared, stared, studied, etc."

What do you want in good critique partner(s)? They should offer changes and explain why. They encourage each other. They don't destroy. They build you up. Equally we teach each other. Who is the teacher? Who is the student? We are both. Where one lacks the other doesn't. Be kind, honorable, and respectful as though it is your own scene, or WIP (Work In Progress), you are offering suggestions on.

Your critique partners are your eagle eyes. Their eyesight is better, more in tune. It's like we see for the first time. And what an experience it is to have 20/20 vision in an area that we were unaware of, that needed more focus and attention.

I can trust my critique partners to teach me to master my gift. If you are one who has not found a critique partner(s), I encourage you to do so. There are many authors who live close by you. They are also at your fingertips on many online e-groups.

Do you want to grow, to perfect your craft, skill, and your gift? Then, FIND A CRITIQUE GROUP. Let's write! On your mark, get set, grooooooooooow.

Crumbs in the Keyboard

The Labyrinth: A metaphor for life's journey
Patricia Crossley

The Labyrinth is a spiritual tool that is used as a centering activity. It is meant to be walked as a form of meditation, and in the walking the spirit finds healing and wholeness. We all feel a need for time for reflection, for moving in concert with our thoughts, for seeking inner peace in our souls. Since the fourth century the Christian Church has used the labyrinth as a walking meditation, but it is a symbol found in many cultures from ancient to modern times. The design appears in fields and in churches all over Europe if you know where to look and now is visible in North America.

If you visit Chartres in Northern France, or Ely in Norfolk in England, you will find the labyrinth pattern on the stone floor of the ancient Cathedrals. The feet of the faithful have walked the path in prayerful meditation since the 13th Century.

People continue to make labyrinths from stones, grass, wood, fishing line, on beaches and in snowy fields. Indoor labyrinths come in canvas and masking tape. There has been a great revival of interest in this spiritual tool in recent years around the world and particularly in North America. Labyrinths can be found on church property, in city parks, in retreat centers, in hospitals, in prisons and in private gardens. People are finding it a powerful tool for spiritual renewal.

Sometimes the words "labyrinth" and "maze" are confused. While both refer to circling patterns, the two are totally different. A maze is a puzzle and thus designed to confuse; walkers must use their reason and cunning to escape. A labyrinth is a single path which leads the walker to the center and back out. There are no hedges, no blind turns, nothing to obstruct the view of the path's destination. In an open, receptive frame of mind, the walker simply follows the path and experiences a refreshing form of meditation. The labyrinth represents a pilgrimage of the soul which follows a long, winding yet purposeful path which finally comes to a center, then winds its way out again. There are no obstacles, no puzzles; it is not a maze. There is one unbroken path to follow.

There are two basic designs, an eleven circuit and a seven circuit. Each design provides a metaphor for life's journey: We can see our goal in the center but the path leads us around, sometimes closer, sometimes farther away. If we persist, we reach the center, survey the path we have trodden and give thanks.

The experience of walking the labyrinth will be different for each person and different each time the path is walked. Many have found it to be a tool to guide healing (of the mind, spirit and body,) to awaken the Spirit within them, to spark creativity. Walking the labyrinth quiets the busy mind and enables a person to see their life in the context of a path or journey. It often gives solace and peace, and encourages action empowered by the Spirit.

Metaphorically speaking, we are all spiritual seekers, on the path together, looking for meaning and purpose for our lives. The Labyrinth provides a symbol that is also quite literal as it presents us with a real path upon which to really walk together.

A true story:

R** was close to release from several years in prison and volunteered to help in the construction of a stone labyrinth in the grounds of the cathedral church in a city close to the penitentiary. The pattern was laid out in masking tape in another area and R** was one of the first to walk it. In his life, he has had little to do with formal religion, but in recent years he has come to respect his own spirit. He will freely tell anyone that he found walking the labyrinth a powerful and empowering experience.

R** worked harder than anyone for ten days to prepare the ground and lay the stones for the permanent labyrinth. From time to time, he would return to the taped pattern and spend some time alone with his own thoughts. When the construction was finished, the crew of five inmates on release, their guard and the three parishioners who had worked together all agreed that R** should be the first to walk the path. He walked it in joy and with a huge sense of achievement.

When R** was released a few weeks later, he came to live close to the cathedral and now spends a lot of time around the green lawns of the church close. He walks the labyrinth almost every day and brings friends and acquaintances. His one regret was that there was not time for him to organize the construction of a labyrinth within the penitentiary before he left. R** may never set foot inside the massive walls of the cathedral, but he has found a way to talk to his God and receive guidance and support.

How do I walk the Labyrinth?

There is no absolutely "right" way to walk the labyrinth. Choose your pace-

-slow, moderate or fast. Most walk alone, but you may choose to walk with another. If you meet someone on the path, pass quietly or move aside and then continue. You may not want to make eye contact, or you may wish to touch in passing.

The walking meditation may be used in several ways according to your needs and wishes.

Here are a few suggestions to help you begin:

Breath deeply, center yourself and enter the path. Begin to move forward and find the pace your body wants. If you have a particular issue you are praying about, hold that in your heart. You may silently repeat a phrase from a hymn or a prayer. If you wish, you can pause now and then to record your thoughts in writing. As you walk to the center, relax and release the thoughts and concerns of life, allowing your mind to become quiet. When you reach the center, stay there as long as you like. Listen for the voice of the Spirit within you. As you walk out of the center, retracing the path that brought you in, allow a new perspective and a new energy to fill you as you continue on your spiritual path in life.

Walking the labyrinth:

Does not require a great amount of concentration in order to benefit from the experience. The sheer act of walking a designated path helps to discharge energy and focus the mind. What seems to work best when preparing to walk is to take a few minutes to reflect on where you are in your life journey, and what issues confront you. You may wish to focus on a particular question that you have been asking yourself. All this helps you into a receptive and quieted state in which insights.

The Writer's Journey

Passing on the Pen and Paper
Cheri Lee Funk

It is quiet and I am sitting at my desk reading my email. I had submitted a story to an online e-zine and was reading many of the positive responses I had received. These comments moved me to consider submitting this story to some print publications. I was working on editing when my youngest grandson Matthew walked into my office. "What are you doing, Nina?"

"I am writing a story," I answered without looking away from my screen.

"What is the story about?"

"It is called "The Shoe Man" and is about something that took place when I was living in Florida and working with children. I am making some changes to it."

"Why are you writing a story?"

I stop what I am doing and I look up. Now there are many among us that ask ourselves that same question every day. I am not sure we choose to write. I think it is more that we are filled with words and are not able to rest or even be happy until we have poured them out onto paper. But how do I explain this to a nine-year-old? So, I think of how to tell him, "Well I write to give a smile to other people. I write to give myself a smile, but most of all I write because I feel I have a story to tell."

"Could I read your story?"

"Of course Matthew, I would love to share it with you."

I print out a copy and hand it over to my new critic. Oh my goodness, how will he feel about what I have written? Will he understand what I was trying to say? Others had praised my words, but will they reach out and touch this very special young man in my life?

I am nervous, so I get up and leave the room. I walk into the kitchen and begin preparations for dinner. Brian, Matthew's ten-year-old brother walks in and wants to know if I know what he is doing. "Yes, he is sitting at the computer and reading a story I wrote." He leaves and I busy myself with the task at hand, making dinner for these hungry guys!

"Hey, Nina how do you spell lizard?"

Crumbs in the Keyboard

Absent-mindedly I rattle off the correct spelling and then return to shucking corn. A few more minutes pass and then I hear, "Hey, Nina, how do you spell Reggie?"

I look up and see Matthew standing in front of me with a pen and pad of paper in his hand. I spell Reggie and then ask what he is doing. "I am writing a story. Brian and I are writing about four lizards. We are typing it on the computer."

I tell them dinner is almost ready and they will need to get cleaned up in a few minutes. As I am setting the table the two of them enter the kitchen with paper in hand. "Can we read this to you?"

"Of course!" I stop what I am doing and turn to face them. I know how important it is for a writer to get honest feedback. And how important it is for us to know we are capturing another's total attention.

Matthew reads the words they put down on the paper and I have to grin. My goodness, it was wonderful, maybe not Pulitzer Prize winning material but pretty darn good! I applaud them both.

"Nina, do you think I could send my story away to someone like you did?"

I assure them that when I get a little more done on my website I will make sure their work is displayed. This answered my burning question about whether my words reached out and touched their heart.

Isn't imitation the sincerest form of flattery? And once again, I realized why I write. I am truly honored that these two very special young men in my life choose to sit down at my desk and write a story. I say a little prayer for the words to always come easy for them. I hope when they were sitting at my desk and writing the story of "The Four Lizards That Ran Into Trouble," they were able to experience a little of what I feel each time I sit down and try to put my thoughts on paper. One day when one of them becomes a published author I can say I possess one of their first works! Now I would like to share it with you.

June 25, 2001
The Four Lizards That Ran Into Trouble
By Matthew and Brian Hutchin

One day 4 lizards saw a poster
but thought it was a toaster
so they ran
and Reggie the leader got hit by a van
we went to see if she was dead,
next thing she knew she was laying in bed

The Writer's Journey

then Lizzie said, oh god look at her head
she said she was better
but she was almost deader
then ever
two weeks later Reggie said,
she was better but she was not deader
than ever
Reggie healed from her broken arm
but never went back to her dads farm.

Crumbs in the Keyboard

What Did I Do—So I Can Do It Again?
Robin D. Owens

After seriously writing for eight years, I finally got an offer from Berkley to publish my fourth book. Naturally after the excitement wore off, I wondered why the universe favored me and what I could do to ensure it happened again. Different ideas have flashed through my brain:

Daily Prayer: I really don't want to tell everyone how long I've been saying my daily prayers for this event, but it's been a long, LONG time.

Feng shui: Last year I put the plaques I won over the years in the proper *feng shui* place of my offices at home and at work to garner fame. I put prints with purple mattes in the right corner to bring money (this worked well at my job, but so did taking on more responsibility). I put a little fountain in my office. I considered getting a monitor arm so that I wouldn't be facing west at home when I wrote my all time most disastrous direction according to one book. (I put a print of a couple embracing in the correct corner of my bedroom, but my love life hasn't improved yet).

Good Deeds: The Thursday before I sold, I saved a pigeon that was flapping around a parking garage and was unable to fly. Taking the pigeon home, fending off my cats, finding a vet that would accept a hurt pigeon and transporting it to the vet (1 trip to find, 1 to transport) ate up an entire evening that I'd intended to write (not to mention what it did to the interior of my purse where I originally stowed the pigeon). I return dogs and cats to their homes. I feed feral cats and take them to vets for low-cost spaying or fixing. I usually save a pigeon every other year. I figure these karma points ought to help when editors see my book, right?

Reverse Psychology: I screwed up my manuscript when I sent it in for the last third of my book, my hero's name was ALL CAPs. I also sent the manuscript without representation by an agent, and without being requested. (The editor had awarded me first place in a contest that required the first ten pages, no synopsis. I marked all over the priority envelope "Awarded first place by Cindy Hwang in Wisconsin Fabulous Five Contest"). Of course an editor wouldn't want it.

Letting go: In the last year it became ok that I wouldn't be print published. I let myself accept that I was writing books of my heart that would not find a market in New York. I could submit to e-pubs such as Hardshell, or small print presses such as the Palladin Group. My work would get out there and I would keep my day job.

I wrote an article for our newsletter on perseverance and ended with the bottom line: Would you continue to write if you knew you would never be published? Yes, I answered. And it is true. I would continue to write my stories.

This year I didn't make my usual BIG Christmas wish that I'd sell.

But the week before my sale, I decided that I would cut down on the amount of time I spent before my computer wrestling with plot and characters and words. There were other things I could be doing every evening keeping up with the new movies coming out, hanging with friends, getting to know my nieces and nephew better, going on day trips or other traveling. Why continue to bash my head against a wall when I had nothing but four books and smiley faces on critiques to show for it? In fact, that snowy superbowl Sunday I actually got the message I sold I was puttering around the house. As I did laundry and cleaned, I thought that it was soothing not to be upstairs struggling to deepen the conflict between my hero and heroine, or revising the chapter my critique group worked on the day before.

When I mentioned this quest to find out what I did right to a critique buddy, he was of the opinion that it was the letting go.

Other things: I haven't looked to see what astrological forces were aligned when I sold. I wear stones and crystals as jewelry, but I'm not always sure of the magical properties they are supposed to have.

I cleaned my desk in September, organizing everything. I was ready to accept an offer that would cover it with work. Maybe I'll get to the computer hutch soon, too, and the rest of the office.

I started a meditation program that is supposed to make me more creative and bring everything else I need and desire into my life.

I decided to finally claim my writing expenses on my income taxes for the first time, letting the IRS know I existed as an unpublished author.

I exercised every day. That should definitely count in my favor with the universe.

The Truth: The truth is that I worked hard at my craft and didn't give up. That I wrote books of my heart, stories I believed in and made as good as possible. That my manuscript landed at the right time on the right editor's desk who loved my work.

I'm just glad that one of my cats didn't die, or I'd be thinking of animal sacrifice.

Crumbs in the Keyboard

Top 10 Things Not To Say to an Editor
Lisa Craig

Excerpted from actual things people said to editors during their editor appointments.

1)"How do I write a synopsis?"
2)"I've never read any books published by your company."
3)"I'm not familiar with your line of books. Can you describe them?"
4)"How many pages *is* 75,000 words?"
5"I haven't written for a long time, but I want to get back into it."
6"I'm not sure how my book will end. Do you have any ideas?"
7)"I don't seem to have time to write?"
8)"Johnny's in cub scouts, my husband works on cars, and my littlest one wants to be a ballerina."
9)"Do you think I should quit my job and write full time."
10)"I'm not sure I'm cut out for writing. What do you think?"

The Writer's Journey

Mama's Five Myths About Writing
Denise Weeks

Mama thought she was helping me when she taught me her five "truths"--actually myths--about writing. Maybe that's because there's a smidgen of truth in each myth. But don't let that fool you; if you subscribe to any of these myths, you'll be unnecessarily discouraged.

Myth #1. A real writer writes from inspiration. Corollary: If you don't produce publishable work the first time out, you're wasting time and paper. This one is a real killer. Eager writers have wasted away waiting for the song from the Muse without realizing that until the seat of the pants is applied to the seat of the chair, there's no chance that inspiration will strike, let alone hang around long enough to finish a work of art. As for the corollary: Did Michael Jordan make every basket the first time he held the ball? No. Certainly he had talent from the start, but he spent years learning his craft and honing his skills until all was perfected.

Myth #2. A real writer can write anywhere: masterpieces are normally produced on the bus or waiting in line at the grocery checkout, and are scribbled effortlessly on the backs of envelopes, around the edges of receipts, or on yellow sticky notes. (Implying, of course, that that's where your deathless prose should stay.) Real writers don't need fancy tools like computers or typewriters. After all, Shakespeare and Milton didn't have them. (Ask Mom if she'd give up her microwave, electric or gas range, and running water.)

Myth #3. A real writer gets published early on and with little effort, because the writing is really good. If only this were true. Sometimes it doesn't matter whether the writing itself is good if the market isn't. Serendipity and coincidence sometimes mean that your potential markets have recently covered the same material as your article, or have just published the only fiction they'll publish all year, and so you don't make the sale. Or maybe you were missing that certain something that would've made your piece appeal to an editor.

It takes an average of five years, according to one survey, to get published. When Mama saw me revising, she naively asked, "Why didn't you just do it right the first time?" Mama didn't realize that sending out my first draft would be like her serving company those burned cookies that stuck to the pan the first time she tried to make that recipe. If work needs a little polishing, that's all right; it doesn't mean you failed the first time, or that you weren't trying hard enough, or that you aren't good enough.

Myth #4. A real writer doesn't need encouragement or validation, and can overcome or ignore all negative input; art (like virtue) is its own reward. The true writer has an inner voice that can go on in the face of discouragement, one that never sounds bitter. Wrong again. Those frustrating early years when a writer craves validation are the norm. Do you have what it takes? No one can tell you, of course, but you'd like to hear sometimes that you do have talent and are doing well.

Myth #5. A real writer is only doing it for fun, not for posterity or for publication. Wanting publication is really just a desire to show off. Why isn't art for art's sake sufficient? Writing isn't fun, any more than training for a marathon or studying for an exam is fun, except in the sense that any effort--even emptying the dishwasher--gives a sense of accomplishment. Certainly the process is somewhat fulfilling in itself, especially when the words flow as easily across your screen as cars down the highway. But the implication here is that writing is like Web-surfing or playing cards, requiring little sweat, and that's misleading. Writing is a lot of hard work. It takes just as much time and effort to write a bad novel as it does to write a brilliant one. And if anyone tells you he or she doesn't care if the work is ever published or read after his or her demise, check that nose; it's probably growing.

All of these are partial truths, but taken literally (pardon the pun) they mislead writers and cloak the deeper reality behind each saying. A real writer may not be published yet--or ever; may need encouragement, especially from professionals, even if it's only "this isn't bad" from a teacher or editor; may need a quiet workspace (and time to sit there), persistence, and self-discipline to give the muse a chance to start her song; and may need tools like a typewriter or PC to be taken seriously at submission time. And may not always find the writing, revision, and submission process unmitigated FUN.

But, as always, what Mama was getting at may have been true at the core: writing is always fulfilling. When we're caught up in our stories and feel so close to the characters we've invented that we might have gone shoe shopping with them yesterday, we're content. To see a poem, novel, or article finished--and to be able to say that you created it yourself, starting with nothing but a ream of blank paper--is something to be proud of, all by itself.

And that may have been all Mama meant, after all.

The Writer's Journey

Writing As An Explorer
Gerry Benninger

Two books I've read have compared writing to exploration.

One, Gloria Steinem's 'Revolution From Within' is not specifically about writing but about self-esteem. She writes: Perhaps we share stories in much the same spirit explorers share maps, hoping to speed each other's journey, but knowing the journey we make will be our own.

In the other book, James Michener's Writer's Handbook, he writes: The basic process of writing is one of constant exploration. (which is) as many adventurers in exotic lands have discovered, a process of trial and error.

The much-discussed explorations of Columbus are an excellent example of what Michener means by trial and error. Columbus tried and he erred. We Americans tried to celebrate the beginning of our country and we erred by assuming it began with Columbus's arrival. My mother's favorite saying (and that of a great many Native American families) was that my father's people came over on the Mayflower, but her people, the Chicaza, were waiting on the shore. The flaw in our celebration of Columbus's achievement has been that we honored him for arriving in a new world, when it was already an ancient home to many, rather than honoring him for making the perilous journey.

That's what happens when we authors honor ourselves only for publishing. We see the arrival in published novel, short story, non-fiction or poetry but it's more difficult to witness the discipline, struggle, work, and doubt that made up the writer's journey.

One of my daughter's is working at sea right now, not her first time before the mast but she says every time is a little like that first time she and her husband sailed a charter alone using their own navigational skills. After many days of open ocean, they almost turned back. They had charts, navigation tools, a radio, good skills but until the end of the journey they didn't really know whether they had put everything together just right and chosen the right course.

And there is no experience in the world to rival that first sighting of land after a long journey at sea. The shore becomes a mythic place like it is in the Navajo oral tradition about Changing Woman, the earth mother, who lives in the west where sea and land meet. These stories contain beautifully accurate images

Crumbs in the Keyboard

of the shore because the desert dwelling Navajo explorers went west and returned to share their discoveries.

Writers are explorers. For most, the journey is less impressive than those of the Navajo or the Carthaginians or Marco Polo or Columbus or the astronauts.

We're more like Robert Frost going out to clean the pasture spring (I shan't be gone long--You come too.) but we need to risk exploring. We need to sail alone trusting our skills and to keep writing without knowing for certain when we will arrive. Sometimes we must allow ourselves to keep writing even without a destination. That's how we arrive at new places and share our maps with others. And that's how we gain the courage to go exploring again.

The Writer's Journey

When the Writing Gets Tough, This Writer Goes Shopping
Barbara Baldwin

What better place to shop for characters for my latest novel than a mall, where people of all shapes, sizes, colors and styles happily gather. Without interfering in *their* enjoyment, I can study and choose from thousands of character traits, personality flaws and secret--free to the discriminating shopper.

I've tried shopping at home with catalogs. It sometimes works for a minor character, but it's hard to tell if I have a good fit without seeing the actual character in motion. All those idiosyncrasies that make my characters special come out in public--their walk, laugh, voice. Perhaps what I'm looking for is the way they hold their head, cling to a boy friend, or talk with their hands. Too much personality remains unnoticed on a still life, one-dimensional photograph in a catalog.

So I settle down to window shop.

My first "purchase" is not your stereotypical hero. His belly's a bit too large; his face is beginning to show the first stages of age. Gray threads his hair and his laugh is a bit too loud. But he also has the nicest smile I can ever recall and the kindest, blue eyes. His gentle gaze speaks of trust and honesty and I immediately realize I want him in my book. He will make the best "best friend" anyone can have.

I turn my head at the sound of male laughter. Cowboys. Are they real or wannabes? They lean against the railing and I study *them* as *they* study girls. I have my pick of sizes, the tallest being well over six foot. If I take a composite of the group, I just might have my hero. Let's see--a mustache from the third guy; the blonde's hair; and the tall one's smile, his lip lifting a little higher on the right than the left.

I like the tall guy's attitude. As I watch, his face never changes expressions; he's aloof, trying to look disinterested. His thumbs are hooked in the belt loops of his jeans. While his body language might indicate he's bored with this activity and wants something more exciting, his eyes tell another story. Twinkling green, slight crinkles at the corners, they laugh and mock and never miss a thing.

As though one entity, they turn to follow a group of girls when they pass.

Crumbs in the Keyboard

Red-blooded, American boys to the core, but I'm still not sure if I can use them, so I study their walks. Only one has the rolling gait of a cowboy--someone who actually spends time on a horse. It's the tall one; the guy with laughter in his eyes and the crooked smile.

I watch them walk away, and he turns and touches his forehead as though tipping his hat. And then he winks at me.

Oh, yes, I definitely need a cowboy in this book.

The Writer's Journey

Walk With Me in the Rain
Barbara Baldwin

I write when the house is quiet; when even the dogs lie at my feet in slumber and there is nothing to interrupt the flow of my words. Then I create a world only I can see. Sometimes, I don't understand the emotional entanglement that occurs when I become immersed in that creative process. I ache for my characters; cry for their heartbreaks and laugh with their joys.

And I walk with them in the rain.

I close my eyes and visualize a world quite different from the concrete one in which many live. As I shuffle beneath an autumn canopy, bursting with crimson, mustard yellow and dusty brown, I long to sit right down among the crackling leaves and listen as the wind echoes through the branches. I write the words to help me remember this day--the gentle caress of the breeze, the call of a bird, distant laughter.

I don't see a tree; I see a young sapling or a towering oak; or an orchard rich with fragrant blossoms. For when others read what I have written, I want them to become part of the world that I created especially for them.

I hope they walk with me in the rain.

I ride down the road, trying to capture the feel of furnace blasts of heat which throw tumbleweeds across the path to make the drive less tedious. I need other words for "hot" because my story takes place in summer and it *is* hot. I take hints from the wilted fields; brown pastures that should have remained green another month. Is it sweltering? Torrid? Bone-melting hot?

Then the rain drowns the summer heat. A warm, soft, summer rain; or an earthshaking thunderstorm, lightning ricocheting across a night sky. Rain is a deluge, a torrential downpour, a miracle, a disaster, a respite. It is the angel of life for barren fields during a drought, or it can wash away a lifetime of hopes and dreams in an instant.

Are you ready to walk with me in the rain?

Can you recall riding through a puddle on your bike as though it were a great sailing ship, lifting your feet high but getting soaked anyway? Do you smell the clean musty earth and feel the mud squish up between your toes?

Crumbs in the Keyboard

Have you ever visited a town where no one lives but where the ghosts will speak if only you listen? Would you dress up in old-fashioned clothes and pretend to be an outlaw's girlfriend, getting a tintype taken in an old time saloon?

This is how I write; caught up in dreams of another time. There is an insatiable need within me to create worlds in which I *know* I can't belong, but to which I am allowed a visit--for another hour; for ten more pages; for tonight.

And always, I will find time to walk in the rain.

The Writer's Journey

We're All In This Together
Cherie Claire

One night, we agreed to help another parent out by offering to babysit his daughter's gerbil while the family vacationed during Spring Break. The father, daughter and younger son arrived at eight p.m. the night before the big trip, all highly energized and talkative.

Everyone except Dad, of course.

We gladly took the gerbil, nicknamed Spot, even though our house contains one loud, smelly, hyperactive dog, a cat with a passion for the rodent family and two equally loud, hyperactive boys. (At least they aren't smelly.) We stood in the kid's room, all six people and three animals, trying to carry on a conversation while the noise level rose higher and higher.

The trip sounded like an exciting one, and I immediately felt envious, especially since our plans for Spring Break included taking in "Rugrats in Paris" on a matinee and a possible trip to the bowling alley.

Our toilet decided to start whistling on us two days before and being the handywoman that I am, I instantly broke off the thing-a-ma-jig that equalizes the water in the tank. My husband took this fix-it experiment one step higher by shutting off the water and causing a leak. So, for Spring Break, our extra finances were handed over one evening to an after-hours plumber, followed by Home Depot for new carpeting.

As Spot's dad began to describe their week-long trip and the youngest member of their family began to talk incessantly and *my* youngest child took this as a challenge to see who could talk the most and loudest, I suddenly wasn't envious anymore. Spot's dad looked around and instantly thought the same thing. A week in a car with two small children?

"I may be back tomorrow night to pick up Spot," Dad said with a laugh.

So many of us working parents think back on our childhoods and imagine something similar to those '50s car advertisements. You know the ones: smiling parents in the front with pressed dresses and suits, quiet, grinning children in the back seats, all of them looking like the Stepford family. And we wonder, "Why doesn't this work for us?"

Crumbs in the Keyboard

I remember when my oldest was three and he performed a usually good temper tantrum during Thanksgiving dinner, like he was saving up all that spit and energy for a special occasion. My mother turned to me, shook her head and said, "I don't remember any of you having temper tantrums."

Did Madison Avenue brainwash us, with those cheerful '50's families in those brand new cars, so happy to be in each other's company that they could tour the world together? Or do our memories leave us as we get older, replacing those horrific car trips and temper displays with angelic views of our children as our calcium levels dip? I certainly remember nightmarish trips with mom and dad and I vividly remember the squeezing arm techniques my mother used when all four of us threw temper tantrums.

John Rosemond, an expert du jour, claims that children today don't listen because the generation raising them are working parents who don't want to make the effort to discipline. We choose the gentler, explain-it-to-them methods of child rearing because they are easier, Rosemond claims. Actually, a spanking is the easiest form of discipline, but Rosemond doesn't go there. Nor does he realize that my mother followed the Dr. Spock parenting style that he disagrees with and look how I turned out. (No comment, please.)

It's much easier to place the blame on a large group of people, to remind us that our parents didn't have these problems even when our own memories tell us otherwise.

What is different from when our parents raised children is the increase of mothers in the workplace. More parents raising children today work, whether at a job or in the home. If you're a writer, like me, you have two careers to juggle, pushing the stress envelope one step further. And those who choose to stay home to raise children are working no matter how you look at it.

We juggle jobs, day care, teacher appointments, karate classes, agent phone calls, vet visits, writer's meetings and haircuts. If one car breaks down, our lives go into an emergency regrouping mode that would put the U.S. Army to shame. We have backups for backups for backups.

We are living on the edge.

And we're doing OK.

No, we're not the smiling '50s family, but I refuse to believe they exist. We have new challenges to meet while our children present the standard ones that have existed throughout eternity, the ones our parents dealt with and their parents before them, sometimes with success, sometimes not.

The Writer's Journey

I once was on deadline for a freelance newspaper story and had trouble getting the final interview. The lawyer interviewee called back at 5 p.m., right as I was giving my baby his evening bottle. I interviewed the man with the telephone cradled between my left shoulder and ear while I propped up the bottle with my knee and scribbled notes with my free hand. When the bottle emptied, I rocked my child with my foot to keep him from screaming.

I got the story. It wasn't a Pulitzer Prize winner, but the process sure was. It was a moment of triumph with no witnesses.

We are all working mothers, both inside and outside the home, who have no witnesses or, sometimes when we do, may not be the positive ones who give us strength. We all live on the edge. And we're meeting the challenge head-on, even at our worst. We need to remember that we are not alone, that there is strength in numbers, that a sisterhood exists if only we can find each other and reach out and hold hands.

Remember the quilts of old, the beautiful scraps of fabric that resembled rags individually but a work of art sewn together? Let us be a quilt of mothers, shining at our worst because we stand together, a rainbow of colors to nurture us and keep us warm.

Because, like our mothers, and their mothers before them, we will survive. And we will leave a creative legacy behind.

Lynne's Book
Diana Lee Johnson

I'm submitting my story at my daughter's insistence. Though I have always believed firmly in God, and in supernatural things, within limits, I've never been captured by aliens or anything. A strange, and heart-warming sequence of events has taken place in the past few days that would make a believer out of most skeptics.

I'm a professional purchasing agent for a local government. I've been in that profession for over 35 years. As such, I must be totally logical, but I must also trust my instincts. Closer to my heart is my life-long avocation--creative writing. Though I always wanted to be a professional writer, I knew I must make a living, thus, when I found I was good at Purchasing, I stuck with it, but I never gave up on my writing.

I began writing poetry at the age of six, and poetry was the bulk of my writing with few exceptions, because it flowed quickly from me in meter and rhyme, thus not taking up much of my time. I love all writing, even technical specifications, complaint letters for friends, resumes and editing college papers for friends.

After divorce, with children nearly raised, I began to write prose, but still had little time for it. A few short stories, and a short story that grew into a short novel convinced me I could write a book. Sixteen years ago, I actually set out to write a novel, then another, and another. It was my therapy and respite from pressure and stress.

I started researching and sending my work out to agents, and publishers, with no luck. I thought perhaps I should join a writing organization. I read about the Virginia Romance Writers, and went to a meeting. I joined it and Romance Writers of America, hoping it might open doors, or at least show me where I was falling short. Where I fell short was that I didn't exactly fit into categories, and by this time, the early 90's, there was a glut of new authors trying to break in.

Being a purchaser, I wasn't very good at selling myself, or my writing. It was very discouraging, but at the Virginia meetings I found a soul mate. Someone only a few years younger than myself, who had the same burning desire, but, like me, hadn't had the time to pursue that desire. We became friends, and often road to the monthly meetings together since they were in Richmond, about 100 miles away. She was in a critique group that could use another writer, so I was invited to join.

The group was an eclectic mix, and broke up after about a year, but Lynne and I stayed friends, though we didn't see each other often. We emailed each other with encouragement and news, and our lives went in different directions.

With seven finished manuscripts, I kept sending query letters and sample chapters out without any luck. In 1998, I was offered a book contract with a publisher in Canada for my favorite of my own manuscripts. Mostly, it was a nightmare, delayed release, mistakes that were changes made after I proofed the galleys, books not getting printed in the quantity contracted, not getting to the distributor…that's the tip of the iceberg.

In July, 1999, though we hadn't seen each other for some months, Lynne drove the thirty-five to forty miles to surprise me at my first book signing. We stayed in touch, and continued to encourage each other. Then in the Spring of 2000, we went to a one-day Virginia writing conference together, driving down the evening before.

Lynne was not herself all that trip, and I was concerned about her, but it wasn't until I got an email in July that she told me she had become suddenly ill and been diagnosed and had surgery for a brain tumor. When I called her after the email, I pointed out her rather bizarre behavior on our short trip, and she realized it was probably related, though it hadn't occurred to her.

She was optimistic, staying at her parents' only a few miles from me, while recovering. We emailed, and telephoned, but I agreed not to come to see her until she was ready to be seen. I could understand her not wanting anyone but family around with her illness, and loss of hair, etc. She'd joke about it on the phone.

I got worried when I didn't hear from her for long stretches, and sent cards and little gifts, like a friendship rose, a poem I wrote for her, etc. Then I'd hear from her. I always told her I would like to visit her, but would wait until she told me she was ready.

As bad as life had to be for her, Lynne always expressed concern for my troubles and illnesses, which I usually only mentioned by way of conversation. She asked me not to spread her condition around to the Virginia Romance Writers, so I kept it to myself with the exception of another member of our

Crumbs in the Keyboard

defunct critique group, who had moved a thousand miles away.

In January of this year (2001), I bit the bullet and called again, fearing bad news, but Lynne answered the phone, and though she was not doing well and the tumor had come back with a vengeance, she was genuinely glad to hear from me. She was still not ready for a visit, and time went by again with no word.

I signed two contracts with an Epublisher in April of 2001, but didn't share that with Lynne. I hadn't had an email for months, but I still sent cards and notes of concern and caring.

Finally, after a long silence, I called her in July. Her mother hesitated to give her the phone, but when she told Lynne it was I, she took the phone. She sounded like her cheery-self part of the time, but part of the time the words were jumbled and senseless. I knew the tumor was doing it's worst.

I wrote her mother a letter explaining my concern and caring on July 29. On Tuesday afternoon, August 14, she called me and said Lynne wanted to see me. I was spread pretty thin that week as I tried to tie up loose ends to leave Friday for my national purchasing conference. I had a doctor's appointment Wednesday afternoon, but told her I could come Thursday.

Before I got home Wednesday, her sister had called and left me a message that Lynne wasn't up to a visitor the next day. I called and spoke briefly to her mother, but learned no more than that. I had such an ominous feeling as I left for the meeting on Friday. I knew I'd be gone a week, and worried I wouldn't be there if Lynne was up to seeing me. I also worried the worst would come to pass, so I'd asked my mother to watch the paper.

I had an all-day seminar on Saturday, but went back to my hotel room to retrieve some papers at lunchtime. While there, I picked up my voicemail from home. There was a message from my mother asking me to call her. I did so, thinking something had happened to my aunt who was ill. My mother told me that Lynne's obituary was in the paper that day. I was numb. It said she had died Wednesday. I assume it was after I spoke to her mother. But no one called me on Thursday, and I left early Friday morning.

I had to go back to my seminar, but couldn't bring myself to participate orally. When I got back to my room, I broke down. Sunday, her sister left me a voicemail.

All I could think was "I never got to say goodbye."

It haunted me. I sat down and wrote her mother a letter, and when I got home I made a contribution to hospice in Lynne's memory, but neither brought me any closure.

September 11 happened, and I felt even more lost and useless. Then my Aunt died and I drove my Mom back to Illinois for the funeral. Everything kept compounding and I couldn't fix anything.

The Epublisher was beginning to make me nervous, and I wasn't hearing good things about them. It didn't pan out, and I withdrew my manuscripts, September 17, but within 24 hours I had contracts with another publisher for those two books.

Lynne and I had often talked about the holiday season and its depression when you live alone as we both did. The fact that it's the time of year my father died, and my ex-husband was killed, magnified it for me. This year I wanted to do something productive. I got most of my Christmas shopping done by Thanksgiving and set about wrapping them immediately. Shortly after Thanksgiving I lost another old friend I used to work with and I kept fighting those blues.

Two days after Thanksgiving, the new Epublisher sent me a third contract for another manuscript. I emailed my first publisher in Canada and asked them if they'd like to "rethink" their failure to produce the contracted number of copies of my first novel, "Too Late for Tomorrow," since I had three books coming out in 2002. I hadn't been able to get any copies out of them for over a year, and it was embarrassing to explain to people who wanted to buy it. They had never fulfilled the "first-run" number in the contract.

Though I had been told a reprint was scheduled for September, nothing happened, and the orders I placed went unfilled. Still unable to get additional copies of it, I sent my last copy to the Library of Congress copyright office to register it myself on November 30. I felt like I was taking control again.

I took a couple of days off work to finish shopping, wrapping, and get some dreaded housework done, Dec. 11th & 12th. The evening of the 11th I was very blue thinking of people I had lost, thinking of all those lost on September 11. I resolved to fight back by posting an email to our troops in Afghanistan and putting up a little Christmas tree, for the first time in 15 years.

The evening of Dec. 12th, exhausted from moving furniture and cleaning carpets, I went to my computer email and there was one from Barnes and Noble apologizing for being unable to fill my September 1 order for three copies of Too Late for Tomorrow sooner. It said they were scheduled to ship on Dec. 13. All other orders I had placed with book suppliers had long-since been cancelled, my

Crumbs in the Keyboard

orders from the publisher ignored.

I decided to look at Amazon.com to see if it was available there, since the publisher hadn't told me any had been reprinted, or released. It wasn't listed as "unavailable" anymore, but as a "special order"; so I ordered two copies, just to see. Up-popped an icon asking me if I'd like to order a used copy. The description went on to say it was autographed by the author.

"Ah-ha," I said aloud. "Which of my friends or acquaintances is trying to get rid of their copy?" Just for the heck of it, I ordered it, through Amazon, at least if the others didn't come, I'd have one copy, and satisfy my curiosity at knowing who got rid of theirs. This was the evening of Dec. 12. At 10:24 AM, Dec. 13, I got a confirmation from a used bookstore in Luray, Virginia, saying the book had been sent. Holiday mail is bad enough, but this year, with all the anthrax scares, it's taking forever here around Washington, DC. Luray is a small town about 100 miles from me. I didn't look for the book until next week.

When I got up Friday morning at 5:00 AM, I checked my email. In the middle of the night, I had been emailed a fourth contract from the Epublisher. This one for the sequel to my first novel.

When I came home last night, I found the used book in my mailbox. I hurried in to see whose copy it was. When I opened the cover, I had to sit down. My inscription, "Dear Lynne, How much you've helped me along the way. I appreciate all the encouragement. Stick with your writing. Love, Diana." A peaceful warmth came over me I can not explain. The only other time I have felt it was when I saw the peaceful expression on my father's face at his viewing after he had suffered long and died from cancer.

How the book got to Luray from here, how I was called to look at Amazon that evening, how it got here by regular mail overnight, and how it was the one from my friend over whose passing I have not been able to gain closure, only God, Lynne, and maybe my Dad, know. I think it was her way giving me closure, making sure I knew that she knew I cared, and that she is still sharing my pursuit of my writing. Maybe it was also her way of getting me back a copy of my book she knew had been so difficult to acquire. It was so like Lynne to be generous.

I will treasure this copy of my book more than the first one I held in my hands, for it was delivered to me from such a special friend, in such a special way.

Mama Told Me There'd Be Days Like This

Pinwheels and Hats
Holly Fuhrmann

Everyone wears a multitude of hats--roles they never give any thought to. At birth I was thrust, unasked, into the roles of daughter, granddaughter, sister, niece, and cousin. As I grew up I voluntarily added student, wife, mother, daughter-in-law, sister-in-law and well, the point is the list is never ending. We are all defined in countless ways everyday and we accept those definitions without thought or pause.

And, yet, sometimes we do ourselves a disservice if we don't really examine the roles others cast us in and then identify the roles in which we'd like to cast ourselves. The beauty of being human is the ability to choose our hats and wear them, not just for function, but for beauty's sake.

Three years ago I did just that and added one of my most profound hats to my collection. I became a writer. Now, you may be of the opinion that writers are born with pens in hand, but alas, you'd be wrong. Writers are indeed created. They tend to be readers who one day wake up mid-book and say, "How I wish I could do that." Now the great thing is, they indeed can do that. Put pen to paper, push mightily and words will flow. Oh, sometimes they're just spatters sprinkling the page, but sometimes they trip over themselves in their anxiousness to find their release.

Now, writing and selling are two separate kettles of fish. But, today we're talking about the act of writing and hats. So, there I was, a thirty-ish mother of four who had played with words for a while and finally decided that she wanted more than just play, she wanted to WRITE. I always saw it in sort of capital letters, bigger than the rest of life.

Unfortunately, with four children, nothing can be bigger. Even though I now feel as if I can timidly call myself a writer, I've found I still must wipe snotty noses, chauffeur children and elderly relatives, and pass out hugs and hollers in turn. I still have to cook (though I'm ever hopeful my family will grow tired of my cooking and suggest eating out every night) and clean toilets and do laundry--and with six people in the house I do mean LAUNDRY with capital letters.

Advancing from a reader to a writer was a profound step and it's impacted

Mama Told Me There'd Be Days Like This

my life in many positive ways, but it's also added a whole new batch of mother guilt. I look at my four year old and wonder if my taking time out of our day will somehow stunt her. I mean, I actually expect her to entertain herself. What kind of mother does that make me?

Today I was in the middle of a stupendous river of thought that was carrying my fingers along, telling the story on its own, when she started screaming, "Mom," in that excited way that only four year olds can.

I stopped mid-stream and turned around. She was standing at the foot of the stairs by a window holding her metallic pinwheel and the sun was hitting it in such a way that it created lightning bolts of colored reflections on the wall.

To a four year old this was magic, and to her mother it was just as magical. My laptop was forgotten along with my story. For a few moments I enjoyed the wonder of light splashed across the wall, but more than that, I enjoyed the wonder of viewing life through a four-year-old set of eyes.

Life is a huge juggling act, like the children's story,'*Caps For Sale* by Esphyr Slobodkina, we walk rather carefully so none of our hats slip. The hats we are born with rest at the bottom and the hats we pick up along life's way are stacked on top. It's a busy sort of life, this collecting of hats, and sometimes they can become quite heavy. At those moments we have to sit under a tree, prop up our feet and rest and take a chance that the monkeys will mess with our balancing act. Suddenly the blue caps, the brown caps, the gray caps and the red caps might be tumbling down, a mixed up rainbow of hats.

Sometimes a pinwheel of light is worth some mixed up hats.

When I decided to add writer to the ways you can describe me, I thought it might be one of my most important designations. Now, don't get me wrong, calling me a writer is fine, but I never want it to get in the way of calling me mom, or calling me wife, or friend, or.

Well, maybe my point is, we have to stack our hats carefully. We have to pick and choose the ones that mean the most to us and put the ones that are too difficult in the closet. What is a writer without a life, without people in it sprinkling their world with ideas and joy? For me there could be no writing without my family --there's not much to say without them. And without writing, my life would be rather stale and flat. Some of the color would fade and I think I would have less to offer to the people I love.

So, I balance. I pick up all those hats every morning and try to make it through the day without spilling too many. And, I try to remember that pinwheels and little girls are worth more than all the pages of dialogue I'll ever write. So are sixteen- and fourteen-year-old stories of dances and boys, and nine-year-old boy's experiments in the basement.

Crumbs in the Keyboard

Like the peddler in the story who "walked up and down the streets, holding himself very straight so as not to upset his caps," I walk carefully, forever balancing my needs and their needs--my fulfillment and my mother's guilt. At the end of the day, I lean against a tree, my hats hopefully still balanced, and close my eyes, knowing I've done the best I can do.

And, who could ask for more?

Mama Told Me There'd Be Days Like This

Sushi Break
Elaine Hopper

"Come here," Johnny's husky baritone implored as he gazed deeply into Kayla's eyes and crooked his finger at her. His muscular frame towered over her, making her skin tingle, making her feel small and feminine. When he pulled her against him, he set her body aflame. He made the rest of the room fade away. The world could explode and she'd never know it, never care, as long as he held her against his heart.

Warm firm lips kissed the tip of her nose. His warm, minty breath tempted her as his lips lowered toward her mouth. Her lips parted on response. Her pulse raced. Nerves in her fingertips became hypersensitive as they slid around his neck and tangled in his glorious silky, sandy brown hair.

No doubt remained in her mind or her heart. "I love you" Pressing against him, lifting her insatiable lips for his soul-shattering kisses, she reached for rapture--

"Mom! Mom!" Ann blinked, trying to ignore the familiar yet alien voice coming at her through the haze.

Like a time traveler, she felt as if she were being sucked out of her preferred world, to another less desirable plane of existence.

"Veronica's on the phone for you." Seventeen-year old Kurt's voice was testy, as if he'd been trying to get her attention for several minutes. He carried a tattered pulp fiction book in his other hand.

Blinking again, mentally shaking herself free from the stranglehold her characters had on her, she tried to focus her gaze on her eldest son who was still blurry around the edges.

He thrust a black cell phone into her hand, muttering about rude older sisters interrupting important phone calls.

Ann glanced at the clock on her computer as she raised the phone to her mouth: 8:47 PM. "Hi sweetie, what's up?" She prayed the kids were going to a movie.

"We're done." Her daughters' sweet voice flowed through her ear. "Can you

Crumbs in the Keyboard

come get me?"

"No movie tonight?" Disappointment tinged her voice.

"Naaa. Most of the kids are broke." Kids joking around and road noise made it difficult to hear her daughter. She had to strain as the cell phone didn't have the best reception ever.

"You're still at the Sushi restaurant, right?"

"Yep, I'll be out front."

"I'll be there in a few." The phone beeped at her when she turned it off.

Kurt snatched it from her, pivoted on his heel and fled.

"Watch the little ones till I get back!" she called to his retreating back.

"Okay." He didn't sound like he was okay, but she would only be gone for a few minutes. "Be nice to your brother and sister." She turned to Sarah and Scottie, her nine-and five-year olds. "Be good for Kurt while I'm gone. I'll be right back."

"Where are you going, mama? Can we come?" Sarah 's beguiling blue eyes pleaded with her as Scottie clamped Ann's knees in a death grip.

What would it hurt? "Okay. But we're not buying anything. Capice?" She shook her finger at Sarah in rhythm to her words.

"Okay!" Sarah bounced up and down, clapping her hands. Thick mahogany hair bounced around her heart-shaped face.

"Yippee!" Scottie danced a jig, his baby brown's sparkling, quite a contrast with his golden blonde hair.

Ann patted Scottie's little bottom and ruffled Sarah's hair. "Run get in the van. " Raising her voice she called to Kurt, "I'm taking the babies with me."

"Okay."

Grabbing her keys and hanging her purse on her shoulder, she ran out of the door. The quicker she collected Veronica, the quicker she could return to Johnny and Kayla and that almost steamy kiss. It was sufficient incentive to break the speed limit.

True to her word, Miss Veronica waited outside the Sushi House, her back pack hanging nonchalantly over one shoulder, her black leather bound artists sketchbook cradled in the crook of her other arm. Shaggy hair hung over her eyes. She waved to Ann and the kids.

"Hi mom!" Veronica scrambled into the front seat of the van, then waved goodbye to her friends. Neon lights from the Sushi House illuminated them from behind. Most everyone carried a sketchbook. Some people drew, some read,

Mama Told Me There'd Be Days Like This

some were writers. Her daughter's world was populated by all kinds.

"Did you have fun?" Ann shifted gears and headed the van homeward. Traffic ran heavy at the movie house so she eased into it.

"Jason broke up with Larissa, but she still came." Excitement laced Veronica's voice.

Ann slid a knowing look to her eldest child. "You like him?"

"Just as a friend." Veronica riffled through her old worn book bag and pulled out some videotapes. "Brett let me borrow more Sailor Moon and Dragonball Z tapes. And Elliott says he'll pay me to draw his portrait."

"Kewl, "Ann drawled, her heart swelling with pride. "For how much?"

Veronica giggled. "That depends on how well I do. Between $15 and $25." That was a fortune to her starving artist daughter who sold fan art sketches for $1 and $2 a pop.

"You'll be famous soon."

Veronica blushed prettily.

"Mama! Mama!" Sarah bounced in her seat, shaking the van. "Can Scottie and I get Burger King?" She pointed at the sign with the golden crown as if she were a pointing Setter.

Ann cursed herself. She should've gone the long, back way home. She met Sarah's pleading eyes in the mirror. The girl had her hands folded under her chin as if this were her most fervent wish in the universe.

"I told you I was not going to stop anywhere or buy anything. I don't know that I have any money."

Scottie chimed in, "Please, Mommy." His big brown eyes reflected in her mirror.

"I have extra money. I sold some anime pictures." Veronica pulled out a wad of singles and a fistful of change that jingled. "You can pay me back."

Gee Thanks!

"Yippee!" Scottie clapped his hands.

Please hang on, Ann implored Johnny and Kayla. *I'll get back to you in a few more minutes. Keep those lips puckered a little longer.*

"Can I get a frozen Coke and a Kid's meal?" Sarah asked. "With a toy?"

"Me too! Me too!" Scottie's jumping up and down threatened to shake the van apart.

"I'll take a frozen Coke, too, Mom," Veronica said.

"You have enough there?"

Crumbs in the Keyboard

Veronica's lips turned up in a shy smile, "I sold a lot of pictures."

The calculator in Ann's mind quickly informed her after she'd paid for all those expensive Prismatic pencils and paper, they were losing money on the deal. But her daughter was nurturing her God-given talent and keeping out of trouble-- even if she smelled like raw fish every Friday and lived for the day she could move to Japan. She was going to be fine.

"Okay." Ann rummaged in her purse and came up with six dollars to add to Veronica's money.

When she ordered, she treated herself to a frozen Coke, too. It was one of her vices. The smell of onions and ketchup nearly gagged her when she passed the food to Veronica to hold. Taking her chances, she passed out the drinks. "Don't spill these, and make sure you brush your teeth when you get home."

Slurping her own frozen Coke, she pulled into traffic and headed home. Finally, they pulled into their driveway and she cut the ignition. "Help the little ones inside and watch them so I can finish my scene," Ann instructed Veronica, then practically vaulted to the computer.

Dismay engulfed her when she reached it. Truffles, their tabby cat, pranced on her keyboard as if he were playing piano.

"Scat cat!" Ann hissed, and pounced for him. He moved faster, and she grabbed thin air. Examining her monitor, her worst fears were confirmed. She'd forgotten to close her story before she left the house. And now, the cats had attacked it. HTML-like code littered the screen.

Leaning over her chair, her butt in the air, she scrolled upward as fast as her greedy fingers, and the computer, allowed. "Hang in there, Johnny, " she mumbled under her breath, praying the cat hadn't murdered him or Kayla.

When her text came into view, she collapsed into her chair in major relief, her heartbeat slowly de-escalating. Highlighting Truffle's uninvited contribution to Johnny's story, she deleted it and saved the story. Then she cracked her knuckles.

"Where were we?"

Skimming the sea of words, she mumbled "Uh huh", "good", "change this", "delete this", "uhm" as she re-read her work. She slurped her almost unfrozen Coke as she read. The smell of onions and ketchup permeated the house now. She tried to ignore it and get back in to the romantic mindset.

"I love you, too" Johnny murmured against Kayla's eager lips. When his warn lips captured hers, Ann typed, *they tasted like raw fish and Kayla gagged,*

Mama Told Me There'd Be Days Like This

her stomach churning. Tearing herself from Johnny, Kayla screeched. "Blech! I hate sushi! I hate raw fish!"

"Well you tasted like raw onions and ketchup. " He pulled a large bottle of minty breath-freshener out of his back pocket and held it out to Kayla. "Try this. You'll taste minty fresh and be kissable again."

Kayla looked at the green concoction, then she shifted her skeptical gaze to Johnny's face. Grabbing the bottle, she tried to open it, grunting.

Johnny took it from her. "It's child-proof. See?" He squeezed the trick cap and pulled it off and handed her the bottle. "You'll smell as good as Sailor Moon."

"You're a jerk!" Kayla yanked the bottle from Johnny's grip and poured its contents over his head. "Now you smell minty fresh , too." She stomped away.

Ann's fingers finally stopped flying over the keyboard. "Ugh!" She leaned her forehead on the monitor full of pure drivel. "I've lost the mood. I can't do this! Johnny's a jerk. Kayla's a shrew. My career's doomed!"

Sarah padded up behind her and began massaging her neck. "It's okay, Mama. Want some chocolate? That'll make you all better."

"Yes, baby girl. I'd like that." Chocolate and a Stephen King movie. Maybe the muse would return tomorrow. Maybe at 3 am. Who knew? He was an elusive muse, that one.

She saved her work and shut down her computer and looked at her kids. They were still there, no matter what.

Scottie, seeing her turn, bounded up to her, crawled in her lap and gave her a giant hug. "I love you, Mommy. " Petal soft lips caressed her cheek. It was a wonderful sensation, filling her with warm, gooey feelings. Even if she smelled of onions and ketchup. Even if his fingers were sticky.

She hugged and kissed him back. "I love you, too, baby boy."

There Are No Shortcuts
Or
I'd Love To Get My Hands On The Person Who Invented The Toilet Brush
Sheryl Hames Torres

A wise person used to hurl clichés at me on Saturday morning. "There are no shortcuts in life so put down that toilet brush." It used to irritate the life out of me. She also said, "you'll understand when you're married and have kids." I hated that one, too. We won't even get into "rise and shine...early bird gets the worm."

The thing was, how could a little thing like using a toilet brush ruin my chances at having a normal life and a successful career? It wasn't like I was going to be a maid, or...gulp...*just a mother.*

No, I was going to do something with my life. This was the day of the bra-burning-we-can-control-the-world woman, and I was going to be one of them. I wasn't going to waste *my* life cleaning toilets and wiping snotty noses. *I* was going to be a *writer*.

She just smiled and said, "Well, tuck your bra away in the back of your drawer and pretend you don't own one. Just see to it that you have to wear it when you leave the house. For now, though, get in there and clean the bathroom the right way. Oh, and make no mistake, we *do* control the world. Ask your father if you don't believe me."

"How can you say that?" I grumbled. "All you are is a mother."

She just smiled. "You'll understand when you're married and have children."

Oh, how I hated that. She just didn't understand. Using the toilet brush allowed me more time for my writing. Why couldn't she understand that? I had an important, absolutely pivotal, chapter to work on. If I spent all that extra time with my hands down in the toilet, I'd forget what I wanted to write.

After all, I didn't like cluttering up my workspace with things like notes, outlines, character sheets. I could write by the seat of my pants and it would be perfect when I turned it into Mr. Strauss on Monday morning. *If* I *ever* got finished with the stupid bathroom.

The following Saturday I didn't grumble about not being able to use the toilet brush. That morning's grumbles centered around those outlines and notes and character sheets.

Why couldn't Mr. Strauss see what a brilliant writer I was? I mean sure, I was no Emily Loring, or Grace Livingston Hill, or Catherine Marshall, or even S. E. Hinton, but I was incredibly good for an eleven-year-old. He said so himself. So why did I have to outline the stupid story? Didn't I get enough of doing outlines in Social Studies?

There are no shortcuts in life, honey.

How did she do that? She was all the way down in the laundry room.

You'll understand when you are married and have children.

Oh, I hated when she did that.

So, I cleaned the stupid bathroom and worked out the stupid outline, and found that with time, I'd perfected both to a lot less time than myriad rewrites and rescrubs. Besides, I could always use the time I spent with my hand in the toilet working out difficult scenes and putting my thoughts in order. So what if my brothers teased me about talking to myself. They were just jealous because no one talked to them.

Now, thirty years later, I have post-it notes framing my monitor, a stack of character sheets, and outlines for enough stories to keep me busy right into the *next* millennium.

And I still talk to myself while I'm scrubbing, as if my own personal muse resides in the rippling waters in that *pristine* porcelain bowl.

There's a little shriek of horror from behind me as my ten-year-old daughter looks on in astonishment. "Mama, why do you have your *hand in the toilet?*"

My eight year-old son rushes out of his room to see what the commotion is about and adds his sage suggestion. "Maybe she dropped something in there. I hear her talking to herself again."

"Well," my daughter muses, "it's a good thing for her, I just cleaned it."

I think I'll call my mother today.

Out of The Mouths of Babes
Julie Pitzel

Shortly after I had joined West Houston RWA, I was with my ten-year old son in the book section of Wal-Mart. There on the shelf was anew book by Susan Wiggs.
"I know this person." I said.
I had been writing a couple of years, taking classes, and leaving Ryan with baby-sitters while I went to classes, meetings, and critique groups.
I took the book off the shelf, amazed I'd actually met someone who'd accomplished something I'd only dreamed of.
"Don't worry, Mom." Ryan put his little hand on my arm and looked at me. "You'll get published someday."
I haven't yet, but I know who I'll acknowledge in that first book.

Mama Told Me There'd Be Days Like This

My Mom Writes Books!
Elizabeth Delisi

When I first started writing, I was married but had no children. I did have a full-time job, but once I had put in my eight hours, my time was my own. I spent evenings and weekends with a notebook in hand or seated at the typewriter, writing one short story after another, immersed in my fantasy world. It was wonderful.

Then, along came kids. I gave up my job to stay home and care for them, and figured an added bonus would be all the extra time I'd have to write.

Boy, was I wrong!

Having a baby instantly triples your workload. Not only do you have cooking to do, but you have bottles and infant food to fix, and you have to nurse the baby. You don't just have laundry to do; you also have dozens of diapers, crib sheets, and sleepers to wash. You have a husband who wants some of your time when he's home, and a baby who wants attention and is home all of the time. It can be overwhelming and exhausting, especially to a new mother.

The first thing I learned was what I call the "Baby/Time Axiom." Although that adorable baby is tiny, his or her needs will expand to fill all your available free time. And I very quickly discovered the "Baby/Brain Corollary"-if you DO manage to squeeze out any free time, your brain will be too fried to turn out anything resembling intelligent writing.

Since I didn't want to give up writing altogether, I had to develop some defense mechanisms and time-use strategies in order to ever get anything down on paper besides a shopping list.

First, I learned to keep my notebook handy or my work-in-progress sitting next to the typewriter. Although it didn't look as neat as I liked, the time wasted in getting out the material each time I had a spare minute to write was worth putting up with the small amount of clutter.

Then, I had to find a way to get more of the necessary housework, laundry and baby care done while the baby was awake, since that time was pretty useless as far as writing went. A miracle device allowed me to do this: a "*Snugli*" brand

Crumbs in the Keyboard

baby carrier.

The baby carrier looked like a backpack of sorts, that I could either strap to my back or my chest and zip the baby inside. I used it mostly in the chest position. There was a small "seat" inside for tiny babies, and when the baby got larger, the outside "seat" was used. I spent many hours with the baby snapped and zipped into the *Snugli*, where there was lots of contact between us with the baby contentedly cuddled against me, but both my hands were free to sweep, dust, vacuum, fold clean diapers, or fix dinner.

I also discovered that grocery shopping was easier with the *Snugli*. I just popped the baby into the carrier as soon as I got out of the car, and shopped with both hands free. If the baby started fussing while I was waiting in the checkout line, all I had to do was rock back and forth a little, and that solved the problem.

Next, I learned to rethink what I considered "enough" time to sit down and write. In my pre-child existence, I didn't dream of writing unless I had at least an hour of uninterrupted time. Post-child, it was important for me to realize that as little as ten minutes could be put to good use.

And the final thing I had to do was to learn HOW to use those ten-minute blocks of time effectively. I could no longer afford to waste ten or fifteen precious minutes assembling my materials and getting "in the mood" to write. If I had only ten minutes, I wanted to write for nine of them.

Ten minutes might only be enough time to allow me to write a paragraph or two, rather than the five or ten pages that I could accomplish in an hour. But writing a paragraph or two once or twice a day would allow me to complete a short story in a month, or a novel in a year. That's something I wouldn't have to show for wasting those ten free minutes every day.

A quick and easy way for me to get back into the flow of my writing was to re-read the last paragraph or two of what I had written the previous time. That helped put me in the mood quickly, and got me right back into the thick of the story. I also discovered the advantages of working from an outline: with an outline, you always know "what comes next."

In addition, I found it helped if I thought about the story and where it was headed shortly before I sat down to write. Since many baby-care chores like changing a diaper or doing the laundry require little mental attention, I was able to work out plot ideas and bits of dialogue in advance. Then, when I sat down with the notebook or at the typewriter, I was "supercharged" and raring to go!

Of course, there were difficult times over the years when trying to write

Mama Told Me There'd Be Days Like This

with small children. There was the time that grape juice was mysteriously spilled on my manuscript pages, and the time when I was so caught up in the scene I was writing that I forgot to pick up my son from his preschool. But the rewards for continuing to pursue my dream were countless, and outweighed all the difficulties.

My proudest moment came when my youngest daughter came home from kindergarten one day, and said they had been asked to tell the class what their parents did for a living. When it was her turn, she stood up and said, "My daddy conducts orchestras, and my mommy writes books."

Her classmates all told her, "You're so lucky to have parents that do such cool stuff!"

I hugged her, and beamed for the rest of the day. After all, isn't that what being a mom, and a writer, is all about?

Crumbs in the Keyboard

Peace Between the Lines
Marilynn Griffith

It was the peak of summer. My house was full of children and my sink was full of dishes. My refrigerator was empty and so was my brain.

My characters in my novel, usually brave enough to come out amid any chaos, took one look around and retreated to the quiet recesses of my mind. My wonderful children kept interrupting my pleas to Brian, Ron and Gail with silly questions like, "What's for dinner?"

I reached for the peanut butter and jelly, insulted that they could think of food at a time like this. Didn't anybody know I had a book to write?

I searched for the bread. There was none.

My two-year-old flung himself to the floor. Mutiny was on the horizon.

"No problem. We'll have cereal," I said. There was air in the space where the milk should have been. I was in trouble now. Big trouble.

I pulled out a limp piece of celery and reached for the peanut butter again. "How about a healthy snack?"

My kids weren't buying it. "Mom, there's no food. What are we going to do?" my oldest daughter asked with tears in her eyes. I made a mental note to work on her optimism.

Two days before, on shopping day, my characters wouldn't shut up. They talked up ten pages. At the time, I was overjoyed. Now, I was hungry.

A car engine sounded in the distance. Dad. I should have been happy to see him, but I wasn't. I was just plain mad. Could it be this hard to write one lousy book?

I scrambled for the keys and squeezed past my husband on my way to the car.

"Get some gas quick, before you run out," he said

I opened my mouth and then shut it again. "Okay," I called back, fumbling at the car door for the right key.

My husband was still in the doorway. He watched me back out with a look in his eye that said, "Make it quick." He didn't have to say it. I already knew.

I made it quick, in fact I almost flattened several old ladies on the bread

Mama Told Me There'd Be Days Like This

aisle. Several frustrated minutes later, I returned home and sprinted into the house with my purchases, ready to soothe the savage beasts.

When I walked in, the house was quiet. My children, well fed on a feast of scrambled eggs and lemonade prepared by their father, were fast asleep.

My husband still in his work clothes, headed for the shower. "You can write now. It's all done," he said, before blowing me a kiss.

I nodded and watched him walk away.

Alone in the kitchen, I pondered the fine line between the urgent and the important. I decided that my characters needed some boundaries to govern their time with me. After all, I was writing a story every day--on the hearts of family.

Everything Has Its Season
Lisa Marie Long

"Mommy, come play with me, *please*." My three-year-old's plaintive cry tugs at my heart.

I sigh and glance longingly at the laptop on the kitchen table. I was hoping to at least turn it on today. Thoughts of unfinished laundry and emptying the dishwasher flit through my mind. A hungry cat rubs my leg. Oh, yeah, and that cat box needs changing. There's always something that needs doing, and it always means putting off my writing.

There are times I feel divided between guilt and resentment, when I wish for the days when my son's naps were every two hours and I actually had time for myself, when I could pursue any of my varied interests, or even write when the fancy struck.

There was a time when I could sit down at the keyboard and write a whole chapter in a chunk, or have the entire afternoon to read half a novel. Those were the days when I had the house to myself all day, the pre-motherhood days. Now, I'm lucky if I get a spare moment to jot down a line or two. I keep a pad and pen next to the bed in case I get any brilliant ideas or lines of conversation to start my writing off the next morning. I used to jot them down by the light of the electric blanket dial when I was struggling with insomnia.

Motherhood cured my insomnia. These days, I don't even remember hitting the pillow before my human alarm clock is climbing into bed with me and telling me to wake up. So much for brilliant ideas.

I'm currently working on my third novel. It's no coincidence that I started it when my son started toddling, and that I'm still writing it. They seem to take longer and longer to write. I spend less and less time actually working at my keyboard, and more time cleaning, picking up after my family, and doing errands. My days are occupied with mealtimes, nap times, swimming lessons, play dates, doctor, dentist and veterinarian appointments, trips to the park and the Children's Museum, the Zoo, and myriad other things that have nothing to do with writing, unless it involves a sticky note reminder.

"Mommy?" My son's expectant face is aimed at me, waiting. It's my move.

I sigh. Then smile. He's my one and only child, how can I deny him?

Mama Told Me There'd Be Days Like This

I once read in Home Education Magazine a reader response to a parent's concern that she had no time for herself while home schooling her children. The reader gave a bit of Eastern philosophy to the woman: " You can't have it all at once. Everything has its season." Those words were a mental slap upside the head that made me take a look at what I had in my life, not what I wished for. After several years of the diaper and bottle grind, and entering the terrible twos (which, I am told, last for two decades), I had forgotten.

I had forgotten the years when I rattled around the house all alone and stared longingly out the window, wishing for the baby that took us eight years to have. I kept the door to the nursery closed, because every visit inside sent me into tears for the babies I had conceived and lost. I had a hole in my heart and I hurt. And then a courageous woman chose me to be her baby's mother.

I became a mother, through adoption. And the hole in my heart closed up.

At that moment, when I first held my little baby boy, I did have it all. But as all mothers know, priorities change. Gradually, I let my own activities and "Me Time" slip away to devote it to my family. But I resented it at times. And the guilt flowed in to make me feel worse. Until I read those wise words.

"Everything has its season." I know, deep down, that I'm not really ready at this time in my life to have my books published, to have deadlines and editing and promotion to worry about. I've got work to do right here, right now, with the young mind and body growing before my eyes. Now is *his* time. My time will come, and then I can direct my energy into my writing and career. Then I can worry about how many pages a day I can produce and deal with the frustration of the endless waiting game with editors while I dream of the glamorous book signings in my future. Then I can have all the time in the world to devote to whatever I wish. Then I can truly be the writer I want to be.

But right now, all thoughts of writing are chased away by my son's glowing smile as I join him on the living room floor to reconstruct his wooden railway. Right now, at this moment, I am the entire world to a certain little boy, and that beats sitting at the keyboard any day.

Another day, another season, I'll continue my dream. It's not gone, not changed, nor forgotten. I'm just not ready to see that dream realized yet. My life is full and rich and I'm happy, even if the most creative bit of writing I do this week is to tell my husband to take out the garbage.

"I love you, Mommy."

And that makes my life complete.

Crumbs in the Keyboard

Grand Theft Manuscript
Carrie Weaver

"It's just a bunch of dumb words on paper." That was the five year-old boy's only defense for grand theft manuscript.

Outrage pulsed through my veins. He'd committed an unpardonable crime and his punishment would be severe.

His eyes glazed with fear. But he drew on all his baby dignity and raised his chin in defiance. His gaze met mine, then slid away. He knew what happened to criminals like him. It wouldn't be pretty.

Gnashing teeth, flying spittle, banshee-like screams of pain.

That's when I saw my distorted reflection in the mirror and realized I'd never be the same again.

I was an author.

With two active boys, every inch of the house was fair game in their quest to destroy. Everywhere, except my desk. It was strictly off limits. No exceptions. Not even my husband dared disturb a scrap of paper or play a computer game on the sly. Because getting caught meant instant reprisal.

Yet, this stubborn child had braved the veins popping out on my forehead, my hair standing on end. Why?

He needed some paper to draw on. And after all, Mom had paper *everywhere*. On top of the desk, under the desk, loaded in the printer, piled by the shredder, stacked on the file cabinet. It was a veritable plethora of artistic supplies. So what if one side had line after line of print? The other side was still good.

Who could blame the boy for coveting all that lovely paper?

I could. It was my dream, my career. My desk area was the only place where I had my own identity, not simply an appendage of someone else. I was an author. Sure, I was still a wife and mother. But there was this sacred creative world I could enter when my other life grew too tedious or overwhelming. Where I could escape, if only for an hour or two. Or a minute or two.

"It's just a bunch of dumb words on paper."

Mama Told Me There'd Be Days Like This

The truth dawned. My family would never comprehend my dream. They might humor me, tiptoe around me as I wrote, give me an occasional 'atta girl.' But they would never understand what it meant to my soul, my very being. How, by some miracle I didn't quite understand, I was able to create living, breathing characters who did exactly as I told them. That was on a good day.

The bad days were nearly as numerous. Characters who fought me, fought amongst themselves, mutinied at every turn.

Then there was the editing. Root canals, pap smears, and parent/teacher conferences were preferable to a day of editing. But it had to be done. Each word, each sentence, evaluated and manipulated until my eyes crossed.

My reward was the finished manuscript, neatly stacked, bound together by dreams. Only to return battered and rejected, but still precious in my eyes.

It was a vicious cycle of creativity and nitpicking. Hope and despair. And I couldn't stop any more than I could refuse a Hershey bar on a tense day.

My family learned valuable lessons throughout the cycle. Never touch anything on Mom's desk, no matter how badly you need scratch paper. Nod and say, "um-hum" when she goes on and on about her latest plot. And never, *ever*, refer to it as "a bunch of dumb words on paper."

Like my favorite romance novels, this story had a happy ending. A few of my manuscripts were eventually published. And the five year-old juvenile delinquent learned the error of his ways. He discovered the magic of the written word and even, upon occasion, read for pleasure. Years later, as he created a hypothetical guest list for a sixth grade class project, whom do you think was the "famous" person he invited? You guessed it. His mom. The woman who put all those dumb words on paper. Pretty nice affirmation from a twelve year-old.

Crumbs in the Keyboard

Day-To-Day Determination
Jennifer Turner

As a mother of three, two of whom are still in diapers, I would have thought becoming a writer would be my dream job. I get to live in a fantasy world, work in my pajamas and eat chocolate to celebrate the completion of meeting self-imposed deadlines. Which on good days could be five thousand words, and on bad, when the craving for chocolate becomes overwhelming, might only be one word.

There are days when I wake up, the bluebirds bring my slippers to me, someone else has made coffee, and I've slept through, blissfully, without a midnight feeding to administer. But normally, I find the cat on my slippers, stubbornly refusing to give up his warm bed. The coffee has been made my two year old, grounds and apple juice in Mommy's favorite cup. And I've spent half the night rocking the eight-month-old back to sleep.

After the morning is over, and the scrambled eggs are diligently cleaned from the ceiling fan, the top of the fridge, and from beneath the placemats. I set the children to play, or if it's been a long night, down for a nap. Finally I'm free to compose, to play with my muse, to--

Answer the phone and delay another bill collector. After the nervous thumbing through of my budget calendar, I'm in no shape to begin writing. I tell myself that I can have a tasty bit of chocolate if I'll only open my novel and edit the last half of what I wrote before. A few clicks later, I'm on a roll. The words are coming together. The story isn't half bad. I finish the edit, and reach for a chocolate when my oldest comes barging in.

"Mom, can we go to the park?" He's hopeful, big blue eyes pleading at me. "Not now, sweetheart. Later, when the babies wake up. " Or starts crying, I think.

He shrugs; he knows the routine. I write one sentence and he comes bouncing in the room. "When we go to the park, can my friend come?"

Mentally, I picture four kids crammed into my small station wagon, two in car seats. "I don't think so, maybe, we'll see."

He groans and looks like he's ready to take it to the next level, but I hold a

Mama Told Me There'd Be Days Like This

hand up and turn purposefully back to the computer. I am working.

The door closes and the characters pull me back in. I am writing! The words are flowing, the blank page is turning into an epic of sweeping sunsets and lovers embracing and wild horses and a baby crying--no, wait, that's *here*.

I pull myself forcefully away from my prose and rush to see the problem. Double diaper duty calls. Twenty minutes later I remove the gas mask and dust the baby powder from my hair, wondering if it's really already that color.

Lunch is served. The babies are hosed off and I'm cramming four kids in the station wagon. The fresh air will surely inspire me. I take notice of the birds, the trees, the way the river glints happily in the sun, the screaming of children in the back seat, the cries of--"Are we there yet?"

And worse, "I have to pee."

I sit with a good book that will give me insight into this thing they call 'the craft'. Like it's a spell to cast, or a bloodline that you must be born into. Finally, it's time to head home. I fasten seatbelts and wonder why, only a few short hours ago, the kids all fit so much better.

A quick whirlwind clean of the house while dinner is cooking. Noodles simmer like the plot lines in my head. Spaghetti sauce thickens like the character's personalities. I don't question my own decision for spaghetti after the previous meals, but I do as I'm mopping sauce from the floor.

Bath time. One, two, three, heads of hair smelling sweetly of baby shampoo. One, two, babies tucked in their cribs, three is watching the latest cartoon offering for thirty minutes before he, too, will fall asleep. And I'm back in front of my computer, feeling inspired and ready for a long night of writing.

One paragraph, two sentences, and the third word ends in a long period, my finger asleep on the key…

Spaces of Time
Jacqueline Elliott

Sometimes writing can be a challenge. Add a husband, two children, and a job to the mixture and it becomes a struggle to find balance. I suppose I'm lucky. The kids are both in school, husband at his job, and I work in the evenings, so I spend most of the day in front of the computer. Then summer hits and my days turn upside down. No more chatting with my writer buddies online, no silence in the house while I try to find another word for 'panted' as cartoons blare in the next room. It's very difficult to pour your heart and soul into a love scene when the echoes of your children's voices bounce off the walls.

Painting an intimate scene with your hero and heroine is very private business. Your heart races along with the heroine's, your palms sweat, and you get those wonderful little butterflies in the pit of your stomach. The last thing you want to hear as you type *'Carlotta shuddered in ecstasy when she slid her palm down Jake's--'* is, "Mom! I'm done!" If you're a mother you know what those three little words mean. Instantly, you're transformed from Carlotta, the love goddess, to Mom, the domestic goddess.

Since the kids are on summer break and with me during most of their waking hours, I've found a system to write by. My daughter, Jayline is now twelve and my son, Jesse is seven. I write as much as I can in the morning before they're fully alert, quit for an hour to welcome my husband home for lunch, chase him out the door at twelve forty-five. Then, for some reason, the kids need attention. We spend a little time outside as I watch how long they can hold their breath underwater in the pool, while I'm thinking of what Carlotta and Jake are up to in the bathtub.

A few weeks ago, I took one of those afternoon writing breaks with Jesse. He begged me to watch him ride his bike in circles. Just for five minutes. I was writing on a self-imposed deadline--I didn't have my manuscript completely polished when I queried a couple of editors. Who knew that it would only take a week for one of them to request the entire story? Maybe writers who are wives and mothers need to live on the edge, so they feel compelled to break that rule, 'completed manuscripts only'. I learned my lesson.

So Jesse rode around in circles while I counted minutes in my head.

Mama Told Me There'd Be Days Like This

"Okay, Jess, I have to go in now," I told my little towhead as he popped a wheelie in front of me.

Jesse climbed off his bike, leaned it over on the lawn, and pushed his glasses up his cute button nose. "Why don't you just quit writing today? Aren't you tired of it?"

"I'm almost done, Jesse," I told him with a sigh.

"How many pages do you have left?" he asked as he sat in the rocking chair on the patio and kicked his bare feet back and forth.

I winced at the sound of skin scraping against cement and remember kissing the soles of his soft little baby feet not too long ago. "I think about a hundred."

His feet stopped. "A hundred? That's a lot of pages. Can I help?"

I smiled at my little ray of sunshine. "I don't think you can this time."

"Are you sure? I'm real good at typing spaces."

I knelt down, gathered him to my chest, and kissed the top of his sweaty head. Tears blurred my vision as my heart raced and butterflies fluttered in the pit of my stomach.

Crumbs in the Keyboard

Steps to Writing Time
Robin Bayne

Being a stepmother is as time consuming as being a natural mom, especially when you have full-time custody of your stepchild. But you can still find time to yourself, for writing, and your family can help. Before you decide to bring in outside help, try to organize your family members into a working team. It's worth the effort, as long as you keep your sense of humor. Before my husband and I married, he brought a young lady over from France as an "*au pair*." He was helping friends who wanted their relative to see this country, and he thought he'd introduce a bit of culture into his home.

Unfortunately, little Timmy never learned a word of French, but we certainly learned a few things. For example, when you employ an *au pair*, be sure to check the bathroom wastebaskets after dinner for your son's green beans, especially when she has her boyfriend over for dinner.

Be prepared to purchase multiple kitchen appliances, because Europeans don't have the same skills with these. Coffeemakers go bad when coffee is repeatedly poured back through the water intake, whole eggs explode in the microwave, range top burners will break off when stretched straight into the air and dryers can clog when large handfuls of softener sheets are tossed in a single load. Europeans drive faster than we do, so don't let her use your five-speed sports car. Keep an eye on the phone bill, and be prepared to eat some very unusual dinners when it's her turn to cook. Think onions.

After we married, and the *au pair* was off and married, I decided writing was a priority and that I needed time after work to pursue it. My husband is a natural helper with laundry and the big projects, like windows and floors, so it was only the daily chores that needed planning. Here's what I have learned over the years: At age 7, children can learn to pick up their toys as a game. They clean them up and hide them from the dog. At age 8, children can learn to vacuum and dust their own bedrooms. Just tell them to dust around anything breakable. Before they suck up the dust bunnies, they can name them. At age 9, children can start learning to sort laundry and start the machines. Make sure they

Mama Told Me There'd Be Days Like This

understand how to measure the soap! At age 10, have them read to the younger kids in the family. Make it fun by having them play teacher and administer a quiz after the story. At age 11, they can clean their own bathroom. Make it educational by installing a clear shower curtain with a map of the world on it. At age 12, children can open cans and heat stuff in the microwave. Make sure they know not to hard-boil eggs in it! At age 13, children can take your place helping your spouse with household projects; holding the nail in place, raking leaves, carrying logs in for the fireplace.

When it's your turn to take the kids to Little League or gymnastics, plan to stay for the hour or two and take your notebook along. You can cheer half the time and scribble the rest. Take the kids to the public library—they're not really quiet anymore, anyway. Get your kids involved with the local theater. It sounds time consuming, but turned out to be a great experience when my son won the part of Tiny Tim in the community college's musical, Scrooge. For months, we went several times weekly for practice. While he sang on stage, I was alone in an empty auditorium with my notebook. Have your spouse stay home with the other kids, and you can be the saint who has to traipse out at night.

When your child tells someone his mom is a writer, it's a great feeling that brings an inner glow. It gives meaning to all the unmade beds, unmatched socks and unidentified containers in the back depths of your refrigerator. Just make sure you buy a little computer vacuum for those 'crumbs in the keyboard.'

Steps

There are steps in my house,
Leading to the room he must clean.
He yells, "You're not my real mother!"
and I retort, "You're not my real son! But I love
you as if you were."
He's surprised,
and he cleans
his room.

Crumbs in the Keyboard

To My Children
Tabatha Yeatts

My children have always been part of my writing. I started a publication about women making a difference in metro Atlanta three months before my first child was due. I remember interviewing someone for it on the day after my due date and hoping that I wouldn't go into labor during the interview. As it turned out, I didn't have anything to worry about because my daughter didn't arrive for another week!

After her birth, I took a one-issue sabbatical, but then I kept going. I loved what I was doing, and I think my excitement and energy carried over into my parenting. I remember the day when I was offered my first book contract. To say that I was thrilled would be an understatement. I was so excited that I had to get out of the house, so I put my daughter (then 18 months) into our baby backpack and went for a walk. The whole time, I was talking to her/myself about how GREAT it was. I even made someone I didn't know laugh by repeating "Great!" so many times! I don't think I stopped smiling during the entire outing. A walk with a toddler may seem like a very simple pleasure, but I still remember it four years later.

Which is not to say that she has always been as excited about my work as I have been. One occasion when she was a couple of years older, I received a check in the mail for my first fiction sale. Having no one else around at the time to share my news with (a common problem for at-home workers!), I tried to tell her about it, but my daughter couldn't even pretend to find it interesting. I explained to her that it was nice to be happy for someone you love when something good happens to them. Now, no matter how boring she finds my work news, she always says, "That's great, Mom!" It may not be sincere, but it's still pleasant to hear, especially when there isn't another grown-up around!

I often dedicate my books to my children, but when I write short pieces and poetry, those are frequently about my children. Here is something I wrote in 1998:

As I await the birth of my second child, I hold in my heart the wishes I have for both my children. I wish them good health. I wish them happiness with who

Mama Told Me There'd Be Days Like This

they are.

I wish them kindness. I wish them a desire for justice. I wish them resilience. I wish them persistence. I wish them optimism. As their caregiver, teacher, and role model, today I will do what I can to see these wishes come true.

Writing and child care can feel like they aren't very compatible, but I think I have had to exhibit many of the qualities mentioned in my "wish list" for my kids in order to be a writer. Persistence and resilience for sure--and if I didn't have optimism, I would have quit long ago!

Crumbs in the Keyboard

Mom's Story
Rebecca Vineyard

I wrote my first book when I was pregnant with my first baby. The baby grew into a beautiful teenager. The book, also a teenager, lives in a trunk. It was so bad I doubt it will ever see the light of day. I like to think of it as my "practice" book.

I had the rough draft completed, but when it came time to do the edits, my baby girl arrived. Writing didn't seem possible, not when there was this marvelous creature around. After six months and a bad daycare experience, I quit my day job and became a stay-at-home mom.

Two years later, I had my second child. The book had long since been stowed away, but occasionally, I'd feel the urge to write. I'd satisfy it with a journal entry, or maybe a short story.

Since I wasn't "working", I ended up babysitting my sisters' children, too. I'd go to the grocery store with not two, but five toddlers in tow. "Are they all yours?" people would invariably ask when they saw my entourage. "Do I look *that* tired?" I would reply.

With so many little miracles around, the idea of writing seemed insane. But, you know, being a stay-at-home mom gets lonely. Little people whose idea of fascinating conversation is toys, food, and bodily functions surround you. Romance is out of the question. It's hard to feel sexy when you smell like diaper rash cream and have formula stains on your clothes.

Such a mom desperately needs an adult outlet. For writers, it's insane *not* to write. Your characters can give you all the conversation and company you need. But how in the world do you find the time?

Well, it can be done, but you gotta *really* want to do it. I started out writing stories longhand on legal pads. My local library offered "story time" for toddlers. Every week, I'd take my entourage to story time, and whilst they were being entertained, I'd either do research or work on my story.

This only gave me just one blessed hour of free time a week, but from that, I was able to build a schedule. I started writing when they napped. Or I'd wait and write after everyone went to bed. When they were awake, I'd work out plot

Mama Told Me There'd Be Days Like This

problems and plan the next scenes in my head. It's amazing how many story ideas a gal can get while folding the laundry or cleaning out the diaper pail.

Another year went by and my entourage got cut from five to three. Still, three active toddlers need a *lot* of attention. It took me two years to finish the second book. I immediately started working on the third one.

My youngest child had joined a T-ball team. I would bring my legal pads to his T-ball practices (never his games though) and tote them with me whenever I picked the kids up from school. . I did some of my best writing in the car.

Wait. My son's school just called. They think he has pink eye. So now, I need to call the doctor and run get the boy. Will write more when I get back.

Okay, I'm back. The boy's on the couch and I'm waiting for the doctors to call back. See? Even when the lil' darlin's aren't at home, they find ways to interrupt their writing mom.

But they won't interrupt very often once they get old enough to realize how important writing is to Mom. If I say, "I'm writing!" they know whatever the problem is, it better involve either blood or illness. Pink eye qualifies. I guess.

Bet I can finish this article before the doctor's office calls. If not, I'll try to finish it there. That's what writing at home is all about. Being FLEXIBLE. You write what you can, when you can. If you know you're stuck in the doctor's office; instead of reading an old magazine, work on your story! So what if the other patients think you're strange? You're WRITING, and that's all that matters.

Today, I have a teenager and pre-teen instead of toddlers. I still spend a lot of time in the car what with band practice, sports, dances and who knows what else. Instead of a legal pad, I use a mini-recorder and transpose my babblings onto the computer later. I try to get everything done while they're in school, but that's not always possible. When that happens, I slap on a pair of headphones to tune out the TV, computer games, and stereo, which sometimes they have running all at once. And keep on writing.

Other than that, not much has changed, except I've now finished six books. Two are currently in submission and two have been e-published.

Did all that writing influence how my kids have turned out? You bet! Both of them enjoy writing their own stories from time to time. They love to read. And a mom can't ask for better than that.

Except maybe a cure for pink eye. So, if you see a woman scribbling away in the doctor's office today, she's not strange. She's me.

I Owe My Career to Burger King
Laurie Schnebly Campbell

I owe my career to Burger King. Not just any Burger King, but the one that installed a ball-filled playground long before those became popular at every fast-food restaurant in Phoenix.

This Burger King, twenty minutes across town, is where I took my son for lunch every weekend while my husband worked at Lens Crafters. Four-year-old Christopher was always thrilled at a trip to the ball yard, where he could jump and slide and cavort among thousands of bright-colored balls while Mommy sat inside and watched him.

Well, yes, I watched but I also wrote. I'd always loved reading, and envied the woman we saw one afternoon who sat alone, sipping her coffee and reading a book from her purse. Someday, I thought wistfully, my son would be grown up and *I* could enjoy that kind of uninterrupted leisure.

Meanwhile, I wrote on the back of the Burger King placemats that lined our lunch tray. Every fifteen minutes or so I'd deal with Christopher's request for a drink refill or runaway ball-finding mission, but during those fourteen-minute breaks I wrote dialogue for scenes to be fleshed in later. Conversation after conversation, dramatic revelation after emotional heartbreak, I scripted my first novel -- a Route 66 romance.

By the time it sold, my son was taller than me. But when I finally got my "author copies" in the mail, I tucked the book in my purse and headed off for a leisurely read with Christopher, at the Burger King.

Mama Told Me There'd Be Days Like This

Oh, the Noise!
Margaret Marr

Oh the noise! Noise! Noise! Noise! Yes, you guessed it, some days I feel like the Grinch. Especially when I'm trying to write and the TV's blaring, the music's thumping (oops! That's me playing Bon Jovi on CD-ROM) and my youngest son is wrestling the cat across the floor above me. Except I'm in my ragged nightgown instead of green fur, and I'm holed away in the basement instead of a cave.

I turn off Bon Jovi and stomp upstairs to barter with my son in exchange for some blessed silence so I can hear my characters speak.

"Josh, why don't you sit and watch this nice, quiet movie?" I flip through the television channels until I come across "The Sheik" starring Rudolph Valentino. This is where I snicker and flash my best Grinchy smile. I'm a "mean one," I know.

Josh's face twists into something only a whole lemon stuffed in his mouth can produce. "I don't wanna watch *THAT* movie, mom," he says and tosses me his, what-are-you-brain-damaged? look.

My oldest son, who is propelling himself back and forth in my rocking chair so hard I fear he'll launch himself out the window, very kindly points out he thinks "The Sheik" plays piano music. I shudder at the thought of piano crescendos blaring through the house. I hope he's got Rudolph mixed up with Charlie Chaplin. But what do I know? I'm too busy searching for that ever-elusive thing called absolute quiet to watch either guy on the silent screen.

I sigh, trudge back to my keyboard and try to pick up the threads of a brilliant sentence that burned so hot the others were reduced to cinders in its wake.

I used to think that when my children started school, I'd have plenty of time to write while it was quiet. But I was wrong. Nothing unusual there. I'm often not quite right. Something in my house is always dirty-the dishes, the laundry, the carpet-on and on and on. I don't even want to think about what might be growing in the bathrooms! Plus, I'm a single mom, so I have to do the outdoor man things like mow the grass, use the weed-eater, check the oil in the car-so on

Crumbs in the Keyboard

and so forth. By the time all of that's done, the kids are home from school again. Of course, they think they need to eat in order to live, so I have to cook supper and clean up the kitchen again.

How do I work in writing? I wait until the shadows grow long, the children are tucked in bed with a hug and a kiss, and the sound of silence dominates. Then I write late into the night and sometimes into the wee hours just before dawn. I don't get any sleep. But who needs it when I'm living an adventurous life through my hero and heroine? Like Bon Jovi sings, I'll sleep when I'm dead.

Mama Told Me There'd Be Days Like This

Hot Sex and Cold Dinners
Carol Zachary

Enrico stares at her, his gaze hot and demanding as it sweeps over Valentina's lush figure. His nostrils flare, like a stallion sensing a mare in heat, and he rips open his shirt. Val throws back her head, uttering a throaty laugh of triumph. She intends to instruct her young lover on the art of pleasing a woman in bed. Rico stalks toward her, determined to prove he has lessons of his own to teach. He holds out his arms and...

...hurls his little body toward me, screaming at the top of his two-year-old lungs. Zac's favorite toy fire truck is jammed under the coffee table. I rescue the truck and comfort my son, realizing my train of thought is derailed. There's no point in trying to get back to my manuscript now. Besides, it's time to make the important decision between hotdogs or toasted cheese sandwiches. After lunch, we'll both take a much-needed nap.

As he pulls her roughly into his embrace, Val's nipples bead against the hard muscles of his broad chest. Rico presses one sinewy thigh to the juncture between her bare legs and lowers his head for a soul-stealing kiss. His hot lips are full and soft and taste like...

...frozen pizza. Again. It's the second time this week, but a key scene is finally coming together and I don't want to stop work just to fix a real dinner. I'm in the flow and really have to finish the great dialogue that appears as if by magic on the computer screen.

Val steps back, allowing the satin robe to pool at her feet. Her body is on fire from wanting him and Rico's rigid desire is painfully obvious against his zipper. He swiftly undresses, dropping his jeans and silk boxers on the floor, and...

...adds to the ever-growing pile of laundry. The 'dry clean only' items need to be separated out before they accidentally end up in the wash. But first, I need to write a good cliffhanger for the next chapter, something to make an editor keep reading.

The harsh rhythm of her breathing matches the pounding beat of his heart. Eagerly, Val arches her body to meet Rico's, her fingers clasping his firm butt. A

Crumbs in the Keyboard

fine sheen of sweat rolls down his sun-bronzed flesh to puddle between her breasts. She gasps in sweet agony. The sensation is pure and explosive and Val sinks into the darkness of...

...complete exhaustion. I've spent most of the night trying to wring every last emotion from my brain and create what I hope is sparkling prose. My muse deserted me halfway through an awkward scene and I'm struggling to tap in to the well of whatever talent I might possess. After staring helplessly at the keyboard for another fifteen minutes, I give up. The clock reads 2:00 am and I need to get some sleep before Zac wakes up at 6:30.

The earth shakes with the power of their climax and, as Val and Rico revel in one another's passionate ardor, the very heavens weep at the depth of their love. The End

Mama Told Me There'd Be Days Like This

My Mother Writes What?
Janet Miller

    Ah, the joys of teenagers. They aren't the same joys of little babies, which warm your heart just by existing, or of young children, with their innocence and smiles. But there are joys to having a teenager around.

    Teenagers are big enough to do their own laundry, to do chores that lighten a mother's load. (When they feel like it, of course.) So, a mother has more time to explore new endeavors, such as writing out some of those tales that have flitted through her brain for the last many years. Tales of adventure. Tales of ROMANCE.

    And so I sit, little orange laptop on my lap, typing madly away. I'm trying to find the perfect words to describe an encounter between two people who have never existed-a sensual encounter. *His hands are large, warm and they are about to stroke the fire of my heroine's most secret spot.*

    "Mom! I can't believe you wrote this!" My sixteen-year-old son has come into the room, and read the last few lines of my epic over my shoulder. Wide are his eyes, and bright pink is the color of his cheeks.

    I'm relatively sure teenagers know their mothers have had sex. They are aware of how babies are created and since at one time, they were all babies--well, teenagers aren't stupid. But somehow, it disquiets a young person to discover that in addition to having a practical knowledge, Mom can actually describe the act. Using words that have the capacity to enflame the reader themselves. In other words, stuff they might want to read, if they could get over who actually wrote it.

    My son no longer reads over my shoulder. He sees a window open on my machine and averts his eyes, less he be blinded like some modern-day Oedipus. And I never have to worry about him poking about in the files of my machine. My privacy is assured, forever more.

Crumbs in the Keyboard

A Day in the Life of a Writing Mom
Lori Zecca

Today began no differently than any other, nor did yesterday end in a manner other than I expected, each day blending into the next, the only difference being the gratification I draw from the individual events. My life is a never-ending series of activities, an ever-growing list of to-do items that never seems to get a day off, much less a vacation, for even these days require lists and preparations.

On many days, I view my life as a perpetual struggle (meant with the utmost love for my very needy family), as I do today, struggling to get my child out of bed, and then struggle to get him cleaned and dressed. I struggle further to get a wholesome breakfast in his belly (or at the very least a Pop tart), while struggling with my own indecision over what to pack in his lunch, followed by the daily struggle of getting his teeth brushed, hair combed, shoes tied, and jacket on.

Finally, the familiar screech and grind of the blessed school bus. I kiss my little darling goodbye as he runs from our home proclaiming his love for me. Our dog, Lucky, sixty pounds of pure love, who hasn't a clue that he isn't another of my children, has his own part in this farewell ritual, giving my son a quick lick as he brushes past. Then, I gaze proudly as my precious baby waves to me from the little school bus window, his face bright and smiling, and I am humbled by my good fortune. This is a solitary moment of reflection, as I watch my offspring head into the structured little life that I helped create, and my heart is full and warm with the fact that he is happy and well adjusted.

I remain at the door. Below me, Lucky continues to watch as well. A gentle smile remains on my face, an expression I'm hardly aware of, as I listen for the screech and grind of the bus stopping at the corner. And, although I can no longer see it, I know it's waiting for a break in the traffic as to safely proceed. I wait, though I am not sure why, until the hum of the engine is too far in the distance to distinguish any longer. Finally, I close the door and look down at Lucky, who is already looking up at me. I can almost read his expression. We are of one mind - our day has only just begun.

Knowing the routine by heart, we get right to it. For me, a perpetual whirl

Mama Told Me There'd Be Days Like This

of household tasks that will take me right through mid morning, taking time for only an occasional sip of my often-cold coffee, the caffeine enabling my quick pace. For Lucky, it's twenty-minutes of following me from room-to-room before collapsing in a centrally located, carpeted area of our house, and taking his enviable nap.

While I nibble on an English muffin (if I've made it to the grocery store within the last few days), I update our magnetic Dry-Erase calendar and make a few house/family-related phone calls before heading upstairs to my miniscule office to check my e-mail. After getting far too wrapped up in my many, if not excessive, mentally-stimulating and vitally-necessary writing-related e-groups, I scold myself for not writing until after lunchtime (an hour I haven't taken since leaving my "real" job in 1989), but I'll write until my stomach rebels, and then I'll grab a yogurt. Maybe.

With the exception of an intrusive phone call or delivery (I do much of my shopping on-line if possible, and incidentally, my post-person and UPS driver are on a first name basis with *each other* as well as with me) I do as I planned, and when my stomach begins to grumble, I stop and read over my accomplishments. If it's good, I ignore my belly and keep writing--if it's awful, it's time to refuel the ole brain--in effect, I'm usually searching the pantry around three PM daily. However, I cheer up after reminding myself that the morning's wash needed to go in the dryer anyway, and my child would be home within fifteen minutes expecting an afternoon snack, which I'll prepare while I wait for the door to burst open alerting me to his arrival.

My son and I chat, Lucky emerges and awaits the stray snacks that will inevitably fall to the floor, and then we are off to various sports, music, medical, dental, vet appointments/practices.

With my laptop in hand, the battery fully charged from the night before, my palm pilot instructing today's tasks, and my cell phone for the inevitable scheduling conflicts, we are out and about for a few hours. If I'm lucky, I sit in the car, the gym, or the waiting room and revise my earlier attempt, offering occasional word of encouragement to my child during the process--if not, I simply kick back and appreciate the ordinary event.

Finally, it's home we go--often via a fast food establishment--then homework, dinner, bath, and bed, though not necessarily in that order. If hubby's in town, I may check my email once more, field a phone call, or two, and possibly finalize today's WIP before calling it a night. Then I'll slip between the

Crumbs in the Keyboard

sheets next to my sleeping sweetie, who would be angry with me if I neglected to wake him. However, if hubby is off earning a living, then I will undoubtedly pour myself a much-deserved glass of wine, and write into the wee hours, usually with amazing results.

And, so it goes.

There is no glamour in this daily routine of cleaning, laundry, and paying bills, but it is all part of this life I have created for myself, a journey that has taken many twists and turns to get me here. It's a treasured life, and I'm grateful for each moment I am given, as well as my ability to recognize this. Life is so precious and unpredictable, yet in our youth we are not privy to such wisdom. Instead, we face adulthood with invincibility and conviction, and learn from the many lessons that occur along the way. If we are lucky, we arrive at the place we were looking for, the place we didn't even know we were trying to find. It is then we realize, that life is not a destination but a journey in itself.

We must stop striving to achieve the next level of greatness and realize that the importance lies in what we already have. It is then we will find the contentment we are longing for, glamour no longer a factor, and we'll take comfort in the mundane tasks of everyday life.

Mama Told Me There'd Be Days Like This

When and How
Jesica Ann Bimberg

I'm a busy woman. What woman in this day and age isn't? Women are masters at juggling duties and roles. At times we drop the balls and scramble to regain them, but we always make it back to the graceful juggling. Okay, I'm not so graceful, but I do it.

I'm a stay at home mom of three. My children are ages four, three, and one. Needless to say, I'm busy. I also go to school full-time pursuing an English degree. In addition to the important roles of student, wife, and mother, I add writer.

Do I get tired? Yes. Do I get frustrated? Yes. Do I ever think of quitting? No. I would never trade being a wife and mother. My family comes first. My kids know that. Even when I'm pecking away at the keyboard, my door is open- physically and metaphorically. The interruptions are at times annoying, especially when the scene I'm working on is really cooking, but I know my kids are at the age they need me. That scene will be waiting for me after I get that drink of water or that sandwich, or after I play Candyland for an hour.

Early on I realized I had to look at writing as a career. Otherwise I would put it off because of those duties in my life. I have to put in the time to reap the rewards. I make sure I write a certain amount of time a week. I make goals and reward myself when I meet them. Everyone in my life understands that writing is a priority for me. My husband takes the kids to the park so I can have an hour of quiet to work on a scene that's giving me a hard time. Even my four-year-old offers to read a book so Mommy can go on the computer for a little while.

I keep track of when I write and what I was working on at the time. I bring my notebook and pen to the park so I can jot notes and ideas down while the kids play. I have a mini-cassette recorder in my car just in case I have an idea while I'm driving. And, yes, I really use it.

Yet, while I consider writing my career, I am flexible. If I don't find time during the day to write, I stay up a little later or wake a little earlier to sit down and work. If I can't write for a few days because one of the kids is sick or something comes up, I don't beat myself up about it.

Crumbs in the Keyboard

Aside from everything, I love to write. I don't remember a time in my life that I didn't make up stories. I'd make them up while doing dishes to make it go faster-often doing a bad job to my mother's disappointment. I'd tell my younger sisters tales every night in bed to help her sleep. I'd scribble stories in notebooks during class and study hall. I just wrote. I found I couldn't stop. The stories are in my head and I just put them in words, on paper.

There was never a question of *if* I was going to write, only the questions of *when* and *how*. And I'm working that out.

Mama Told Me There'd Be Days Like This

Creative Moms Have No Down
Cherie Claire

Down time. That's the current buzzword in my household. Having burned my candle at two ends for several months now, Mom is slowly burning out. Now comes advice time.

All of my friends keep telling me to take time out for myself. My Canadian writing buddy, Susanne went so far as to quote Stephen Covey in his "The Seven Habits of Highly Effective People," as if an authority figure would carry some weight. As if.

"If you don't look after the goose that lays the golden eggs," Susanne said in Covey's words. "Soon there'll be no more golden eggs."

My mother gave me a motivational tape. "Take time for yourself, sisters," this woman commanded her listeners. "Take time for yourself!"

OK, this is good advice. My question is *when*?

I'm one of those crazy artistic types with a day job. I love being a journalist, find it interesting and educational, in addition to keeping the lights on and the children fed. But, I also love to write fiction. Within the last two years, after countless years of endless rejections, I have finally counted myself among the published. My first novel came out last summer, followed by a novella. Soon I'm launching the first of three books in a series for a new line of historical romances. And that's where the problems lie. In order to be part of the line's "launch," a prestigious position for a new writer to be in, I have to write three books within one year. Impossible, you say? Well, you're right. But when have I ever said no to opportunity, especially when it took half a lifetime to knock.

Two books are finished, both in production, leaving me one last book to write for my next deadline, which quickly approaches. Mind you, I still have to attend my day job and be 'mother-of-the-year' when I come home. So guess who loses in the battle for time?

I've become the living burnout barometer of all my friends. I believe they are secretly taking bets on which day I will crash and burn and be admitted to the insane asylum. I'm praying it will be sometime *after* my deadline.

But until then, I have to listen to an endless stream of good advice.

Crumbs in the Keyboard

"Take some time to nurture yourself," friends tell me. "Pamper yourself."
"Take a quiet, bubble bath." "Go for a long walk."

Sure. I'll take a nice quiet bath and forget that the neighborhood boys are camped out in the living room, ready to bolt into my bedroom at any moment, always forgetting that a woman lives there. I'll stay in the tub for hours and forget that people need to be fed or nursed or supported through homework. When the dog runs out the front door and chases the meter man--I'll let *Calgon* take me away.

A long walk? No problem. I'll take an extra long one after the children get on the bus in the morning, while rush hour is at its peak. I'm sure my boss won't mind me showing up sometime around lunch. Or how about when I get home at night, power walking through the dark neighborhood with a crowbar for protection?

My answer to all this advice is BE REAL. Even if I didn't have an extra career, it's hard finding time for yourself until kids say those final, magic words: "I'll call you when I get to the dorm."

Working moms and dads are like long-distance runners. The clock goes off and we hit the floor in a trot. We don't stop pumping the pavement until the little ones close their eyes. And if you're like me with ambition that goes beyond the 9 to 5, the careers that don't come with a steady paycheck, downtime is non-existent. My kids' bedtime, for instance, is the precise moment when I sit down to write. I will live until I meet my deadline. I may crash the next day. Or somehow, somewhere, I may find the time to sit quietly and be at peace for a few moments.

Until then, I shall do what I did when I was a new mom and was told my son would sleep through the night at two months. I have to laugh.

Mama Told Me There'd Be Days Like This

Shadow Stretches
Amy B. Crawshaw

I am a full-time mother of four children. A mother as well as a writer, I prefer to pen romances. Four years ago, I started writing with the aim of eventually being published. I've mainly been concentrating on my historical novel since then, but I have completed a short story here and there, trying my wings in other genres. The novel's story line I got down in a period of eighteen months, but rewrites, corrections, and editing lengthened the time between the beginning of the endeavor and its completion.

Long before I started writing, I'd collected titles. I couldn't resist toying with a good one, a title that captured my imagination. I scribbled my thoughts on tiny pieces of paper and stuffed them into folders. I typed them on the computer and saved them in my writing folder. I collected them in the corners of my imagination.

Then I started putting a story down on paper. In the beginning, I hid the evidence of my pastime under my bed, not willing to let anyone know about my ridiculous dreams. It was eight months before I finally let someone in on the secret, and several years elapsed before I told my children.

My daughters Caitlyn and Erin, immediately wanted to read the book. I told them "no" in no uncertain terms, thinking they were too young.

But evidently Erin had looked at the forbidden material.

So begins my lesson:

"Shadow Stretches, wouldn't that be a cool title?"

"Yeah, that's good, Mom."

I look over at my twelve year-old daughter, Erin, who reclines in the passenger seat, one of the four children I endlessly drive to this event, or that lesson.

I spend a lot of time in the car.

"Yeah, I like that title. What do you think the story will be about? I can just imagine a romance between--"

"No, it's a horror story," Erin inserts quickly.

But I don't do horror. I cringe even at the thought. Good-naturedly, though,

Crumbs in the Keyboard

I question, "You think it would be a good title for horror?"

"Yeah, definitely horror. " Only Erin's "yeah" sounds more like "yeh."

The conversation moves on then, my mind still half on a future book.

Later that week, as I drive my daughter and her friend, Katelyn, to the middle school, I foolishly utter words I quickly regret. "Let's write a story using the title." At that point, "Shadow Stretches" does a quick metamorphosis from a horror title into a title of a book with the content being a giggling recitation of my unfinished romance novel.

How many times has she read the darned thing, anyway?

Well, I guess to save my children's tender sensibilities, I should have saved my story in an inaccessible area like a floppy, but it's so much easier to click on a story from the hard disk, avoiding the hassle involved because I neglected to label the diskette. So, what I get when my story sits on my computer, bright and bold, under Amy's file in "My Documents," is overly educated pre-teens.

As I listen to my daughter's quite accurate recitation of the story line, I wonder--

How hard is it to write horror?

Mama Told Me There'd Be Days Like This

The Juggling Act
Shirley Kawa-Jump

A friend recently asked me, as a fellow mom and full-time writer: "How do you juggle work and being a mom and make sure you're doing a good job at both? I feel guilty when I work and guilty when I don't. Well, all except for at night. But the work I can get in from nine to midnight just isn't enough if I want to do this full time.

My answer: You don't.

I'm not trying to be flip about this, just realistic. There are going to be times, *no matter* how hard you try, when you feel like you are only doing a good job at one or the other, times when you feel you should get the "World's Worst" award for both. It never balances out-ever.

But here's the kicker. It doesn't matter what you are doing with your time during the day, whether it's baking cakes or working a job or writing or mowing the lawn. You are ALWAYS going to feel like you can't balance both equitably.

Nora Roberts, who is probably one of the most prolific writers in the world, started out writing when her kids were very young. She is often asked how she managed to balance both. She said that in the juggling act of life, you have to decide what things are glass balls and what things are rubber balls. The rubber balls you let drop so you can catch the glass ones. The glass balls are obviously the most important things in your life: children, husband/wife, writing. The rubber balls are the Tupperware parties and the pristine house and anything that smacks of Martha Stewart.

In short, you have to let some things go in order to attend to your priorities. I'm not telling you anything you can't hear on an "Oprah" rerun. This makes sense, and it works.

But it doesn't solve the problem of *feeling guilty* for working when the kids are around and *feeling guilty* for playing when you should be working. That isn't going to go away. I battle it daily. *Guilt* has a starring role in my house. Heck, I'm even thinking of giving it a bedroom of its own.

A few things that I do when the balance is tipping precariously in one direction or the other:

Crumbs in the Keyboard

Let the kids fend for themselves: I know, it sounds cruel. What do you mean, not make them a sandwich? Not bathe them? Not put away their laundry? Yes, that's exactly what I'm saying. My daughter, at nearly eight, is pretty proficient with the microwave and knows how to make soup from a can. My son, at three, has attempted his own sandwich. He can change his own clothes. They do many things for themselves. To me, it's not a bad thing. It teaches them independence and makes them feel proud that they can "do it themselves."

Pass the guilt trip to someone else: Think you feel guilty? Think about your spouse, who is probably working more hours than you and spending even less time as a parent. Share that guilty burden. Don't be a martyr.

Involve them: My daughter and I play "Mancala" while I answer e-mail. My son colors at my desk while I work. It doesn't always work out, but if my task is light, their company is nice.

Walk away from work: I do this when the kids least expect it (keeps them on their toes.) There are times when I have to say no to playing a game or watching a video, but I try to temper that with just as many yes times. I counter this by sleeping less and working during their sleeping time, but it works out okay.

Show them you love them: I leave notes in lunchboxes, put lipstick kisses on hands, bring home the occasional treat, dispense hugs no matter what I am in the middle of, and tell them I love them all the time. It's not a substitute for being with them, but it reminds them that I think about them all the time.

Last of all, accept that you will *never* have that perfect balance. If you weren't writing, you might be at a full-time job, or going to school, or spending your time knitting. Everyone needs something for themselves, whether it's a job or a hobby. That time is time well spent because you are investing in *you*.

And isn't that a great lesson to teach the kids?

Mama Told Me There'd Be Days Like This

Stealing Minutes
Cathy McDavid

With a long, suffering sigh, I shut my office door, lean my shoulder against it and close my eyes. Now, at last, I can write. I'm alone for the first time since my hungry cat knocked over my beeping alarm clock more than six hours ago. My husband, always more chipper than I, hastened my rising with a gentle shake and a sunny, "Up and at 'em, sweetheart. Time for work."

I really dislike morning people.

While toweling off after a quick shower, my son bangs on the bathroom door.

"I'm not dressed," I shout.

"What's for breakfast?" he shouts back.

"Whatever you're fixing."

"Moooom!" He draws out the one word over a good three syllables, already perfecting that annoying male whine at a mere twelve years old.

"Honey, you're a big boy now. You can make cereal and toast." Someday his future wife will thank me for teaching him to be self-sufficient.

Seconds later, another knock sounded. "Yes?"

"It's me," my daughter's muffled voice came through the bathroom door.

"I'm not dressed," I moaned, feeling like a broken record.

"Can't I come in? We're both girls."

This struck me as rather funny because it's the line I use on her when she ducks in the closet, refusing to let me see her newly budding naked body. I suppose the same preteen hormones responsible for her sudden onset of modesty are also responsible for our constant disagreements over clothing and hair styles choices.

"What is it?" I asked with exasperation, refusing to give up the sanctuary of my bathroom.

"I need two dozen cupcakes."

"What for?"

"It's my turn to bring refreshments for the student council meeting after school."

Crumbs in the Keyboard

"Not today!"

"Yes, today," she informed me in a small voice.

Later, while my family ate the soggy cereal and burnt toast my son had prepared, I spread peanut butter onto saltine crackers.

During the drive to the bus stop, my daughter pouted. "I can't believe you're making me take peanut butter and cracker sandwiches. Everyone in student council will laugh at me." She wailed loud and long. "I'm going to die."

"You won't die," I assured her, remembering some vague incident from my own youth when I suffered unbearable mortification at the hands of my mother. "And maybe next time, you'll remember to tell me sooner when you need something for school." I had the distinct feeling the lesson fell on deaf ears.

"I'll eat them," my son offered. He rivals the Coneheads from *Saturday Night Live* in consuming mass quantities of food.

My daughter, guarding her treasure from the threat of scavengers, clutched the sack of peanut butter and cracker sandwiches to her middle.

As a working wife and mother, I steal every free minute that comes my way to write. This includes brainstorming into a micro recorder when I take walks in the evenings, scrawling longhand notes while my husband drives, outlining scenes on my AlphaSmart in the waiting area at the piano teacher's or, like today, dashing off a quick couple pages at the office during my lunch hour.

Laughing giddily, I make my way to my desk and plunk myself down in my chair. After a full morning of distractions, I'm finally free, charged up and ready to write. Last spring I made my first book sale on proposal. I've marked this historic event by missing my deadline. A whole month to date and counting. My editor has gone from patient understanding to mild annoyance. During our last conversation, I promised her she'd have the finished manuscript next week. Only ten more pages to go and I'm done. If that isn't motivation to write, I don't know what is.

With fingers poised over the keyboard, I empty my mind and call up the characters. Let's see. Where were we? Last time, the hero and heroine had just discovered the missing papers that would prove--

The phone intercom rings, shattering my concentration. I'd asked the receptionist to hold all my calls.

"Yes?" I struggle control my annoyance.

"Cathy, I'm sorry to bother you but Tom from Valley Contractors is here and needs your approval on a change order."

Mama Told Me There'd Be Days Like This

I handle the problem, return to my office and once again shut the door. Three sentences into the page, I'm interrupted when one of the accounts payable clerks barges into my office.

"Sorry. UPS is here with a C.O.D. delivery. Where's the petty cash box?"

I give her back a dirty look when she leaves and decide to model the villainess in my next book after her.

It's thirty minutes later and I'm on a roll. I have to be careful not to rush the ending because I'm so excited about finishing. Words are pouring from me at such high speed, I can't type fast enough.

Once again the phone intercom rings, and I want to scream with frustration. I'm almost done. Can't they just leave me alone!

"Yes," I bark, not caring if I'm rude.

"It's the school nurse on line three."

My characters fade like rising smoke as I pick up the phone. "This is Cathy McDavid."

"Mrs. McDavid, your son's been hurt. He's all right, but we need you to come down to the school right away."

"What happened?" I ask, my heart lodged in my throat.

"He broke his finger playing kick ball at recess."

"I'll be right there."

On the way to the school, I call my neighbor on my cell phone and make arrangements for my daughter to go there when she gets off the bus.

* * *

After four hours at the emergency room, my son and I head home. He's proud of his splint and races off the second we pull in the driveway, eager to show his friends. I stumble inside, exhausted and weak with relief, and collapse on the couch. My darling daughter has thoughtfully made a dinner of Ramen Noodles and hotdogs. Who am I to complain? My husband comes home from work, and he and our son have one of those male bonding sessions, swapping war stories and showing scars.

The next afternoon, I leave work early and take my son to the Orthopedic Surgeon, who sets his finger and casts it. Even though we have an appointment, it's a long wait. I think there's some kind of unwritten law that states you can't get into see the doctor right away. My daughter, forced to accompany us, complains grumpily and then buries her nose in a teen magazine. Luckily, I brought my AlphaSmart. While my son is having X-Rays taken, the characters

Crumbs in the Keyboard

come alive in my mind. By the time we leave, I've finished the manuscript. This, I feel, calls for a celebration. We stop at 31 Flavors and splurge, remembering to buy a pint of Pralines and Cream for Dad.

As we're laughing and licking the melting ice cream off our fingers, I'm struck with inspiration for another story. I can hardly wait to get home and make some notes. But wait, my writer's group meets tonight. Oh, well. There's always the micro recorder and a few minutes to steal.

Mama Told Me There'd Be Days Like This

A Two-Page Day
Maureen McMahon

Amanda turned and ran frantically from the room and into the entrance hall, sobbing uncontrollably. In her blind haste she did not see the tall gentleman propped casually against the stair post until she collided forcefully with him. The impact buckled her knees so that she would have fallen had he not caught her up against him...

"Mom, I'm home!"

"Be with you in a sec, dear!" *Now, where was I?* I scanned the page, *Oh yes...*

He held her easily, supporting her firmly so that she was pressed full against...

"Oh, here you are! What are you doing?"

I hit the 'shrink page' button on the computer and smiled at my son who peered over my shoulder at the screen.

"I'm working on my novel."

"What novel?"

"The one I've been trying to write since--"

"What's cooking? Is that dinner? Mmm. Smells good!"

"Yes. Dinner's in the oven. Why don't you go get changed and have a snack."

He shrugs and saunters off.

I bring up the page again, closed my eyes for a moment, then began to type: *... his lean muscled form. She sucked in her breath sharply as her eyes traveled rapidly from white, ruffled shirt up into a rugged, exceedingly handsome...*

The front door slammed, rattling the windows.

"MO-O-O-OM?!!" my daughter's voice shrilled.

"Out here, dear." I listened to the approaching scuff of feet.

"Sara broke my watch!"

"What?"

"*My New Watch*, Mom! I just let her try it on and she broke the band!"

"Let me see." I inspected the item, "It's okay. I think maybe I can fix it. Leave it and I'll have a look at it later. How was your day?"

"Terrible! Janice snubbed me all day! I didn't even know why, and when I

Crumbs in the Keyboard

asked her, she said Sara said I'd said something mean about her brother, even though I didn't and I don't know WHY she thinks I did…I really think it might have been stupid Georgette who said it, but she won't listen to me, so now we're not friends anymore."

"Mmmm." I rubbed my temples where a dull throb was beginning. "Darling, can I talk to you in a few minutes? I'm right in the middle--"

"Sure! Well, it wouldn't really matter to YOU anyway!"

I listened, chagrined, as her stomping footsteps ended in another resounding bang.

I turned back to the page and re-read the previous paragraphs.

"…face. She was momentarily stunned. His hair was dark, nearly black, and tousled rakishly with no inhibiting oils to tame it. His hands, where they gripped her shoulders, were strong and tough, obviously used to hard work. He towered over her, making her feel like a child's doll in his hands. Her eyes met his and their deep penetrating blue, a color quite startling in contrast to his weather-browned complexion, mesmerized her. His dark brows--

Suddenly two large, warm hands covered my eyes, causing me to nearly faint with shock. " Hey there, gorgeous! Guess who?"

I shoved the hands aside and reeled in my chair, my heart beating in my throat. "Don! You scared the daylights out of me. Don't EVER creep up on me like that!"

I watched my husband's smile fade and turn swiftly into a scowl. "Well, if that's all the welcome home I get!"

I was instantly sorry and reached out a hand to him. "Don, please…I didn't mean…it's just that you startled me."

"Yeah. Okay."

I watch ruefully as he disappears, knowing I'd have to tend hurt feelings later.

Nevertheless, I am determined to finish this scene. Only a couple more paragraphs and I can call it quits for the day. I try valiantly to ignore my now pounding headache and re-read again. I take a deep breath, place my hands on the keyboard, and--

Suddenly the room erupts in a commotion of hissing and squealing as our tomcat, Boris, enters the room and drops a struggling rat at my feet. The rat instantly skitters off behind the bookcase, with Boris in hot pursuit. This attracts the attention of our dog, Lucy, who begins barking to let me know that she'd been right all along about that stupid cat, and now look what he'd done!.

"Don! Michael! The cat's let a rat loose in my office!"

Silence. I hesitate, eyeing the cat who has positioned himself in front of the

Mama Told Me There'd Be Days Like This

bookcase, tail twitching. Lucy looks at me questioningly and, seeing that I am not leaping out of my chair, ceases her barking and decides on a 'wait-and-see' approach.

I face the monitor once more, mouthing the words. Then I continued:

"*...were arched in surprise.*

"Ho there!" he exclaimed, steadying her on her feet and eventually putting her away from him. He looked down at her slightly taken aback at the tears streaming down her face. "Are you all right, Miss?" He spoke English with a smooth tone, with just the hint of a drawl.

She did not answer but began to weep once more.

The phone began to ring. I squint my eyes, forcing my concentration to remain unbroken.

He pulled his handkerchief from his coat pocket and handed it to her.

"IS SOMEONE GOING TO GET THAT?!" Don's voice boomed.

"MO-O-O-M!! WHERE ARE MY JEANS?"

"Hey Mom, what's Boris got down there? Wow, there it goes! Atta girl, Lucy, go get 'em!"

"Aaaiiieeeee!!!! MOM! THERE'S A RAT IN THE HOUSE!!"

"WILL SOMONE GET THAT PHONE!!!!"

I refused to shift my eyes from the screen. My fingers ran frantically over the keyboard:

She stared at him curiously for only a moment before snatching the proffered cloth and pulling herself away to race, sobbing, out the front door and into the cool night air.

I let out my breath. I'd done it! TWO complete pages in one day!

"Hey everyone, GUESS WHAT?" I called. But there was no response.

I sighed. There were more important things to tend to.

There Resides In Me
Stacey L. King

There resides in me a wonder woman of sorts. I believe I owe who I am today, in part, to my daughter, my miracle child. Several years ago, three months after she was born, she was diagnosed with a congenital heart defect, which required open-heart surgery. She would die otherwise.

Before this, I had enjoyed the blessing of an extremely healthy and happy baby boy, who had joyously welcomed his new sister to the family. I loved both of my children intensely and thought that if anything bad ever happened to them, I would die.

My daughter had the surgery and did not die.

And neither did I.

In fact, sometime during that week in the intensive care unit, my entire perspective on life changed. I learned that I am a lot stronger than I ever knew. I learned that not a lot of stuff really truly matters. I learned that faith and a prayer will pull me through anything.

And I learned that I was extremely fortunate. I found deep compassion for other mothers in the ICU who would not be taking home healthy babies.

There resides in me a wonder woman of sorts.

This one only occasionally dons skimpy little outfits and wields a lasso. Most often this wonder woman is kissing boo-boos. Listening. Taking to and picking up. Doing laundry. Writing. Drawing. Vacuuming. Painting. Decorating. Reading. Coding. Arranging. Cooking. Photographing. And writing some more.

I still love my children intensely, but now I know that, whatever comes, I am equipped to handle it.

Until then, I will try to find that invisible jet. It would be really handy for carpool.

Mama Told Me There'd Be Days Like This

Napkin
Pamela Gayle Smith

The baby's down for a nap,
I have a little quiet time.
Maybe I can, quickly,
compose a new rhyme.
Now where are those lines,
I jotted down yesterday?
I remember carefully,
putting them away.
They're not on the counter,
nor on the refrigerator,
I wrote them on a napkin,
to be recopied later.
It was such a good line,
to start a wonderful verse,
I can't believe I've lost it,
maybe I stuck it in my purse.
That was a waste of time,
no folded napkin there,
maybe it will come to me,
if I sit quietly in this chair.
As I sat there,
I let my mind go back,
as the piece of napkin,
I tried to mentally track.
Then came a glimmer,
in the corner of my mind,
how could I be so silly,
it wasn't hard to find.
As I rose from my seat,
I walked across the floor,

Crumbs in the Keyboard

picking up the diaper bag,
lying by the door.
It wasn't a napkin from home
that I'd been looking for,
it was a Long John Silver's napkin,
wrapped around some fish and more.
I hurried to unwrap it,
I threw the fish away,
and there was the verse
I had written yesterday.
I got my note book,
sat down with a sigh,
then from the other room,
I heard the baby cry.

Sometimes It Takes Grit

Crumbs in the Keyboard

No! I'm NOT Just a Housewife
Lisa Marie Long

"Do you work?"

"Are you an at-home Mom?"

"Oh, you're still doing that writing thing?"

Sound familiar? Wanna throttle the next person who says anything remotely close to any of these? Me too. I've found that gaining respect as a writer is rather difficult for an unpublished, stay-at-home-mom.

Since before I can remember, I wanted to tell stories, to write, to transport readers like I was transported by the books I constantly read as a child, and when I stopped working in 1996 to pursue a writing career, I guess I expected the world to bow at my feet.

Reality check. Oh, I know a few people who are inflate-my-ego impressed with what I do. They are interested and ask questions and want to know how my latest manuscript is going, or if I heard from a publisher, yet. I think they are the ones who have always secretly wanted to write a book, but never took the leap to actually do it. Then there is the rest of humanity, including my darling husband, who couldn't care less that I pour out my heart and soul each day, create people and whole communities, create a world full of justice that will let two people fall in love and have hope for the future. They don't care about a world where, with a lot of persistence and hard work, I might someday transport a reader. Most folks just don't get how special my job is. And they aren't shy in letting me know.

"When're you gonna be done? I'm hungry."

Sigh.

It's hard enough some days to get respect as a woman, even harder as a mother who chooses to stay home and raise her child. But tell people that you're a writer, and they look at you with tolerant, condescending eyes that seem to say, "Sure, honey." They must expect a writer to look more glamorous than I do. Not that I can be called glamorous.

But I wonder if they realize how many writers go to work in their sweats.

Lately, I feel like Rodney Dangerfield--I can't get any respect. My 30th

Sometimes It Takes Grit

birthday hangs ahead in the not-too-distant future, and I pray a small measure of respect might follow it, but I won't hold my breath. I was labeled the "smart kid" in school, but I find that as I get older, people's expectations are higher. Why don't I have a career? Why don't I have a job? Why don't I have a degree? I'm at home with my child; I must be a bit dull or something. If I were the manager of some corporate division, or a lawyer, I know I'd get more respect than I do now. I'd be treated as a professional. I *am* a professional, but people don't recognize it.

That's the problem with having a home-based career, and being an unpublished writer. People don't take us seriously. They measure success with dollars and job titles.

I measure it with how many pages I've written today, what obstacles my characters overcame, and how many submissions I have out there. Never mind that I wear sweats to work.

I have the drive and discipline it takes to start writing a novel and finish it. I've done it more than once. Those of us who have had the joy of typing "THE END" know a rush of pride in accomplishment that few people will ever know. Only one percent of the population will ever write and finish an entire book, and we are among them! To me, it's better than climbing Everest. When my characters look deep into each other's eyes and declare their love for each other, I weep with joy.

But when I look into the eyes of the clerk behind the counter who just asked me, "What's your occupation? Homemaker?" (What, is that tattooed on my forehead?) I cringe and stutter and eventually give in. I am at home with my son, but I do so much more, darn it!

And it's time I let the world know. No one will respect me unless I first respect myself. It's time we all stood up and claimed the respect we all deserve as women, as professionals, as writers of the biggest-selling genre of mass-market fiction. As WRITERS--period.

Join me in taking pride in our occupation. Put "writer" under your name on your business cards. Fill in that occupation box with "writer" or "novelist." When someone asks your occupation, tell him or her, "I write historical (or contemporary, inspirational, etc.) romantic fiction." Put a sign near your writing area that clearly states to your family that you are working. Make it clear that until a certain time, you do not wish to be bothered. But be sure to stop at that time and pay attention to your family. It's only fair, after all. The muse can have

Crumbs in the Keyboard

her time, but she must get back into her box when time's up. That how she'll get her respect.

I recently made a deal with my husband that has made him take my writing more seriously. He gets two afternoons each week to do whatever he wants--which nearly always involves a Cummins diesel engine-and I don't ask anything of him during that time. In exchange, he comes right home after work two days a week and cares for our toddler son so I can write. By my respecting his time to relax after work, he is forced to respect my time to pursue my career.

It works out for him, because I don't get mad when he's out fiddling with his trucks anymore, and it's great for me because, well, it's obvious-more time to write!

I stood up for my right to be respected, and you should too. Don't be shy, don't be embarrassed, and don't make excuses. You are a writer; say so. Hold your head up high, look the next person in the eyes and tell them, with no apologies, "I'm a writer, not a homemaker."

Sometimes It Takes Grit

Life is Good
Sharon Porpiglia

I was morbidly obese. That's right, me, the fun loving, easygoing words on a screen that no one can see. I joked and laughed, wrote funny stories, and often folks had the impression I was something other than huge. Hugely afraid of anyone finding out my horrible secret, I should say.

I'm not sure why being overweight carries so much stigma, but it does. To my good fortune, I found a venue for my work in which I would not be judged by the size of my body, but instead, by the size of my mind, my characters and my "self." My rhythm matched that of other faceless writers who penned their hearts for others to scrutinize.

Words came easily. I believe it was because I'd received a death sentence, for surely one doesn't survive long when their heart and lungs and body are taxed daily by the heft of their own girth. I felt the need to be heard, to leave something behind should my bulk cause my untimely demise.

I was being realistic. I knew that my days were numbered with each pound that heavily weighed against me. Yet, I could not seem to change it.

I find myself today, healthy and happy with my new life, yet unable to express it sufficiently enough to record it with quill and parchment until today.

Surgery changed my life, gave me back a life to actually live gave me a whole world I'd denied myself for far too long. I sit here writing on this sunny fall morn, contemplating the now endless possibilities of my life. I've been resurrected, reborn. Still, instead of having more than enough time to write, I find myself unable to find the time most days. And it scares me.

What does one do when they have spent nearly a lifetime hiding, keeping themselves at arms length from imagined dangers? Broken heart, broken spirit, broken dreams all contributed to what I once was. Now that I am "normal," there are seemingly no more defenses from those shadowy ghosts that haunt me. I fear they will chase me my entire life. The difference now, is that I can run like the wind, hold them at bay, laugh at their attempt to keep me a prisoner of my own making. And the best part…just as my size is no longer my shield, so too, my writing. It has become my sword.

You Don't "Work"
Nancy C. Lepri

Freelance writing can be lonely. Working in a small, usually "make-shift" office in your home, there's nothing to distract you. It's lonely and quiet. Or is it?

I started freelance writing ten years ago. At that time I had a full-time "real" job and attended college, but something deep inside made me want to make my mark on the world; to create something to leave behind. A couple of years of writing for local newspapers and magazines, I decide to pursue writing full time. I was full of spunk and determination, had received my BA, and thought I had it made!

When I decided to work at home, well meaning friends and relatives seemed to pour out of the woodwork like termites. My services were volunteered for one thing or another after the comment, "You don't do anything during the day!"

Like I had nothing better to do than watch soap operas and eat candy! Where society got the idea that women who work at home do nothing but this, I don't know.

Through clenched teeth, I'd decline, reiterating I was "working." I got some "Humphs," and "ah ha's" but let them roll off my back.

Engrossed in my book, I'd find myself curtailed by dirty laundry, grocery shopping, cooking meals, or other errands. It soon became easy to procrastinate. Nothing is worse than being on a roll, only to be interrupted to perform mundane tasks. Creativity is not like a faucet; it can't be turned off and on. Once the juices flow, no one wants to be disturbed or interrupted. Unfortunately, this is a fact of life for those who work at home.

One morning I had intentions of accomplishing a great deal. My head was into creating and I was determined not to get waylaid. I threw a load of clothes into the wash and headed for my office, ready to take on the day. The phone rang.

"We want to thank you for last year's donation to the Cancer Fund. Can we count on you this year?" I benignly told the operator to sign me up for $20, and I'm back to work.

Sometimes It Takes Grit

Soon my attention-seeking feline saunters into my office, jumps on my chair, rubs against me, meowing piteously, wanting food. Okay, down the stairs to scoop out more Fancy Feast, and while there, put clothes in the dryer and the second load in the washer. I decide to make some coffee, and can't forget the fist full of M&Ms. Gotta keep the energy up!

In the office the computer hums quietly, only to be overpowered by the ringing of the doorbell. UPS delivering a package for a "working" neighbor who's not home. Hmmm.

Back in my office, I crack my knuckles, settle down, and read what I had previously typed. Before I know it words are flowing from my fingers like lava from a volcano. I'm on a roll! Excited and happy by my progress, I try to ignore the phone as it shrills. No luck!

"Hi Mom; watcha doing?" My daughter was on her lunch hour and wanted to chat.

"I'm working," I sigh.

"I won't keep you. Can you hem a pair of pants for me?"

"Do you think I have nothing else to do?" I ask tartly.

"Well, you're home all day. I thought you'd be bored, and you're cheaper than a seamstress!"

Is there a store where mothers can return our offspring when they annoy us?

Finally disentangling myself from a lengthy discourse of how hard it is to have to work a "real job," I get back to my writing.

Where was I?

Brrrr! The dryer signals. Before I get involved in my work again, I empty the dryer, put the other load in, and put the dry clothes away. Then I notice the time--3:00. Ugh! What to make for supper? Rooting around in the freezer and fridge for another ten minutes, I throw potatoes on to boil, make a hasty salad, and put chicken in the oven.

Heading back to my office, the phone rings.

"Hello, Mrs. L! How are you today?"

"Hmm," I grunt.

"I'm calling to inform you, you can now have replacement windows for your home for less than you'd think."

I drummed my fingers as she droned, trying to find a way to tell her I live in a new house and don't need new windows. After her long spiel, I finally tell her I'm not interested, hang up and head back upstairs. But not before making

Crumbs in the Keyboard

another cup of coffee. Need that caffeine!

Sitting at my desk I read what I had composed that day, which wasn't much.

The dryer signals again. I haven't gotten into new writing, so I head back down stairs. While there, I set the table and check on dinner. My stomach rumbles.

Coffee and no sustenance. Won't be long till dinner! Dragging myself back upstairs with the late afternoon slumps, I flop in my chair, gaze at the computer monitor, and groan. I'm too tired to do any more!

What did I accomplish? *Zip!* Holding my head in my hands, the phone rings yet again.

"Hey, Hon, I'm on my way home, do you need anything?" hubby sings cheerily over the line.

Yeah, like about two months of uninterrupted time, peace, and quiet, I want to scream into the phone, but calmly answer, "No, thanks. See you soon."

I give my computer one last disparaging look, save my work, and shut down for the night. Closing the office door I decide, tomorrow I'm utilizing the answering machine and having pizza delivered!.

Sometimes It Takes Grit

Still Learning After All These Years
Kim Cox

Like our characters, writers are always evolving, growing and learning. I've always been a by-the-seat-of-my-pants writer with no certain time to write and no plotting. I would just sit down with an idea and start writing. But I'm finding it harder and harder to write like this.

I wrote my first finished book, *SUSPICIOUS MINDS*, in three months by-the-seat-of-my-pants, but the revisions and rewrites took almost seven years, off-and-on between rejections. The only thing that kept me going was determination, or those closest to me would say, *hard-headedness*.

Now that my book is slated for publication that determination has faded somewhat.

These days, writing related work fills my time, and I need to regroup, to find time to write. I work a full-time job, just finished serving a two year term as treasurer of my local RWA chapter, serve as contest coordinator for the same local chapter and serve as treasurer of World Romance Writers, another writing organization. Then there's promotion time to consider, and not to mention all the Internet listservs I belong to. I find less and less time to actually write, and more and more reasons to procrastinate.

It disappoints me to realize that I only have one book finished in seven years, although I have begun five others. The very first book I started has five chapters, my second book has only three chapters, my finished book is the third one I started, my fourth book has only three chapters, my fifth book is almost finished and my sixth book is still in the planning stages, as it's been for the past four years. None of this is to say I haven't been writing at all. I've finished ten short stories. Ideas aren't the problem; the writing is where the difficulty lies.

So what am I doing about it? For one, I'm reading the multitude of the books sitting on my bookshelf about writing and I'm buying more. I read *GMC: Goal, Motivation and Conflict* by Debra Dixon which made me to rethink my WIP (work in progress), and I came up with an even stronger conflict. I'm also finding Phyllis A. Whitney's *Guide To Fiction Writing* very helpful in learning to document and plan my novel. The next books I plan to read will be on

Crumbs in the Keyboard

characterization.

I've scheduled writing time for myself, and so far I'm sticking to it. I started a notebook to get my thoughts in order. Simple things are hard to remember sometimes, and I can relate back to the notebook instead of reading until I find the information I need.

A writer never stops learning his/her craft even after the contract is signed. It's only the beginning of their education.

Sometimes It Takes Grit

Rise and Shine
Laurie White

Every weekday morning at four a.m., either the sounds of a too peppy pop song, or a very annoying commercial blaring from my clock radio tears me from a sound sleep. No, I don't work at a hospital or the early shift at a factory. I'm a writer dealing with one of those things called a "day job."

I'm not really a morning person, but I get up early anyway, because I have to write. I want to try my hardest to realize that dream of some day seeing my work in print. So, I have to make the time to sit down in front of that computer and get those words down. With only a couple of precious hours a day, the process for me is often painfully slow. Sometimes the words just don't come, almost driving me to tears of frustration. Other days I can get a lot accomplished in that short amount of time, which makes the satisfaction even sweeter.

Someday I hope to have the luxury of being able to write full-time, but until then I have to make time when I can in the mornings and on the weekends. I rarely watch television, and haven't been to a movie in ages. Dust gathers on the furniture, soap scum builds in the bathtub. To me, though, following my dream of being a published author gives me much more fulfillment than a clean house!

If you really have the desire to write but find it difficult because of family or work obligations, or both, MAKE THE TIME. Even spending only an hour a day writing is better than no time at all. Try writing before the kids get up, or steal an hour while they're at school. Take your manuscript with you wherever you go, and do some editing while you're waiting at the doctor's office or the car repair shop. If you have a very tight schedule like I do, every minute is precious. Make them count.

I recently submitted my third manuscript after over a year of work. The satisfaction was worth all the frustration and lost hours of sleep. Will it pay off? Who knows, but I'll keep on doing it in pursuit of my dream.

Crumbs in the Keyboard

So You Think You Want to be a Romance Writer?
Pamela Arden

How many times have you read a book and before you finished you were telling yourself you could write like that, or better? How many times have you started stories in your head or on paper? Maybe you wrote a few pages, maybe even a whole chapter. If so, you aren't alone. Millions of people have thought about writing a novel. Hundreds of thousands have even put some words on paper. But the number dwindles drastically when you talk about that relatively small, elite group of people we call "authors."

To me, a writer is someone who writes. Anything. It may be fiction or non-fiction. But just because they "write" doesn't mean they finish. An author, on the other hand, is one of those few people who actually complete what they start. They don't have to be published for me to consider them an author. Anyone who can write a 300 page readable and understandable work deserves the title.

It isn't as easy as it looks. Just because you can read a 275 page romance novel in four hours doesn't mean you can sit down at your computer and pound one out in the same amount of time. If you're fast, know what you want to write, understand the basic "rules" of writing, and have a support system, you might accomplish that task in a month or two. More than likely, it will take six months or more. Then you need to be prepared for the fact that it may take months, or even years, to sell that book and see it published.

I was one of those readers who said, "I can do that, and probably do it better. It doesn't look that hard." Let me tell you, I was wrong. Not about being able to do it, but about how hard it was. When I started, I was home schooling two teenagers. We live on a few acres in the country, miles from the nearest town. A "quick" trip to the grocery store takes an hour. I have a large garden and greenhouse to take care of, as well as seven dogs, thirteen goats, and over a hundred chickens. Feeding them takes more than an hour a day. I also fix a full home-cooked meal every night. So how do I find time to write?   I make time.

I open my manuscript first thing in the morning, as soon as I turn on the computer. That way, if I have an idea while I'm weeding the garden, I can run in,

Sometimes It Takes Grit

jot it down in Notepad, and go back to work. When I need a break from working outside, I take it at the computer, a tall glass of iced tea at my side. When it gets too dark to work outside and dinner is over, that is "my time." I write from nine p.m. until I can't see the screen any longer, which may be three a.m. Then I get up at six-thirty and start over again.

Once you start writing, you'll have a greater respect for published authors. You'll understand the trials they have endured to bring you that novel you finished reading in less than a day. They have poured their heart and soul into that book, sometimes at the expense of their marriages. Their life revolves around writing, promoting--including online chats, book signings, appearances, teaching at conferences, paperwork, research, queries, submissions, rejections, contracts, and taxes. It doesn't leave much time for a life.

Finding time to write can be a trial all its own. For a wife and mother with small children at home it can be nearly impossible. You get up at six-thirty to fix your husband's breakfast and pack his lunch. The kids are up by seven, so there is no time to write until naptime. Maybe you can squeeze in an hour or two of writing then. More likely, you need to do laundry, start supper, dust, vacuum, or one of a hundred other chores. By the time you finish, the kids are awake again. The rest of your day is shot until the kids go to bed at night.

Many serious writers get around this problem by getting up at three am. Yes, you read that right. I know several who do that every morning. On the weekend, if they're lucky, they might grab an hour or two to write while the husband watches the kids.

Then there are the single mothers and those who work a full-time job outside the home who still manage to squeeze out time to write. I don't know how they do it, but I salute them. Anyone who can finish a novel under those circumstances deserves all the accolades we can shower on them. I cannot imagine the incredible stress they endure. I think I would buckle under the strain and give up.

So, do you still want to be a Romance writer, now that you know there's more to it than typing out a few words, then sitting back and while the money rolls in? Good. You just may have what it takes. I wish you the best of luck.

Broken Promises
Pamela Gayle Smith

He promised to love and protect me,
to keep me safe from all harms.
He promised he never would hurt me,
I'd always be safe in his arms.
He promised he'd never abuse me,
our future looked permanently bright.
He promised he'd be there for me,
any time morning or night.
He promised security for me,
with money, a home and a car.
He promised he'd forever love me,
but forever didn't go very far.
I didn't think he could punish me,
but today I found that he could.
I didn't believe he meant it,
when he said it was for my own good.
I didn't think he would hurt me,
but today he grabbed my arm.
I didn't think he would bruise me,
but my arm is all swollen and warm.
I didn't think he would push me,
but today I clung to the rail.
I didn't think I'd be frightened,
but next time I don't think he will fail.
I didn't think he would slap me,
but today there's a print on my face.
I didn't think this could happen,
oh how did I get to this place.
I didn't think he would punch me,
but today I'm doubled in pain.

Sometimes It Takes Grit

I didn't think it was possible,
that he could act so insane
I didn't think he would beat me,
but today I'm all black and blue.
I didn't believe he could hate me,
what causes it, I haven't a clue.
I didn't think he would leave me
but here I lay dying alone.
I didn't believe he would kick me,
as I struggled to reach for the phone.
I didn't think he would shoot me,
but today I lay by the door.
I didn't think he would kill me,
as I drew my last breath on the floor.

Crumbs in the Keyboard

Road Warrior
Trudy Doolittle

I am a Road Warrior. Some people even call us Cowboys or Cowgirls. In the last 30 years, I have worked in twenty or so different cities across the US, and for as many Fortune 1000 companies. I get on the plane Monday morning and seldom return home before midnight Friday, logging more hotel and airplane frequent flyers points than I get the chance to use.

"Have laptop will travel," chant my colleagues. "We are consultants. We implement computer systems." Our friends are our fellow workers and our clients residing throughout the nation. Often on weekends, we repack our suitcases and instead of going home, we trot off to visit these friends in other cities, refraining from returning to our lonely homes. Our nights out of town are spent eating out, drinking, and visiting local theatres. To compensate for the high-life, some of us pull out our tennis shoes, shorts and t-shirts and exercise on the equipment is the hotel's stuffy gym or run in strange neighborhoods.

Not being physically fit and being the iconoclast that I am, I urge my laptop to work overtime. I send my brain off into tangents of the unknown, dreaming of being a normal person. I am an author. That's my excuse. My hotel room is cluttered with heroes, heroines and villains. I carry on conversations with them, trying to make them conform to my wishes and desires. Of course, they have minds of their own considering the fount from which they were spewed.

Now I work for one of the Big Five. If you don't know what I'm referring to, suffice it to say it is one of the largest conservative full service companies in the world. Up until recently the uniform of the day was dark suit, shirt and tie. Women were men look-alikes. But the leaders saw the light and we too have opted for business casual.

It would seem that writing romance and working for a conservative firm mix about as well as oil and water. That was my take on it and I vowed to keep my nocturnal scribbling a secret. Not true. In a meeting of the entire office, my boss held up the copy of the book that included my short story and told them that I write romance. They all applauded, several standing in line to get their own signed copies. It doesn't hurt that the said short story was about an overworked

Sometimes It Takes Grit

Road Warrior.

My friends are scattered throughout the world. Many I haven't yet met face-to-face, since we know each other only through the Internet lists. My friends are also authors. We chat online, communicate through email and share our writings. We support and motivate each other. In each new city I visit I try to take the opportunity of meeting one of these online friends.

Being a Road Warrior has provided me with plenty of fodder for characters, plots and scenes. Through this lifestyle I've had the opportunity to meet great friends. I wouldn't change it for anything.

Crumbs in the Keyboard

Writing with Pain, Fatigue a Fuzzy Brain
M. Kathleen Crouch

It's morning for everyone except me. I'm finally going to bed after taking another dose of my pain medication. Living with the pain from Post Polio Syndrome and Fibromyalgia for the last fourteen years should have taught me to take the medications earlier, but I was so involved in writing that I forgot to take them on time. I was one of those children who was bitten by the Polio bug back in the mid 50's; but except for having to wear a back brace for eighteen months, it didn't slow me down one bit. In fact except for a funny walking gait, I didn't seem to have any problems growing up.

So, what's Post Polio Syndrome? Well, according to Dr. Richard Bruno, of the Post-Polio Institute of N.J., Polio survivors now have to deal with overwhelming fatigue, new muscle weakness, pain and cold intolerance.

Fibromyalgia is a syndrome distinguished by chronic pain in the muscles, ligaments, and tendons, around joints. It is called a syndrome because it includes a set of conditions that always occur together. It is a dysfunction of the biochemical informational substances (hormones, neurotransmitters, peptides, etc.) and a pain amplification disorder.

Back in the late 80's my body was telling me to slow down, that I was getting older, but I was only in my mid-forties! Old was when you reached your late seventies. I was too young to be getting old and not able to do things that I enjoyed. Only my body didn't agree with my mind and I soon learned that I couldn't do the things I wanted to do. I loved to dance and even taught ballroom dancing while I was in college, but dancing left me so tired I couldn't move. Walking in the woods was another favorite pastime that had to go as well. The leg muscles in my left leg couldn't or sometimes wouldn't respond like they used to when I was younger, it was the new muscle weakness that was responsible, not to mention the new fatigue and additional pain when I overused the muscles.

Like many women, I thought of myself as 'superwoman', able to do anything thing I wanted anytime I wanted. It was a shock to realize that I had to limit my activities in order to conserve my energy. The realization that I would have to limit my activities and that I would probably need pain medication for the

Sometimes It Takes Grit

rest of my life sent me into a spiral of depression and determination to prove that I could still do everything I wanted to do and it nearly caused me to be wheelchair bound instead of being able to continue with a normal life.

I had three things that kept me going. One, my determination not to let anything keep me from doing what I really wanted to do; two, my Siberian Huskies who needed me to take care of them and three, my faith.

Of course, I had to first decide what I really wanted to do. That took a while to figure out, but in the end, I decided that I wanted to write more than anything else. While I enjoyed dancing and long walks, I didn't like the pain I suffered as a result. Writing and mild exercise limited the amount of pain I had to deal with on a daily basis.

My Siberian Huskies--Bear and Tia--looked to me for their welfare. I was their 'ownee' and it was my responsibility to see that they were loved and taken care of every day. Many times, Bear would stop me from doing something that I thought was important, begging to be loved on. I finally caught on to his tactics. He would usually interrupt me when my body was hurting and I had blocked my mind to the pain I was feeling. His interruptions made me realize that I had to take short rest breaks during the day. In many ways, he became my guardian angel.

My faith in the Great Spirit also kept me going. I knew that He wouldn't give me more than I could handle and that He knew me better than anyone else. There were days and sometimes weeks that I didn't feel as if I could continue, but I managed and in the end, I learned.

I learned that pain didn't have to control my life. I learned that I didn't have to go full tilt all the time. I learned that others were willing to help provided I let them know I needed the help. Most of all, I learned that life is wonderful when you have friends who care about you.

My long-term goal is to finish a novel. I have many stories that I have started but haven't finished because when I get brain fogged I can't remember what I wanted to write. The characters don't help either…they hide from me and only appear in my dreams which I have trouble remembering the next day.

My short-term goal is to write at least three to five hundred words a day. Some days, just getting out of bed and taking care of myself, two cats and my Siberians is all I can manage though I do try to write something every day even if I can't write at the computer. I keep a notebook by my lounge chair in the living room for when I get a great idea or to answer questions that arise about my

Crumbs in the Keyboard

characters or the story. Some days, I seem to spend in limbo, not wanting to do anything or having to use my brain to think, much less write. Thankfully, I enjoy reading and my bookshelves are full of books waiting for me to re-read and lose myself in someone else's world.

I joined a small group of women who were writing romance stories (RWU). I've learned a lot from them and I've become better at critiquing and in the process, I've become a better writer. I still get frustrated when I can't participate as much as I would like to, but I take it a day at a time and sometimes an hour at a time.

Sometimes It Takes Grit

What Goes Around Comes Around
Barbara Donlon Bradley

There are some days when you just don't want to get out of bed. That's the way I felt about the year 2000. Oh, don't get me wrong. It started out great. I learned I had just sold my first book to Hard Shell Word Factory, which had me on cloud nine. I had also finished my third manuscript and decided that I would take a quick break from writing.

Like most of us, I've been driven to write. I worked during the day then spent time with my son in the evening, but the moment he was in bed I flew to the keyboard to write for a couple hours and had been working that way for years. At least until the year 2000.

That year was a very hectic one. My husband lost his job about seven months before and instead of him racing out to find another I talked him into going to school to get his Associates Degree in computers. It was what he really wanted to do and I knew if we tightened the old purse strings we could do this.

I worked almost full time for one company as a manufacturer's representative and then freelanced, doing the same thing for several other small companies to bring in extra money. On a weekly basis, I normally worked fifty to sixty hours and still managed to write. I think knowing it wouldn't be forever gave me the motivation to keep writing. I knew once my husband graduated and found a good job I'd be able to limit myself to one company and have more time to write.

The trouble started in March. I was working in one of the stores I covered and ran into another rep. She filled me in on a bit of gossip. It seems the company I had the most hours with had hired a new regional manager.

I did a double take. That was my job title. I hadn't given my notice, so why were they looking for a new rep? After informing my husband of the problem I called the president of this company.

The owner was his late sixties, he believed in using scare tactics to motivate his employees. Whenever I saw an e-mail from him I cringed. He was a yeller, and his posts always upset me. Each week I turned in a report then waited. I always got a critique back and folks you think getting your manuscript critiqued

Crumbs in the Keyboard

hurts, try having a boss who in one memo said I told him too much and then in the next said I didn't tell him enough. One time he even went as far as to say my reports were too mundane because I didn't have any trouble to report. Excuse me? I thought that was a good thing.

So, I called and basically said I heard I needed to be looking for a new job. He told me he hadn't decided and I learned he hadn't hired anyone, but had been interviewing for my position because he wasn't happy with me.

As we talked, he started a tirade that upset me so much my husband wanted to take the phone and tell him to take the job and…well, you know. He told me I wasn't pushy enough. I did too much work for the stores I covered. I worked for his company and not for the stores.

Somehow I kept my job, I'm not sure how. I never begged to keep it, but I continued to get a paycheck so I continued to work. His attitude, however, and the way he treated me had a devastating effect. I found myself pushing off my writing. It was hard to slip into that fantasy world because sooner or later I'd have to face the real world and an abusive boss once again.

I would have imaginary conversations with the man, hoping to word it just right so I could make him see how much the retail world had changed. But I never came up with the perfect dialog. And those hateful e-mails kept coming. It didn't matter that my sales were up thirty-five percent over all and I had the fifth largest sales worldwide.

My poor husband didn't know what to do. I was angry all the time. My ready smile disappeared and the worst part--I stopped writing. He knew I had to quit this job when one E-mail made me so angry I grabbed the nearest thing to me, my car keys and I threw them against a wall. The tinkling sound as the key ring broke open and the keys clattered against the tile floor had a wonderful calming effect on me, but the fear on my son's face made me realize that I should start thinking about leaving the company. Yet, I knew I only had about six months to go before my husband graduated. There was a light at the end of the tunnel, all I had to do was maintain until then.

It all came to a head at Romance Writers of America's National conference that year. After spending five days surrounded by writers, gaining new friends and great knowledge I broke down. I didn't want to go back to work. I hated it that much. I felt like a rag doll. My emotional well had been drained dry, and I knew it. Life had lost its luster and it was all because of my boss. That emotional breakdown made me realize I had to change things.

Sometimes It Takes Grit

The first thing I did was go to the doctor to see if I was just over reacting. We talked about my job and even my doctor said I needed to walk away. My health was more important than the money. She prescribed some pills for a slight hormonal imbalance, but cautioned me that my emotions probably wouldn't balance out until I left the job that caused all the trouble in the first place. The medication worked wonders, yet the president's e-mails continued to get to me. It was time to cut the cord.

I was scared to death. How was I going to make ends meet? I feared not being able to make my bills every month but no job was worth the heartache I was being put through. So, I started to pick up more part-time lines on the side. My husband had gotten a part-time job, too, that brought in a little more money.

I'm so glad God was watching out for us, and started sending these little jobs my way. The president of the company had hired a twenty-five year old boy who had no experience in this field to take over my position. The president didn't fire me, nor did I lose my salary, but I was bumped down to merchandiser, basically doing the same thing but with no title. I knew if I stayed the new guy would get the credit for all my hard work.

So being the writer I am, I plotted and I plotted well. Once I felt I could walk away, I prepared to leave the company the same way they would have fired me, with no notice. Goodness, I felt good! I was in control again.

The day I left I packed up everything that belonged to the company, placed it in my car and prepared my coup-de-grace. I sent the following e-mail: "By the time you get this e-mail all company property will be at the office. I quit. I have found employment elsewhere where they know how to appreciate their employees."

I heard he went ballistic when he received it. I couldn't help but smile.

I've been away from the company about nine months at the time of writing this. I'm a lot happier now and I have time for my family, my writing and me. I have completed another book already.

Oh, and I still keep taps on that company. It's hard not to in my business. The company has lost a lot of business since I left. Salespeople who had worked fifteen years or more walked out, taking manufacturers with them. Other manufacturers just got tired of his attitude and walked away too. In fact, I represent some of those lines again because they ended up with some of the new companies I now work for.

No one should put up with scare tactics and verbal abuse. Life is too short and we should live it to the fullest.

Crumbs in the Keyboard

A New Perspective On Rejection
Lisa Craig

Not long ago, I received yet another rejection letter. I did what any normal writer does. I cried for hours, feeling as though my dream had been shattered. What was I doing subjecting myself to pain, criticism, and rejection? They'd rejected my work! My best writing yet! When the immediate shock wore off, I answered my own question. I'm a writer. I write because I love it, because I need to. I write!

When my husband came home from work, he asked me what was wrong. Like he didn't know. I told him, as tears burned my eyes, stung my face. What he did next changed my life, altered my perspective and changed my attitude. He congratulated me. Yes, that's right. He held out his hand and shook mine. My initial reaction was shock and anger.

"You don't get it, do you?" he said, in his all-too-familiar husky voice.

No...I guess I don't, I answered secretly.

He continued, "Success comes with failures. Every day you write, you're climbing the ladder of success. Some writers never finish the first book. Some never submit their work to a publisher. Some never try. I'd say you're a success."

I thought long and hard about what he'd said. He's right. Sure rejection feels more like a knife in the heart, but without it, how would one know she's on the right road. The road to success, that is.

I took his ladder analogy literally. I made myself a success ladder. The outer frame serves as the base. You build the foundation by understanding the basics of writing. For each book or partial I've completed, I add a rung to my ladder. Every submittal and rejection gets another rung. Now, I look at my ladder and know I'm climbing it.

Some writers may only need a step-ladder, and others a 20 foot extension. The ladders are individual, just as the journey is individual. No two journeys are alike.

Since I received my last rejection letter, I have submitted other work. Regardless whether I finally reach my goal of becoming a published author, I

Sometimes It Takes Grit

continue to build my ladder of success.

Even after I reach that sweet goal of publication, I will continue to add to my ladder, strengthen it, and hold it as one of my most prized possessions. Rejection can't take away my ladder. To stop writing can!

Thanks to my husband's wise words, I now view rejection differently. Yes, it hurts, but not near as much as not writing at all. I suppose it comes with the territory.

In the words of a very smart man, my true-life hero: "You're living an adventure. Enjoy. The experience is what careers are made from."

Crumbs in the Keyboard

Write to Survive, Survive to Write
Robin D. Owens

"There is not much danger that real talent or goodness will be overlooked long," says the tab on my teabag (Louisa May Alcott). My reaction to the quote mirrors my writing life. Most of the time I believe it--my golden ships will be steaming into port any minute. Other times I snort with disgust. So how do I continue writing after years of rejection? How can others?

First, define yourself as a writer. Once your personal identity is tied up into a goal, you don't abandon it easily. (We know that the motivation of our characters centers on an issue/event that threatens their self-image.) I'm not a daughter or a sister or an aunt or a paralegal. I'm a writer. I've arranged my day job to let me focus on my writing. Fellow workers and other friends know how important writing is to me. When my family and non-writing friends ask me how I'm doing on my "book," I usually say I'm on my fifth, my fourth is under submission and it takes time.

Practical Supportive Techniques:
1. I use crutches when I'm feeling low and to quiet the "inner critic."

Daily affirmations: "Every bridge I cross brings me to a higher level of achievement." Little cards called Never Quit. The one on my bulletin board says: "Listen to your dreams--those are the sounds no one else can hear," Kobi Yamada. The current one floating around on my desk is: "Grant me the courage not to give up, even though I think it is hopeless." Chester Nimitz.

I love the book *Walking on Alligators* by Susan Shaughnessy, geared for writers. It has a quote, a writing exercise, and an affirmation to help jump-start daily writing. (I have followed this format for my web-page and update monthly).

2. I keep compliments and look at them for reassurance. This includes critique group smiley faces and comments and praise from contest judges.

3. I practice my craft daily: revising, plotting, brainstorming, doing writing exercises. I belong to three critique groups and work with The Observation Deck by Naomi Epel. Sometimes the weekly exercise only inspires a journal entry.

Sometimes It Takes Grit

However, I've also written four scenes, cleared up the motivation of two characters, the plot line of one book, and gotten a new story idea. I moderate a monthly "Book in A Week" bunch which is great for setting goals and getting support.

4. I enter contests that I believe might further my career, and continue to submit. My last book is at one small press, one New York print publisher and one e-pub. (It has since sold to the New York publisher).

5. Most of all, I garner support from other writers. I stay in contact with my writing communities and talk frequently with my closest friends, my critique group. I whine about my lack of publication and receive encouragement. I ramble on about lots/characters and obtain input. And I let them hold the faith for me that I am a good writer and will get published when I no longer can believe it myself. Talent and craft aren't enough. Dedication and determination are equally important.

After the crash of my last serious relationship, I decided to do something for me. My creative life was dismal; I felt guilty for not pursuing my writing dreams. So I took a "How to Write Romantic Suspense" class. The course was in April and by a conference in September, I'd written the book without benefit of critique (I still have my first draft. It is not a pretty sight). About 15 people took that course with me. Only two of us showed up at conference. I am the only one still writing. Perseverance is as important as talent.

Write to Survive: The worst time in my career came two years ago. The previous winter I noticed that the senior editor for THE publisher was judging a contest. I entered two proposals. The editor placed me first and second in the contest and requested the first book of my series. I did everything right, I continued writing the second book, kept in touch with her and informed her of my progress. She passed my manuscript to another editor who didn't want it.

End of story. It hurt and depressed my spirits so much I couldn't write for weeks (months, but I don't want to sound like a wimp). All my friends were incredibly supportive. They and the writing itself got me through. I had stories within me that wanted to be told, and a miserable hero struggling half-way through a book (the crushing of my hopes while I was writing this story affected it).

Poor hero, he needs to come to terms with his fatal flaw, escape execution and win his lady. He won't be silent. Nor will the other characters who populate

Crumbs in the Keyboard

my brain. Six or eight people (romances deal in twos) keep chiming in.

"*Here we are!*" they shout. "*When will you tell our story?*"

"*I'm stuck on a cliff, ready to suicide,*" says one prospective heroine.

"*I'm brooding in my office because my grandmother hated me and hid my lady. How will I find her?*" says the hero of a different plot.

The stories in my head got me through the depression. I wrote to survive as a creative person, and so survived to write.

Bottom Line Questions (to write or not to write): There are two questions I ask myself, as long as I answer "yes," I will be a writer. Are you a happier person when you are writing than when you aren't? Yes. The best thing that can happen to me in a day is the writing taking off. The worst is losing pages. The absolute bottom line: "Would you continue to write even if you knew you would never be published?" Yes. I write, therefore I'm a writer.

May your writing dreams come true.

Sometimes It Takes Grit

A Career Based On Two Words
Pamela Johnson

My entire writing career is based on two words: Potential and Possibility.

Anyone who knows me very well understands this much about me. And I see this not only for myself, but those around me as well.

I suppose on one hand, you could say that's an arrogant trait or one that demands the constant glare of "tooting one's own horn."

But it is quite the opposite. Let me explain.

Potential and possibility are often, in their humble beginnings, two seeds planted when nothing else exists. When you feel life has thrown you the worst kind of curve, not just the lemons, but the whole lemonade stand--lock, stock, and barrel.

It springs from a heart so desperate for hope where there seems no hope.

It emerges like a tiny point of light in a blackened, stormy sea, known as despair.

Tricky things, potential and possibility because they make you face yourself full view in the mirror--they challenge the null and void of a weary heart. They demand a vision of something beyond the sequestered walls of resignation and disillusionment. They set your heart and energy on a quest for the happily ever after.

They are the very life-blood of a great many artists--including authors.

And yet, so have I discovered, those creative qualities--potential and possibility—do indeed 'exist"(used or unused) in each one of us. It is not an age--related condition, nor is it privy to race, creed, color or gender.

One step. One contemplative look in that mirror and the reflection you see can set you on your own discovery of the potential and possibility that lies inside. You are a gift to be celebrated.

Crumbs in the Keyboard

Playing Tag With
The Muse

Crumbs in the Keyboard

The Other Woman
Leslie Burbank

I have a split personality. Actually I have multiple split personalities. I am not meaning to make light of those with severe mental disabilities; I'm just trying to be honest. Or perhaps there is another description that explains why I hear voices in my head and as the saying goes "I do what the voices in my head tell me to do?"

Being a writer means being another person literally. While most people know me as the mild mannered Leslie Metcalf, when I write I become the wildly adventurous and supremely sensual Leslie Burbank, hostage to the whims of her characters.

I can whip up dinner, clean the house and work a full time job by day but when night falls it's a whole different ballgame. That's when the writer comes out and takes control. She speaks about things LM doesn't know and she writes about things that would make LM's parent's blush.

LM leads a pretty average life fraught with the mundane things one does to exist, pay bills, clean the house, shop for groceries and wash the car. There is no real link between LB and LM except they live in the same body and use the same brain.

LB' s life is much more exciting, always writing about exotic destinations and feats of daring. She has ridden with knights, sailed with pirates and dabbled with vampires. She revels in getting two people to recognize their deep love for one another even though they may very well hate one another at first glance. So, I guess she's a matchmaker too. Yet, although LB can have a wicked sense of fun she is also very serious about her craft. Discipline? She' s working on that, but serious, most definitely.

My father knows LM and has known LM all his life. He hasn't met LB just yet. She wouldn't be good in social situations where decorum is called for. She wouldn't simply mention the weather or what the average stock price for IBM was. Oh no, she'd come out with something sure to curl even the straightest person's hair.

I think my fiancés is in love with the 'other' woman, but then at this point

Playing Tag With The Muse

who would blame him? LM's conversation revolves around how much money was spent on the electric bill this month while the topics du jour with LB have to do with the art of licking honey and the 101 things one can do in a forest clearing?

So, a sage word of advice to the struggling writer. Never let the other 'you' out at a family gathering after a few glasses of wine. Keep her on a tight leash. There are just some things your relatives do not need to know about you. Trust me when I say not everyone is so enamored with your vivid bedroom scene descriptions, even if they're only in your mind!

The Muse
Joni Seabolt

Words spoken in my ear
from that quiet part of me
Secrets that only I can hear
until I set them free
Whispers without a voice
in the rhythm that I feel
Heard without a choice
truths that seems to heal
Pure insanity spoken sane
embraced just like a friend
The paper calls my name
that's when I begin

Never Plan a Day of Writing
Pat Snellgrove

Finally. Husband and kids have gone out the door, cats out, dogs fed, clothes are on the line. Now it's time to write.

Bring out the typewriter, sit down and begin to--Damn. I knew I'd forgotten something. The phone. Forgot to turn on the answer phone.

My writing time is ticking away, but I answer it. Its hubby, could I possibly go and collect some things for him during the day as he needs them for work next morning?

I swear under my breath, and in my sweetest voice say ' of course I will, darling. Now, back to the love scene.

"Darling, I really do love you."

"And I love you." Craig sighed as he pulled her gently down onto the bed.

"Show me." Melinda's nerves leapt in anticipation.

At last I am getting into the story, getting this love scene, which has been hovering in my brain for days and nights, down on paper.

Uninterrupted writing time, what bliss! But I spoke to soon.

What the hell is that *noise*? Sounds like someone is killing the dog. I get up to investigate and find that the dog has been involved in a fight and is now dripping blood all over the carpet.

At this stage my language is getting quite ripe. One day for writing when everyone is out of the house, when I can write to my hearts content. But does it work? Of course it doesn't.

Out with the car and down to the vet's with a very subdued dog. *Keep him quiet* the vets says. *Don't let him go outside and make sure he has these antibiotics every two hours.* Does he know what he is asking? Of course he doesn't. He thinks I'm one of those women who stays at home and does nothing. I nearly tell him, but decide it's a waste of time.

Two hours later, we are home again and I am back at the typewriter. This time I manage two hours uninterrupted writing. Bliss. Then I remember husband's errand. Why didn't I do that when I went to the vet's?

Out I go again.

Crumbs in the Keyboard

As I climb back into the car, arms full of parcels, I remember that I have no bread for lunches tomorrow, so a quick stop at the supermarket to pick up the bread and necessary fillings for the lunches.

Another hour down the drain.

Now, is that everything? Silently, I list off all the chores that seemed to have gathered during my WRITING day. Yes, I am sure that's it. With a sigh, I sit down again.

Now, with my hero and heroine at a very precarious stage in their lovemaking, I need peace and quiet to get this just right.

Slowly his hands slid down her body to come to rest at the very heart of her womanhood. With trembling fingers--

"Mum, where are you?"

Oh hell, is it that time already? The kids are home from school and my peace and quiet is gone for another day. WHAT PEACE AND QUIET?

There will be no more writing today. Kids need the table for homework, and I'd better think about dinner or I'll have riot on my hands.

Oh well, I guess there's always my day off next week, or perhaps I can persuade hubby to take the kids to the movies on Saturday. Now, there's an idea.

Why are we writers? Why do we put up with these interruptions? Why do we keep at it?

Because we love what we do and couldn't exist without our fix.

Did I keep on writing? Yes, I did. Did I get published then? No. It wasn't until my children had left home, and I gave up full time work that I managed to devote more time to writing and finally hit the jackpot.

Now, shall I tell you about having a husband who works from home? After all, they are big kids, aren't they? No, perhaps not, that could be another story.

Playing Tag With The Muse

A Writer's Moon
Barbara Baldwin

A full moon illuminated the night, shining over fallow fields and dancing across the pond like a thousand fireflies. It beckoned me to sit outside on the lone prairie, cuddle up next to my lover, and listen to a favorite melody of songs. But most of all, it whispered to me in the night. *"Come with me and listen to my story. Let me teach you to love."*

The winter moon rose high in the sky, full and bright against an ebony backdrop. It took determination to keep me from pulling over to the side of the road to write instead of pushing on to the class I was to instruct that. I realize many people have recorded the moon's mysticism long before I picked up a pen, but no matter where my characters reside, no matter in what century they have lived, it remains the one constant. That glorious globe of luminous light follows an eternal path across the starlit sky while it creates an exotic aura that causes my characters to fall in love, create songs and poetry, or sit in silent companionship.

What enchantment does that night orb hold that makes me dream of lovers, or write of romance and intrigue? After all, in rather non-scientific terms, the moon is merely a chunk of rock. It doesn't even produce its own light, but simply reflects the sun's rays. And yet, in the dark of night exotic thoughts converge.

Even though the moon consists only of reflected sunlight, it calls forth an entirely different set of verbs. The sun scorches, but moonlight caresses. The sun's rays blister and char, but moonbeams dance, soothe and delight.

Moonbeams, moon glow; a hunter's moon, a harvest moon; phases of the moon, once in a blue moon. I can promise my heroine the moon, think my hero magnificent enough to rope the moon. Witch doctors and sorcerers may chant incantations to the moon while singers swear "by the moon and stars in the sky, I'll be there." (John Michael Montgomery, *Kickin' It Up*, Atlantic)

At times when I sit at the computer and the words won't come, or when my characters rebel against my direction, I want to howl at the moon. It doesn't matter if it is a full moon, a sliver of a moon or no moon at all. My feelings can't be changed by a crescent moon, or even when clouds obscure the moon.

Crumbs in the Keyboard

There may be a man in the moon, but he can't compare to my hero when the moonlight glitters off his golden locks or reflects the passion in his eyes.

Though steadfast in the night sky, the moon is an inconsistent character in my novels--sometimes romantic, sometimes teasing. Like a candelabrum in a breeze, moonlight flickers and plays against the shadows to tantalize our senses. Every once in awhile, as it waxes and wanes, it takes on yet another demeanor as a symbol of intrigue.

Most often my characters consider the moon a romantic orb of light. However, if they are betrayed, it morphs into a reflection of their disappointments and failures, becoming cold and solitary.

The greatest writers in history have faithfully administered to the moon's ego, singing its praises and inconsistencies with eloquent words. It's impossible to forget the majesty of Shakespeare's *Romeo and Juliet:*

Romeo: *Lady, by yonder blessed moon I swear,*
That tips with silver all these fruit-tree tops--
Juliet: *O! Swear not by the moon, the inconstant moon,*
That monthly changes in her circled orb,
Lest that thy love prove likewise variable.

Lest we forget the tragedy the moon has witnessed, Alfred Noyes reminds us in *The Highwayman:*

The wind was a torrent of darkness among the gusty trees,
The moon was a ghostly galleon tossed upon cloudy seas,
The road was a ribbon of moonlight over the purple moor,
And the highwayman came riding --
Riding -- riding--
The highwayman came riding, up to the old inn door.
[He offers eternal love and promises to return for her later]:
I'll come to thee by moonlight, though
hell should bar the way.

It makes little difference that tragedy ended both these love affairs. The moon must have its say, reminding us it oversees both the love and laughter in our lives, and the tragic termination of our most tender feelings.

So beware! No matter the course of your writing--romance or tragedy, mystery or myth--the moon will exert its primal pull. Without conscious thought, you will find yourself incorporating that masterful overseer of human emotions into your manuscript. I encourage you to take heart. You are not alone when

Playing Tag With The Muse

you disguise the moon behind a veil of clouds or see its face shadowed by trees. Don't be concerned as you proclaim your characters moonstruck, moonblind, moon-eyed, or moonish; or when they exclaim over a moonflower, moonscape, moonseeds, moonstones, or a moon shell. Continue to scatter your writing with moon dust and moonbeams; enjoy each and every moonrise or moonset. You are in very good company, for in the sixteenth edition of *Bartlett's Familiar Quotations*, there are over 130 references to this chunk of rock I affectionately call *A Writer's Moon*.

Crumbs in the Keyboard

The Muse As A Puppy
Linda Voss

Time is not the real obstacle to getting your writing done. I discovered this the week I had set aside for drafting. The challenge is capturing fleeting thoughts on paper. This involves two things: moving your fingers to the rhythm of the scenes unfolding in your head (with pencil, pen, paper, or keyboard) and seeing those images in your mind's eye. The later is the realm of the muse.

My muse is very much like a puppy--a live, fun-loving energy that does not respond to rationality or explanation and won't patiently wait around while you're trying to figure out how to *do* the writing. Getting into relationship with your muse is very like getting into a productive relationship with your puppy. You don't want to squelch her spirit, but neither do you want her peeing on the rug.

Puppy training class provides a case in point. At 5 months, Misty was the youngest puppy in her class, but she was doing better than most. There are many things you have to handle at one time in a puppy training class--correct with the leash, give treats and commands, physically put your puppy in position, keep the puppy on track and attentive, keep the puppy from fighting with the next dog, listen to the instructor, and perform the exercises.

People who were training for the first time were stuck on trying to do the exercises literally: say heel, walk your puppy around the cones, plant your left foot for the left turn, bring your right foot across to make the puppy fall back in the heel, etc. They were getting tangled up in their leashes with the dogs and having a hard time with the cones.

Having previously mastered my training skills, I could hear what the point of the exercises was and apply my own style of training. There were a myriad of things going on in my mind all at once. It is impossible to think through the specific steps of the exercise and handle the furry, moving bundle at your feet at the same time. The only way to get the job done is to focus on the ultimate goal and pull all your learning, at whatever stage it is in, into getting the job done. You have to throw out some of the "rules" to get into that flow of handling the dog, giving the guidance, and moving through the exercise to get the job done.

Like puppy, the muse can be bribed, drawn out, psyched up, coerced, and

Playing Tag With The Muse

played with. She can be persuaded to cooperate once you've built a common language and as long as you give her affection as well as correction. Guidance and discipline are required. But your muse will not do anything for you if you're just trying to pull her around by the leash. The Latin root for the word "obey" comes from the verb "to hear." You will not be able to capture her vivacious energy if you take too long, think about it too much, or don't listen to her.

In writing, too, that energy can be harnessed. It's all about motivation. You have to loosen up and enjoy the flow. Some things you may have to throw out to do the writing (making sure all your bills are paid on time, your house is always clean, you've thought of everyone else's birthday). Perhaps you don't have to be at your computer, or need so much time in certain places.

Try doing whatever it takes to capture a thought. Your brain just had a thought about how your heroine should react when the hero does what he just did to her.

When I broke through to achieve my highest number of pages written to date, I threw out considering whether this was deepening the love story, wondering about the consistency of the character development, making sure the setting was described, checking my plot points, and trying to think the action through all the way to the end to make sure it fit with my plan. I just wrote whatever came into my head.

When I set aside the thoughts and considerations and just typed as wisps of images formed, I got to the point where the words started coming. It was fun! The story was engaging. And a lot of words were accumulating. I wanted to get back to it and follow up with what was happening between my characters. It changed my relationship with the manuscript. It lifted the heavy, built-up sense of the impossibility of finishing the manuscript in this lifetime.

The surprise and discovery lie below the line of consciousness. A writer's gift is to mine that barely conscious terrain and bring some of that richness to light. For this, you have to negotiate a trusting relationship between your creative muse and your responsible productive side. All other obstacles-finding the time, selling the manuscript, making technology work for you, deciding on the right font-melt away when that creative connection engages and you're off on a creative adventure. Your reward, should you succeed, is some of the muse's waggly puppy energy may rub off on you.

Crumbs in the Keyboard

The Blair Writing Project
Lori A. McDonald

I believe it's true, that one should write about what they know and have experienced. One of my story plots came about after a night of letting my imagination run completely wild.

My Blair Writing Project took place at a secluded retreat in southern Indiana. I had attended writing workshops in summers past that were very informative, but left no time for writing. I decided to try out the Mary Anderson Center for some peace and quiet. The old brick building looked deserted, but well kept. As soon as I got there, I saw an entry table with an envelope bearing my name and my room key. I carried my luggage upstairs and decided to walk back down and investigate this house.

The only other resident I found was a black cat with a gleam in his eye that made me very nervous. He followed me all the way back to my room, and turned out to be very friendly after all.

Even though I knew I should get busy and put the pen to the paper, fatigue from the long drive won out and soon I was dozing. I was awakened by a knock on my door and woke to the sight of eerie shadows dancing in the remains of the setting sun.

I was relieved to open the door to smiling faces, two other folks that turned out to be weekend residents. They gave me a complete tour of the house and the cafeteria where we were to have our meals. There was another resident that I'd not yet met as he stayed in the confines of his room.

Three wonderful days of nothing but eating, writing, eating...did I say that already? Ahh, chocolate, what a motivator!

On my last night at the retreat, my friends decided to take me into the city to see a movie. We saw *The Blair Witch Project*, which seemed to bother me more than it bothered them. When we returned, the house looked very dark and ominous. I'd not noticed in the daylight just how big the woods seemed to look out in back of the property. I told my friends goodnight and promptly locked myself in my room.

I tried to get my mind off of the scary movie I had just seen and tried not to think about the big dark house, the empty hallways, and the woods out back. I flipped on my little TV to watch Jay Leno for a while, and decided I was just

Playing Tag With The Muse

being silly. Still I jammed the desk chair up against the door and settled in for a long night's rest.

I was awakened by a noise at almost 3:00 AM. from someone banging on the door downstairs. There were no overnight staff members in the house to answer the door. It was up to one of us to go downstairs and see who it was. I did the only thing that I could do; I pulled the blankets up over my head, held my breath and listened. The banging on the door stopped, only to be replaced by the sound of someone trying to open the window one floor below me.

When I crept out of my bed and sneaked a peek out the window, I saw no one.

The next morning, I found out that all the noise had been created by the mystery resident. He'd only locked himself out of the house. Still the experience served my writer's imagination, sparking a plot for a story about a writer on a weekend retreat.

I won't spoil the ending. You'll have to buy the book!

Crumbs in the Keyboard

Soap Bubble Rhetoric
Barbara Baldwin

Reading my latest copy of a writer's magazine reminds me I haven't written anything for quite a while. *Anything* does not include bill paying, completing rebate forms and making grocery lists.

Oh, I have lots of ideas. That's why I'm writing on top of the washer instead of folding clothes. Regardless of the fact I punched the hot button for a load of bright colors, when an idea bubbles forth, I grab a pen.

As an educator, I have developed numerous ideas and activities that my students love, so I have been sending queries to educational publishing companies and periodicals. But alas, I can decorate the laundry room with rejection slips. The most ingenious states, "due to a paper shortage, we must return your manuscript."

Why is there never a laundry shortage?

While I may run out of stain remover, I always have another publishing company on my list. So I begin again. Sometimes my articles have been accepted, but I haven't gotten paid in the traditional cash method. Many educational journals are forums for professional advancement, and writers contribute articles in return for a byline and a few contributors' copies. While that is fine up to a point, I've found it difficult, if not embarrassing, to pay my grocery bill with a copy of my latest published article:

"Oh, you got published (finally)! That will be $41.50, please."

Now, I shouldn't be wishy-washy. In addition to contributor's copies, some educational publications do pay contributors in merchandise. But have you ever tried to use an apron that says, "Teachers are neat" to barter for bleach?

I've even gone so far as to make presentations at state and regional conferences, because I *know* notable speakers always sell books, *and* get paid to speak. Again, I became agitated. Not only did I have to pay my expenses to a conference, but I usually had to pay the registration fee to be a presenter.

I pour fabric softener in for the next load and a fantastic idea materializes. Why not write an article about the fact that educational associations and publications get more than their money's worth because they don't pay for what they get?

Playing Tag With The Muse

Great--drop the jeans and grab a pen!

Midway through the second page, I have an appalling thought. *Who* will buy this terrific article that is taking precedence over my children having clean clothes? No educational periodical will touch it since I state they don't pay for what they get. Educational publishers will hang me out to dry if I belittle them for paying only in contributor's copies. Another great idea down the drain!

As I analyze the problem, I realize I'm writing for the wrong market. Instead of submitting to educational publications, perhaps I can interest *soap manufacturers* in putting little activities on the sides of their soapboxes to keep kids busy at the Laundromat. Little Bobby can help Mom pour soap into the washer and get fun games like "How many words can you make out of *Proctor & Gamble?*" or a word search for items of clothing washed only in cold water.

I could create entertaining stories as inserts for detergent boxes with titles like, "Soap Bubbles Whisk Grass Stains in Water Polo Finals", "Detergent Detectives Collar the Dirt Ring."

My hands negligently fold socks as I mentally assemble my next dirt fighting, biodegradable creative effort. The washer gyrates in the background, unaware of my neglect as my mind floats away on a soap bubble.

Dreams
Janet Lane

Dreams
Like dawn mists on the surface of a lake
Untouched by the penetrating rays of the sun
They hover.
Delicate, they swiftly vanish
In the harsh light of day.
Dawn is the key
Or darkness, then.
Like a nocturnal creature,
I will fly on my velvet wings
In a time of silence.
Fingers on the keyboard, softly clicking,
Following, like a delicate echo,
The beating of my heart.
Words, my dreams
Rise like the mist, great warmth from within
That whispers through the noise in my life
Yearning for release.
I will hug my dreams,
My dreams, like the dawn's mist
Hugs the earth.

Playing Tag With The Muse

Caller ID and the Neurotic Writer
Laurie Schnebly Campbell

Okay, picture this. The editor says, "I'm not sure about this new story idea, see if you can fix etc, etc--and if you want to run it by me again, call before I leave for the holidays."

Gulp. "Sure will," I say.

So I fix etc/etc and plan to phone her Friday. But Thursday night I'm rehearsing, reading my pitch and realizing it stinks, it's got holes the size of Texas and it feels like the whole thing is (to quote my husband) "held together with spit and baling wire. " I can't read the editor this!

Except I don't want to sound like a flake who said I'd call and then didn't.

Hey, I know! Since she rarely answers her phone anyway, I'll just call and leave a voice-mail implying that I WANTED to read her this wonderful idea, but darn it, guess we didn't connect. That'll give me until after the holidays to come up with something else.

On the off-chance that she MIGHT answer her own phone, I'll have my finger positioned ready to hit the disconnect key, so all she'll hear is a dial tone -- and if that happens, I'll just try and reach her voice mail later on. (Am I well-prepared, or what?!) So the receptionist rings me through and--oh, *shoot she answers her phone.*

SLAM down the disconnect key.

Whew. Close one. But--oh, good heavens. What if she has caller ID?

What if she recognized my area code and wonders why I'm hanging up on her?

I feel like such a WUSS that I dial all over again, get connected, and read her the spit-and-baling wire idea and she likes it.

She likes it!

I'm still shaking. I call my critique partner to ask when I became so neurotic and she observes that "you aren't neurotic, you're a writer."

I guess she's right. But for now, it's back to the keyboard with a quick prayer of thanks for Caller ID.

Crumbs in the Keyboard

Where Do You Get All Those Crazy Ideas?
A Guide For The Despairing Writer
Denise Weeks

When asked (for what must have been the billionth time) "Where do you get all your crazy ideas?" Harlan Ellison reportedly said, "From a crazy-idea factory in Hoboken." Other writers are likely to retort, "I wish I knew! I'd go right back and get some more!"

But there are a few of us who feel there just aren't enough years in a lifetime to write all the novels that we'd like to finish. (Although we'd also say, like Woody Allen, "I don't really want to live forever through my work. I want to live forever by not dying.") We're filled with story ideas that just keep coming to us, and we despair of having enough time to work on them all, to keep them alive and exciting in the backs of our minds or notebooks until the current project is complete. What's our secret--if there is one?

There's a secret to it, all right--but it's not so secret. It's nothing more than learning to recognize and cherish the great ideas that bombard us every day from all corners, and being unashamed of writing them down, no matter where you happen to be. You can learn to preserve and use all those story ideas that escape your notice every day, but you must be methodical and persistent. I suggest using four steps to uncloak the mystery of finding those story ideas and then to conjure the courage to put the plan into practice. I write fiction, but the same method could be applied to finding article topics.

Don't buy the hype. The act of creation only seems esoteric and mysterious to us because it has so often been advertised that way by instructors (and reinforced by the eccentric film and television portrayals of creative people.) It seems that unless you experience some magical "inspiration" all at once, you aren't being creative. Everything has to leap forth fully formed like Athena from the mind of Zeus, and it must be as dazzling as "Creation," the Sistine Chapel fresco with God's hand touching man's, or it's not Art. No second try with that slab of marble: you carve it right the first time. No wonder that's daunting to many people, who think (or have been told by educators--professional educators, who "must know what they're talking about") that they're "not creative." Unlike

Playing Tag With The Muse

being not-female or not-Chinese-Irish, this is more a state of mind than a permanent condition.

Sometimes the spontaneous Song from the Muse does fill my ears, and when it does happen, it's wonderful. (Often it's Thalia, in charge of comedy.) But the rest of the time, it's more practical for the working writer to remember what Einstein said: all great inventions result from 10 percent inspiration and 90 percent perspiration. Creating a novel, poem, story, or essay "out of nothing" is a fantastic accomplishment, whether or not it ever sees print. It seems weird, extraordinary, difficult, tiring, an act of God (though I'm not saying it isn't all of these--at least just a little). It's something that could never happen to you.

Not unless you let it.

I might compare the way I come up with a story or story idea to with the mundane act of deciding whether to ring a doorbell. First, I hesitate on behalf of the people inside: should I bother them? Shouldn't I have called first? What if I'm interrupting something? My fingertip goes slowly forward; hesitantly, I touch the bell. But, at last, there's a moment of heedless courage when I experience the flash of decision--*Just do it now!*--a moment when I give myself permission to reach out and BEGIN.

I have to be typing or penning something--anything; a shopping list, titles of books to read, baby names--before I can hope to capture those ideas. Sit before that blank page. The idea is coming--give yourself permission to freewrite, to succeed, to fail, or just to amuse yourself.

First nothing's there but the "ether"; then, all of a sudden, a phrase, scene, or situation is ready. *What if...that old man sitting on his front porch as I drive home every evening were really a spy in disguise...a visitor from another planet...a Nazi war criminal, still in hiding? Has he ever left this little town? Will he ever? Does he sit there all day, just watching? Or waiting for someone? Anyone in particular, or would I do?* Hundreds of possible ideas could come out of this "I wonder." Yet most of us would dismiss it all with, "But it's been done. I can't do anything new with that idea."

Don't extend that thought to its concluding absurdity, saying that, since "there is nothing new under the sun," you couldn't possibly invent a different slant on it. You are a new and unique person. Start typing. You can always recycle the "good parts" later on if it doesn't work out; at least you'll have *something*.

To get started, type out one sentence out of a newspaper article, a joke told on the elevator, a chance remark you overheard down the hall at the copier. If it's

Crumbs in the Keyboard

written down and allowed to germinate, to change, to percolate through the wrinkles in the gray matter, it can become the basis of a short story; inspire a scene, character, thematic idea, or some other part of a novel; or even lead to an article like this one.

Hope your family and friends aren't as nosy as mine. But if they are--

Start today. I used to put off everything so long that by the time I was ready to start writing it, either the deadline had passed or the freshness of the idea was just completely gone. It was dead, and it was like trying to make grass cuttings into a fragrant lawn full of interesting bugs: it just wouldn't work. So don't let it all get away. Let the stream of words flow freely now and edit later. Make time today for those things that have set you aflame.

This is the simplest of the four rules, but so often it is the one ignored. "When I get the time--" can turn into "if I'd only *used* my time" before you realize it. Remember the doorbell analogy: there's no catalyst but yourself. Set the alarm for 3 AM and write for those hours before work. Do whatever it takes. How badly do you want to write? Or do you just fantasize about having written a bestseller, without desiring the act of creation itself?

Nobody will remember tomorrow whether you vacuumed the carpeting or folded the towels. Possibly not even in two hours, after the kids have tracked in mud and the cat has made a bed out of the laundry basket. But your writing has the potential to speak to future generations and give you literary immortality. Which is more important?

WRITE things down! Somewhere, right when you find them. You might have the germ of an idea that you think you'd never forget, but if you don't write it down right away, it is gone. Even if you're working on something else at the time, you must record these ideas.

Once I kept a little notepad in my purse on which to jot down these things, but I'm ashamed to say that, after many scuffles with the family (who would steal it for phone messages, or just read it and snicker), I changed my methods. I think I invented coded speedwriting after the morning my husband announced to the contents of a crowded van pool, "What do you mean by, 'She's all over me like baby poop?' We don't even have a baby." (He had read one of the "interesting colloquialisms" I'd recorded for later use.) In fact, I used that line of dialogue as the first line of a short story for young people; eventually, it was "tightened" out, but it had started the whole thought process that led to the story "Mademoiselle Kate."

It would've been even worse had he found the list of elf names for my fantasy trilogy. Trust me on this one.

These days, I also hide gems like these electronically: they reside on my

Playing Tag With The Muse

computer's disk in word processing files I name sequentially, such as "Ideas. 001" (002, 003, etc.) When I'm driving, I also write ideas on yellow sticky notes and stick them in the zippered pocket of my purse. (I pull over first.) They survive the trip back to the computer much more often this way.

Actually, you probably shouldn't even let the wrong person read the first draft of your pieces. It can be quite uncomfortable if while they're reading your story, they think they're the models for the bad guy, while you were about to ask them to please do the laundry. There are many people who won't comprehend (or can't handle) your subject matter, and can ruin your story in its incubation stages--before the caterpillar has unveiled its gossamer butterfly wings, if you will, or has at least turned into a moth, if such be its destiny.

I once experienced a terrific scene when my mother read some stuff I'd left lying on the sofa by mistake after a full night of editing:

"Where in the world are you going to send these crazy stories?!" she yelled in exasperation, waving a sheaf of papers as I walked in bleary-eyed (this was before breakfast, and normally I don't get up before eleven unless it's Christmas morning and I heard reindeer on the roof the previous night; I don't even see in color until noon.

"Like this one about the two LDS missionaries who walk in on the meeting of the snake-handlers' church. You can't exactly send this one in to the Baptist Standard!"

"Relax," I said. "I'm working on a novel."

This sent her into a serious vale of tears, as she apparently had hoped to hear I had an interview at Penneys that afternoon. "Get a job!" I could hear her moaning through her sobs.

This ugly scene could have been avoided if only I had kept those early drafts out of sight. And, please, don't ask people who don't read for pleasure to read your work! If they can't be amused by anything that moves slower than MTV on fast-forward crack-cocaine speed, how can you expect them to give you any helpful feedback on the romantic beginning of your historical novel set in Italy during the Renaissance? Most of your co-workers, unless you know them to be leisure-time readers, will develop the attention span of a three-year-old when confronted with a sheaf of boring old manuscript pages. They are the types who walk into your living room where the bookshelves are and exclaim in astonishment, "Have you really *read* all these books?!" And they're serious. Trust me on this one, too.

Don't waste it on "telling" or kill it with over-research. These two are insidious. I've been so excited about some of my ideas that I rushed right out at lunchtime and blabbed the whole storyline to shocked or appalled co-workers.

Crumbs in the Keyboard

DON'T do it. If they don't completely discourage you with their complete apathy ("Uh-huh. What?" "That's nice, dear," or maybe "Aw, mom! I'm trying to watch TV"), they'll either think you're strange, or they will pick away at flaws in the unformed idea as if they were helping rid you of an old scab on your knee, so fiercely that you go away thinking your great idea was completely stupid.

Also beware of the allure of endless research. (Don't we all love libraries?) You may find you need to ask a question of someone who knows about snakes or plumbing or whatever (this is called either an "interview" or an "imposition," depending on your viewpoint), but be careful.

For example, say you need to ask a computer whiz whether, when you delete a file on a certain type of PC, the file is actually erased, or is just marked for deletion later. Your fictional detective needs to "undelete" a file to catch the killer, and you need to put it on the proper computer. I'm not telling you that if you have a difficult part in a tale that you shouldn't go to an expert and ask, but I don't recommend you let on that "it's for a story." (Asking is the lazy way out, because everybody knows you should really research this in the library--but I try to stay away from the library during months in which I hope to get some work done; they appreciate it, too, because then someone else has a chance to check out some books.)

Go ahead: ask your expert--how about that co-worker who happens to be an enthusiastic computer hobbyist?--those enticing leading questions. Only keep the reasons for asking to yourself. Just imply (in the perennial student's famously vague and preoccupied way) that you need to know the answers for school or work--a research paper, or something; match the reason to what you think the person being questioned would consider "worthwhile" (translation: "real work"). Not everyone is willing to answer questions if you let it be known that you ask because you're writing a story: to many, that's an open invitation for them to start asking you about your publication credits or to start laughing because you are "wasting your time with that." There are so many ways to flatter a person with a question that you should have no trouble getting an enjoyable ten-minute lecture on the subject, if you have chosen your teacher.

If you ever had parents, you already know how to do this. My mom, for example, has little time for novel-writers and story-crafters, but will drop anything to tell you all about any one of her diverse areas of expertise, such as wallpaper hanging or bread baking or finding the area under a curve or what Hamlet's tragic flaw is--*if* she thinks it's for something "legitimate" like a term paper, a book report, your continuing education class, or (in my case) if you've really changed your lazy ways and are ready to learn homemaking at last, after all! You know how to do similar "adjustments" to the truth without exactly

Playing Tag With The Muse

lying--after all, you will take that college course one day, won't you? If not, you're a writer--use your imagination. Once you know so much you're sick of the entire subject (or when your hidden tape recorder runs out of tape), thank your helper. Then smile enigmatically.

And don't do all the research up front; just circle or underscore the facts you need to check, and continue with the flow of the words. After all, how do you know you won't edit that out before you need to know whether all flamingoes are the same shade of flamingo pink? (They aren't.) Then you know all the things you'll need to find out about after the first rough draft is finished. I know research can be slightly embarrassing. In fact, I'm known around my workplace and my neighborhood as a nice but slightly eccentric person who's apt to pipe up after church, "Does anybody know the easiest way to pluck a chicken?" But they're used to me now.

As a result of my bravura and curiosity, I've learned even stranger things than that. I can't spend any more time discussing it, though, because now that I've given the secret away, it's working for me again. I can't wait another moment to begin the tale of the little girl who just appeared in the doorway of my imagination, and said, "Come quickly! I need to show you something."

With my finger on the proverbial doorbell, I begin to write.

Another Point of View
Candace Sams

"You think she remembered this time? Do ya?"

"Will you stop drooling all over the place? And quit wagging your tail. You're knockin' stuff off the shelves and she'll blame *me* again."

"Can't help it. That's what puppies do." Tug pants. "Do ya think she remembered to buy the treats, Goblin? You know, the ones with the chewy centers that taste like bacon?"

"She didn't buy anything to eat except the regular stuff. Her mind has been on this stupid book. " Goblin pauses to look back at the computer screen. "Dogs! They're God's answer to leftover, moving parts."

"At least I *move*. I'm cute, lovable, and do whatever Mom wants. Cats just lay around and look bored."

"That's because I *am* bored. If you could read what she's going to submit *this* time, you'd be bored too. Now, let's see what she's got here." Goblin's golden eyes move over the text.

"*Torvald sauntered toward Rotunda. Their eyes met. He wanted her. She wanted him. They would not be denied. He led her deeper into the forest, picked her up and placed her gently on the ground.*"

"Great crud!" Goblin shakes her head in disgust. "She doesn't actually think somebody's going to *buy* this does she? I mean, where's the *pacing*? There isn't enough conflict between the hero and the heroine. They don't even meet until page eighty-four. And get *real*. I know Mom writes fantasy, but two human beings can't physically get into *that* position. I don't care *what* reality they're living in. And no human, in their right mind, is gonna' *do it* on the ground."

Goblin lifts one paw.

"Grrrrrr, you'd better not do that," Tug growls and buckles her front legs. "She'll go totally ballistic. Really *postal*."

"Go chew some furniture! I'm doing this for her own good." Goblin proceeds to walk across the keyboard, making sure to put in a few hard page breaks. When she finishes, there are lines and lines of garbled letters and symbols all over the page. The whole thing would have to be deleted. "There.

Playing Tag With The Muse

That's better. Now she can start over, and work on her goals and motivation. Clean up the plot a bit."

"You're gonna' be in so much trouble!" Tug barks. "She *hates* it when you do that."

Goblin jumps off the desk, glances back at the computer in disdain, and stretches out on the carpet. "Maybe I'll just let her think *you* did it. After all, you *were* up in her chair again."

"I wanted attention. Puppies need lots of attention and she keeps forgetting the treats. You *know*, the ones--"

"Yeah, I *know* already. The ones with the chewy centers."

"Listen, Mom's home. Ohhhhhh, I can't stand it! She's home, she's home. I'm gonna race to the front door. I'll be there when she opens it. And I'm gonna pounce, dance, and tinkle aaaaaall over the place."

"Get a grip!" Goblin watches as Tug races to the front door, barks hysterically and jumps up and down. "What a complete waste of energy. She won't have the treats. She'll pet us once, walk over to that computer, and open a bag of chocolate-covered caramels. We'll have to wait for her to notice the food bowl is empty again. For *that* I'm supposed to get up and act excited?" Goblin sits on the floor and watches the puppy make a complete fool of herself. "If you only knew how *stupid* you look."

"She's got the key in the door. Hurry, Mom. Hurry, hurry!" Tug shakes in anticipation.

The door swings open and Mom walks in.

"There you are," I croon in ridiculous baby-talk. "How are my precious baby-wabies? Did you miss me, Tuggems? How about you, Missy Goblin?"

"Get a *life*." Goblin turns her head away, and doesn't bother moving.

The cat pretends not to watch as I distractedly pet the puppy, smooth a hand over her own black head, then settle myself before the computer.

"See. Told ya," Goblin complains. "It's the same thing every night."

Tug hangs her head, and pastes a pitiful expression on her face. "I thought she'd play tonight for *sure*."

"Well, get over it! We're way down the list where her priorities are concerned. And you just wasted a whole lot of energy for nothin'," Goblin smugly responds.

In complete frustration at losing an entire evening's worth of work, I turn toward the animals. "All right, who's been walking on the keyboard again?"

Crumbs in the Keyboard

Tug and Goblin look up in unison. The puppy's tail wags, Goblin purrs loudly.

For several long minutes, they watch as I study the ruined work on the computer screen. "What a mess!"

"You can do that later. Come and play. *Pleeeease?*" Tug dances around, hoping to get attention.

I watch as Tug tries to put every ounce of cute, puppy gleam into her eyes. She moves forward wagging her tail so hard it threatens to shake off.

Goblin jumps up, and winds around my legs in that figure-eight pattern I pretend to hate.

"Come on, Mom. Your characters aren't going anywhere. They're still trying to get outta that weird sexual position you put 'em in. Come play with us," Goblin begs.

I sigh heavily, then squat down to their level. "Okay, you win. Let's go find the ball and the catnip."

"YES!" The puppy hops around wildly.

I see her race around the house looking for her favorite toy, the tennis ball.

Goblin leaps to the back of a kitchen chair and shows off her graceful balancing skills.

"Why do you need to spend so much time writing anyway?" Goblin presents a wide-eyed, innocent expression. "We're a lot more cuddly than some old manuscript."

Goblin's deep purr rumbles, and she bumps her head against my arm. I pick her up off the chair and go searching for the hysterically, barking puppy. Resigned, I know I'll have to wait another day to finish the further, amorous adventures of Torvald and Rotunda.

Playing Tag With The Muse

The "Muse"-ings of an Author's Cat
Vurlee Toomey
(With a little help from Socks, the Cat)

Great. Here she comes, straight for this comfortable chair and me. Double great. She has that maniacal writer's gleam in her eye. Her "muse" must be cooperative this afternoon. Why my human depends on a mythical creature for inspiration when I'm right here is beyond me. That "muse" is as fickle as that smooshed-faced kitten that runs around the house, thinking she owns the joint.

"Come on, Socks. Move, baby, so I can sit down and write."

Ugh. I'm getting too old to be moving me from the soft confines of this chair to the cold, hard floor. Darn! That dratted mutt is circling my human, looking for a place to sleep. She always takes the blanket under the desk.

Sigh. Guess I'll just curl up next to her feet. Her so-called inspirational figure will depart as she normally does, and I'll take over, as I usually do. What *would* she do without me?

The tap tapping of the keys has stopped and my human drums her claws on the desktop. Not a good sign at all. I suppose I'd better see if I can get her back on track. It's worse than I thought. She's got that roller coaster game going. How am I supposed to give her inspiration and help if her concentration is on some silly game and not the task at hand? These humans are such complex creatures. Not at all like us cats. We're so simple and easy to get along with. Well, I am at least. Those other two cats are such nuisances and almost as brainless as that worthless creature wagging her stub of a tail under the desk.

But I digress. My human needs me.

I'll just curl up on the paper strewn across the desk and paw through them. Maybe I can find something she can use. Hmmm. Not bad, but it's missing something.

"Socks, don't play with my papers. I had them organized."

Hrumpf. Like anything on this desk is organized! It looks like a tornado blew through and left chaos in its wake; or maybe those *other* cats chased each other over the top of the desk. It looks more like the messes they cause around here. How can she work with all this clutter? Books stacked on the floor; magazines and other tomes opened and piled on one another, marking pages to

Crumbs in the Keyboard

read; sticky notes stuck on the walls, desk and monitor; hand written memos scribbled on anything that holds ink; pictures of flying machines and maps taped to the wall. *Sigh.* It looks like the litter box after that princess of a kitten has visited it.

Good. She's turned off that game and returned to her writing. But all she's doing is staring at the screen, her fingers hovering over the keys. What has her stuck and looking so disgruntled?

Hmmm. Good. Not bad. Better. That could use some work. Scratch that. What's the problem here? This isn't so bad.

Oh, my! If we cats could blush, I believe I would be doing so right about now! No wonder my human isn't writing. The mating ritual of these creatures is very complex, indeed. How do they do it with all those arms and legs and no fur? If they didn't have all that lip touching and grooming and rolling around, it would be so much easier. Humans are difficult, aren't they?

Wait. Now she's turned on the music. Hopefully, this will help. Oh, yes, there's Sarah Vaughn belting out "'Round Midnight". What lovely sound. Perhaps she was a cat in a former life. And now, the low and sultry tones of Miss Ella Fitzgerald pour from the speakers with "Come Rain or Come Shine".

Yes! Her fingers are flying over the keys and the words are materializing on the screen! NO! Don't stop! What are you doing?

Oh, okay. You can stop to pet me if you wish. I'll allow it this time. Just keep thinking about the story. Are you stuck again? Let's take a look-see, shall we? Good. Good. Funny. A bit rough, here, I think. Good.

"I've been told I have the voice of an angel," Vicki purred.

Need a good come back line there, don't we? Let's see, what would work? The two female humans are acting like a pair of jealous cats fighting over a Tom. And that Vicki character isn't being too subtle about it, is she?

That's it! Now, how do I get the idea across to my human? *Puuuuuuuurrrrrrrrrrrr.*

Darn! All that's doing is making her pet me. Which I don't mind, but we need to focus here! What's that noise? We can't be distracted from our work.

Great. It's that little she-devil of a kitten. What is she doing lounging on top of the monitor, her fluffy tail twitching back and forth, like she's the Queen of the Nile?

Hiss! Go away, you scrawny excuse for a cat! Leave my human alone so she can work! And leave my tail be! It is NOT a toy! Hiss! Hrumpf! That's

Playing Tag With The Muse

better. Now, maybe we can get something accomplished.

"That's it! Thank you, Socks. I've got it now!"

Why, you're welcome, but what did I do? Not that I don't mind taking the credit, but I have to make certain it's worthy.

"And all the tact of a cat in heat," Colleen muttered.

Why, yes. I do believe I will take the credit for that little come back and stroke of brilliancy. Well, I guess my job here is done. I've accomplished my good deed for the day and now my human is busy at her keyboard, typing away as intense as that smooshed-faced kitten chases moths.

But I suppose I should stay close by--just in case my human needs a real muse.

Crumbs in the Keyboard

Inspiration When We Weren't Looking

Crumbs in the Keyboard

It Never Occurred To Me
Ariana Overton

"You've got cervical cancer and we don't know if it's spread or not."

These were the words that assaulted my mind while I sat in my doctor's office after a checkup in the Fall of 1979. I was 29 years old and thought I'd never hear these words. I'd already heard too many words like them, like 'you're a diabetic' and 'you have a bad heart,' but, it never occurred to me to give up.

I had long ago given up having more children after I gave birth to my daughter Danielle in 1968. After six miscarriages, my doctor told me he had no idea why I kept losing them and suggested I give up before my health went downhill. I had no choice and was given a tubal ligation. I was sterilized and had to give up my dream of a dozen kids.

Still, I didn't give up.

Now, less than a year later, I was being told I had cancer. I handled it the only way I knew how. I asked, "What do we do now?"

Within days, I was in the hospital and recovering from a radical hysterectomy. I cried but it never occurred to me to give up. From that day to this, twenty-one years later, I have lived my life with passion, honesty, and a respect for life and other people. It has served me well. I went back to college and got my degree at age 30. I've traveled all over the United States and managed to experience many things that most people don't find or make the time to do. I've met some fantastic people and some not so great. Yet, all have value.

Four years ago, I lost my job and, for the first time in my life, I went on unemployment. That's when I decided it was time to fulfill my life-long dream of becoming a writer. I swallowed my pride and I wrote "*Trapdoor*". It was contracted in 1997 and that set me on the road to writing.

During this time, while researching for my second novel, "*Tapestry*", I launched a search for a special tropical plant. The contact name that came up was Max Overton, teacher of Botany, Biology, and Zoology in Queensland, Australia. I wrote to him and, within weeks of our 'meeting', I received round trip tickets to Queensland with the attached invitation, "Come and see for yourself."

Inspiration When We Weren't Looking

I didn't hesitate. I sold everything I owned, packed what I kept in two big suitcases and I went to Queensland. With a heart and head full of happy anticipation and the joy of being an adventurer thrumming through my veins, I was not at all disappointed.

I met Max and fell in love with him. We were married on July 4th of 1999 and we've been happy ever since.

I stayed in Australia for 2 ½ years. I wound up doing a comedy radio show with two crazy Aussie guys who ended up being close, dear friends and that radio show introduced me to Townsville, Queensland and its citizens.

Everywhere I went, I heard, after saying something in my 'yank' accent, "Are you Ariana?" A grin, a hug and an exclaimed, "I'm so glad to meet you! I listen to you every morning and you never fail to make me laugh. Thank you!" inevitably followed my answer. Those were some of the happiest years of my life.

When I first decided to go to Australia, my daughter asked me, "Doesn't it scare you to go to a strange country and start over again?"

My answer was simple, honest and very much me. I told her, "Honey, just having a life to start over with is a miracle. I'm not going to throw away any opportunities to live it to the full. I don't know what will happen but, whatever does, it's a gift I won't turn down."

I now have 7 books published, a husband who is truly my soul mate, a daughter, a son-in-law, two grandsons that I adore, and an Internet full of close friends that are as close to me as family. I've made book covers for others and rejoiced at their pleasure in my work. I've edited books and glowed when an author told me they respect me. I've done my best and given freely, openly and with a full heart. And it's come back to me many times over.

I'm a happy woman.

All because it didn't occur to me to give up.

Crumbs in the Keyboard

Dreams vs. Reality
Su Kopil

Any dream can come true if you want it bad enough, whether that means publishing a book or finding your true love. Back in the days of the depression, my grandmother, the oldest of five children, fell in love with a boy while she was working in a cigar factory. His parents didn't think she was good enough for their son. Her parents thought she was too young to marry.

But they loved each other. So instead of waiting, they drove to a bordering state and eloped. He bought her a simple white gold band and had the date engraved inside. That same night they drove back home. He dropped her off at her parent's house and he went home to his parent's house. But one thing had changed. They were now bound together forever. My grandparents remained married and in love until my grandfather died leaving my grandmother a widow at age fifty. She never remarried.

I always loved listening to my grandmother tell this story. For me, it had all the makings of a fairy tale romance. It showed me, not only was love possible, but dreams were, too. Somehow, I knew even back then that my lifelong dream of becoming a published author would happen.

Being a voracious reader until her eyesight gave out, my grandmother understood my dream. When my first story was published in a magazine, she proudly wrote to her friends, bragging of my accomplishment.

Years passed and I saw my stories published in an anthology soon to be followed by a second anthology. With the second book, my publisher allowed me to dedicate one of my stories, The Sweetbriar Inn, to my grandmother. I could hardly wait to get my hands on a print copy to show her. But as will happen in publishing, delay followed delay.

By this time, my ninety-one year old grandmother had been in a nursing home almost a year. Being five states away, I'd only been able to visit her a handful of times. I knew her mind was going, yet I clung to the hope she'd be able to understand my dedication to her. Finally, the week before we were due to go home for Christmas, the book arrived.

But the news wasn't good. My grandmother's mental state had deteriorated.

Inspiration When We Weren't Looking

When I went to visit her, I left the book home.

Christmas Eve, the night of my last visit with her before returning home, I'd also been shooting the cover for a new anthology using old photos of my grandfather. A month later, I learned my design had been accepted. My grandfather's picture would grace the cover of a romance book. What a kick my grandmother would have gotten out of that. But she would never know because she passed away a few weeks later.

My writing partners have been extremely gracious in suggesting we dedicate *Seasons of Romance* to my grandparents and their great love. A dream come true, being able to dedicate a book to my grandmother and the grandfather I never met, though I can't help but wish it had happened a little bit sooner.

I've learned dreams can come true if you want them enough but wanting is no longer enough. I now set goals and reach for them everyday. A sticky note on my computer reminds me to keep my dream in sight. Even when life throws a curve ball, I try to stay motivated, focused and determined. Most of all, I've learned to cherish the people who offer me encouragement and inspiration. Though my grandmother may be gone, her stories remain with me ever-fueling the journey to my dreams.

Crumbs in the Keyboard

Spun Yarn
Terri Hartley

To my dad, Small Salt

One often wonders "why" we choose to take a certain path in life, or "who" or "what" influenced our decision. As a young girl, I would listen intently while my dad would tell stories of his adventures upon the ocean as a younger man.

"Gee, Dad, the last time you told that story, the water wasn't coming over the starboard bow!" One could almost see the whales approaching, hear the water splashing against the sides of the seine boat and smell the salty sea air. When he began to tell one of his stories, anyone within earshot would stop talking and become mesmerized, hanging on his every word.

I found myself "following in my dad's footsteps" one summer afternoon. During a long walk to the beach, my younger sister said, "I'm tired of walking. Are we almost there?"

"Almost," I replied. Something sparkled under the hedge that bordered the road. "Look what I found!" I exclaimed to my younger sister, "A magic quarter!"

"Really?" she said as she looked at me rather dubiously.

"Yes, really! The tooth fairies must have dropped it last night on their way home!"

"Is it a genuine tooth fairy quarter?" she asked.

"Oh, I'm sure of it!"

"Well, how do you know that?" she inquired further.

I turned the quarter over, and showed her the "lady" on the back of the quarter.

"See, there's a picture of a tooth fairy which makes this a magic quarter." As we continued walking toward the beach, I began to "spin my tale." My sister listened intently to the story, and had completely forgotten how tired she was from walking!

Since having my own children, I have told many a bedtime story. It was seeing the excitement in their faces, (just as in my younger sister's face many years ago), that encouraged me to continue creating stories.

Like so many of my sister and fellow writers, life's responsibilities need to be attended to first. Often times, I hear my son say, "Mom! Do I have any clean

Inspiration When We Weren't Looking

jeans?" Next, my daughter is looking at me saying, "How can I wear my red shirt without my matching red socks?"

And, let's not forget dinner! Like so many of us, I have probably cooked over 10,000 chickens in my lifetime. Contrary to the singing commercial, "I don't feel like chicken tonight!" Actually, nobody does it better than the "Colonel!

When my household is finally "quiet," I can take a little corner of my life and escape to my keyboard. Once there, I can journey to different lands, go back to a time long ago and let my imagination soar. Through our gift of being able to "paint a picture with words," we open the door to an entirely different world.

As writers, we bring smiles, laughter, happiness and contentment. We have the ability to fill the romantic "poets cup" within each of us. I believe that if we listen to our hearts, we will find our own unique path. When we are driven to write with a passion, it is then that our spirit shines through brilliantly, illuminating the words on the pages as our stories unfold.

As I sit here twisting open my double stuff Oreo cookie getting crumbs everywhere (please don't tell my kids), I'll answer your question. Did I choose writing? Hmmm...for me it was the contagious enthusiasm with which my dad told a story that gave *me* inspiration. I guess, in a certain sense, you might say, writing chose me!

Crumbs in the Keyboard

One Moment in Time
Laurie Alice Eakes

My hand shook as I set down the phone. Then I sat motionless, numb, and incapable of feeling if I was still shaking. All I could hear were the words to a song so old it was an oldie when I was a kid. "So they tell me that a friend is dying..."

My dearest friend, my soul mate, the kind of person with whom I'd always wanted a female friendship and waited so long to gain, had less than six months to live. I had an indeterminate number of years to live without her insight and guidance.

In writing classes, I've often been told that the story pivots on how one moment in time changes a character's life. The events that make up a story begin with this moment. Little did I realize that, with that phone call, my own story would begin in that one moment in time.

As part of the grieving process, I considered what my friend had intended to do and what she was never able or never allowed herself to do. That led to me thinking about all the things I wanted to do, would not allow myself to do, thought I could never have. Like my friend, I was on a path set for a life with many material comforts and few comforts for the heart and soul. I had security and even a good measure of luxury. I did not have closeness or much hope for life getting better. I imagined myself with only six months to live, and knew I wished for, yearned for, a different existence.

Be careful what you wish for are words whose meaning have struck home with breath-taking force during the past year. Within a month of deciding I needed to take Fate into my own hands and make the changes myself, I realized I could choose either to remain where I was, uptight, frightened and all but reclusive, or risk going out on my own.

I gave up the security of a reliable, if boring, job, the knowledge that I would always have a roof over my head and would probably have a trip to Europe every year. I moved to a city I had never seen before where I knew only one person and had no job prospects or even a place to live.

A year later, I have a wonderful place to live and a more promising writing

Inspiration When We Weren't Looking

career ahead of me. I am back on track with my education, a track denied me in my previous life, and, most importantly, I have the kind of romance in my life I thought only existed in books.

None of this has come easily. My decision has put me through situations I can't even bring myself to make my heroine's suffer. Yet, I have never regretted my decision to take charge of my own life and be the actor rather than the acted upon. Through all I have endured, I possess strength in the knowledge that I am in charge of my own destiny, and am moving forward because of that one moment in time.

Crumbs in the Keyboard

The Value of Human Life
Karen L. Syed

Every day another life is lost. That person may not be physically dead, but their will to succeed and thrive may have been horribly impaired, if not broken altogether.

As a writer it is my pleasure to create lives filled with joy and happiness. Though these people are often forced to overcome huge obstacles, I can make it possible. This is not always the case in real life. Domestic violence is one of the most horrible crimes ever perpetrated against another human being. I know. I've been there.

Many years ago, I met and fell in love with a beautiful man. Eyes the color of a summer sky and a smile that could melt ice in the Arctic. After a whirlwind engagement we were married. This time that should have been the happiest of my life became a nightmare. I had married an abuser-a drug abuser, a people abuser, and a life abuser.

I had only recently begun my journey as a writer and I found myself slipping deeper into my make believe worlds to escape the threats and insults inflicted upon me on a regular basis. Though I'd lived a life of love and encouragement from my family, I let that slip away. I grew deaf to the words of support they offered to me and I became blind to the abusive words hurled at me with such bitterness and rage.

I lived to write. I sat at my computer for hours on end, avoiding the physical contact of a man who dared to tell me I had no beauty or value to humanity. Day after day I found myself going to work, only to dread coming home for another round of "You will never amount to anything!" I closed myself off from friends and family and sunk further into the depths of worthlessness. Then one day I reached the bottom.

Finally succumbing to what surely must be the truth, I made the heart-wrenching decision to stop the charade of becoming a writer. I had no talent, I had no ambition, and I had no value to humanity. My muse had deserted me, leaving me empty and unfulfilled. Hadn't it?

I gathered all of my written words and research, accumulated over two

Inspiration When We Weren't Looking

years, and I angrily shoved them into garbage bags and carried them to the curb outside. Surely, this would be the answer. If I stopped kidding myself, I could spend more time devoting myself to becoming a better wife and person. Distraught and broken, I said a prayer and fell into bed. The next morning I awoke with a clear head and a newfound determination.

I stumbled from my room and out to the curb to find everything gone. The words and characters I loved so dearly and who had never let me down had been stolen from me. It was, as I recall, my first epiphany. I had let another human being steal my heart and cast it aside like useless trash. It took some time, but with the support of several fellow writers and some very dear friends, I was able to find myself. I found the strength and the determination to rebuild my life.

As a single person, I have had many struggles, from working multiple jobs to begging food from friends. I have maintained my desire to write and touch people's lives with my words and characters. Everything I do now is for me. I am strong, I am brave, and I am successful. I don't have the money of kings, but what I do have is of far more value. I have the spirit of life.

My writing is a part of me, as much as my arms and legs. Though I know I could survive without any of them, I will fight to the death to keep them all. My body is my own and I find pride in it. My mind is also my own and I find peace in it.

The value of human life can never be measured. The wealth of love can never be diminished. No human has the right to steal another's spirit or desire and with the support of those we love, nothing is impossible.

There is good in every person and with the proper nurturing and faith, that goodness can be enhanced and shared. With love the value of human life can always be increased.

Crumbs in the Keyboard

I Found My Lights
Rae Shapiro

I recently went to a writer's conference where a keynote speaker mentioned that everyone needs someone to hold the light to help them find their way to success. I am fortunate enough to have two beams, one over each shoulder. They give me different kinds of support and encouragement. One is my husband of forty-five years, who never ceases to amaze me, and my very dearest and oldest friend in terms of time, Elaine Galit. We have been holding beacons for each other for fifty years.

Our history goes back to high school, where we met. She was my inspiration to make as many A's as possible. (My exception was PE. I have never been cut out for running, jumping or hitting balls with sticks of any kind. She got A's in PE too, with little effort.) We weren't really competing; we were both very goal oriented and our main goal was to be the best.

Elaine moved from Los Angeles to Houston in the '70s. A trip there in 1999 granted me unbelievable bonuses. At that time, Elaine was already a published writer and way ahead of me in this game. When I purchased my computer in 1998, she said, "Now you have to write."

My answer to that was, "Sure, why not. I can do that." So I started writing. I found a terrific writing group at a Seniors' Center here in the San Fernando Valley where I live, and a short story class with a great teacher at the junior college.

In October of '99, I visited Elaine in Houston, bringing some of my stories and essays at her request. She read my work with a terrifically critical eye. One essay in particular was a favorite. "Enter this one in the Houston Writers' League Conference contest. I really like this piece," she said.

The rest is history.

I got the essay in just under the deadline, and then decided if I had an entry, I really should be at the conference. So I asked Elaine to get "my" room ready again for another extended visit. I never travel for just a weekend if I can help it--all trips must be real visits or they don't count. I found the registration form on the Internet, filled it in, and wired my reservation for the whole conference, then

Inspiration When We Weren't Looking

started to plan my trip in March of 2000. Before I even got my luggage out, I received a letter telling me that I was a finalist in my category, heady news for a beginner!

My next hurdle was to pack my bags, including the wonderful letter, and then off to Houston for a life-changing trip.

The venue for the Conference was the Westside Marriott, a terrific place to congregate. The check-in table was well organized. When I opened my packet, I found a special ribbon that said "Finalist," which I was to wear throughout the Conference, attached to my nametag. My "checker-inner" helped me put my ribbon and name badge together and congratulated me. After giving her my thanks for everything so far, I began to walk around and mingle.

While in line for a cup of coffee, I compared experiences with another person new to writing conferences. She asked how I got to be a finalist. With a big grin, I answered, "I entered, and then prayed a lot."

Another life changer was taking second place in my category. I was nervous, but not overly so. I love desserts. But when the fourth, and then third winners were announced, I pushed away a really scrumptious looking pile of something gooey loaded with chocolate, stating, "Now I'm just too nervous to eat that!"

My hands were shaking as I accepted the certificate and trophy for second place. My old friends and new ones were clapping furiously and cheering for me as I came back to the table. I felt like a celebrity.

At conferences, one speaks with publishers, editors and other writers. The people I met gave me the courage to say again, "Yes, I can do that. " An enthusiastic Texas publisher accepted a story for an anthology, my first sale! My light, Elaine is in that anthology too, which makes it doubly special.

I have since been accepted for two other anthologies. Elaine in particular, and all the great people I met in Houston gave me the assurance that age is no barrier to new experiences. What could give me a greater high than that evening in Houston? Since it was a first-time event for me, it will probably never be equaled until I sign my first full-length book contract. However, now that I have received that "warm Houston push," I'll never stop trying.

And I still have those beams over my shoulder, lighting my way.

The Nature of the Beast
Kathryn Smith

I had a discussion the other day with a friend of mine about writing, specifically, the type of writing which shows the more unpleasant aspects of life. My friend believes it is our job as writers to rise above human nature, to write in such a way that the horrors of life are bypassed and we only present what is safe, acceptable and 'proper'. After all, he said, we don't want to take a chance on traumatizing our readers.

This raised large questions in my mind on why we write. What is proper and acceptable? Just what is so bad about human nature anyway? Sure, humanity produced Adolf Hitler and Al Capone, but it also gave us Leo Tolstoy, Marie Curie, John Lennon and the little girl next door with blond ringlets and eyes like bluebirds who trills hello to me each morning.

It isn't our job to produce characters that are above human nature. To create stories that resonate, we must people them with characters ripe with humanity, characters which try and fail and try again. We must create characters who speak to us, not from lofty heights of heavenly perfection, but whisper in our ears while plodding along next to us on our well-worn paths of angst, guilt, fear, and insecurity. If we deal only with idealistic concepts and situations where nothing bad ever happens, will we reach anyone? I've never met anybody who has experienced only good things and never been exposed to unhappiness.

We lament over that aspect of human nature that makes us slow down at car accidents and stare raptly at movie screens as bombs explode and characters die. Why do our headlines focus on earthquakes and wars rather than flower displays and puppies? Perhaps it's because the joys of life far outweigh the sorrows. We have many things to be thankful for. Yet, would we see the beauty if we didn't have the ugliness? Would sunrise be so precious if we hadn't lived through hours of darkness? It is contrast that gives us the perspective to appreciate the good in life. Without those dire headlines and sad stories, would we realize how lucky we are?

All well-crafted stories have one thing in common: emotional truth. This is the driving force behind the story that enables readers to connect with it. We

Inspiration When We Weren't Looking

can't forge an emotional link to perfection. We are not perfect. The struggle to overcome our shortcomings fills our lives, our hearts. As we move through the patterns of life, working, playing, striving, it is our dreams that keep us going through the humdrum routine, adding that fillip of anticipation that keeps us from sinking into despair and futility. This is what we can all identify with. As readers progress through our stories they form a bond, however temporary, with our characters as they go through this common struggle.

This is why we must write about the negative aspects of life. Not to glorify them, but to celebrate that part of human nature which strives to meet each challenge. How we choose to present it, whether explicitly or implied, is up to each writer, but it must be present in order to give readers what they are looking for.

Our characters do not rise above human nature, they reflect it. Human nature isn't a pestilence to be wiped out. It's an integral part of each one of us and we must embrace it, because that is who we are.

In my writing there is sometimes more of me than I've ever shown anyone face to face. Writing is an outlet for a lot pent-up emotions. This doesn't mean the story is true, only that the emotions depicted are in some way true for me. Emotional truth is what readers identify with; it's what makes a story ring true. I think this is what is meant by 'opening a vein' when we write. We don't write from a vacuum. Our experiences and emotions find their way into our stories.

Why have I opened these private places in my soul, exposing them to others who may never understand? The answer goes to the heart of why I write.

We are never alone. In our darkest moments there are others there ahead of us, others who will follow. We are all part of the human tragedy. Some of us experience more, a lucky few get by with less. I don't write to shock, anger or upset others. I write to share. Not everyone will want to read what I've crafted, but I hope those who do will, for a brief moment, cry with me, laugh with me, celebrate with me. Through my stories and the characters I've created from the patchwork of my life and my imagination, I tell of the things that touch me. What touches me will touch others. The message isn't that all is dark, or even that everything is good.

Rather, I want my readers to come away with a feeling of hope, the realization that others have experienced their pain and survived. That they too, can survive. I want everyone who reads my words to know that none of us are ever alone.

That is why I write.

Crumbs in the Keyboard

Subtle Delights
Kate Walsh

Sitting in his favorite winged-back chair, my uncle says, "Well, will you look at that! A body might think she could read already, and she's only three!" Black letters shined on white pages; an odd, lovely perfume rising from them, creating unforgettable delight.

This is the earliest of my book memories. Others include the August challenges presented by the Ragweed Season, sitting up in bed with a generous supply of soft cotton pieces cut from old sheets--"so as to not tear up your poor nose; oh, just look at the puffy eyes on that child!" Waiting. Finally, the back door opens and my beautiful godmother (a real one) moves across the kitchen floor toward the bedroom I gratefully occupy since my grandfather's death. She balances the stack of books carefully. A piece of cake for her, because she does much the same thing all day long at her library.

Along about 1937, someone said to her: "Well, Miss O'Leary, you do have a fine record and degree from St. Francis College. But, you cannot teach in the Chicago Public Schools. We cannot have a *deformed* person in the classroom with our children, don't you see?" Hunchback is the word folks used to describe her condition. (Say it to yourself three times; remember that game? Repeating words and phrases over and over shows either their loveliness or how goofy they are). She fell from a high place at a very young age. The substitute doctor who put her body in a cast didn't do it quite right; thus, the hunchback status.

What does one do, after encountering such stinging rejection? Anne O'Leary took herself right back to St. Francis College for a fifth year of study. The Chicago Public Library would, "of course, be very pleased to have you in our employ upon completion of a Library Science Degree." Somehow, they either missed or didn't care about the variation in her body shape. Why is that? Was it something in her eyes, those endless blue rivers, reflecting the possibilities in this young woman? We never knew; Anne never discussed it; I never asked.

For more than forty years, Miss O'Leary brought information, delight, encouragement and beauty to her 'patrons' Preparation for work received the same attention that performers give to current engagements. Auburn hair in an

Inspiration When We Weren't Looking

upsweep with a spray of forehead curls framed her face. Special platform shoes, in an array of colors, came from Joseph's Salon on Wabash Avenue. My grandfather's splendid black 1936 Oldsmobile sedan, with its ostrich-leg stick shift rising up from the floor, was her classy chariot.

Anne O'Leary read voraciously. History. Novels. Biographies. Periodic Head-librarian's reports kept her head-bent over the dining room table for days. No time to work on them at the library, as every hour belonged to the community of patrons and staff members.

When anyone asked, "Annie, what do you want for your birthday?" the answer was always the same: "Peace and Quiet; that's it." The answer came with a smile or light laugh, as she'd look up at you over her book or newspaper. For others, though, a magical parade of boxes came out of her deep-set closet. Finding just the right gift for family and friends gave her great pleasure.

What might happen, when a child grows up in the presence of such a person? There is a good chance that she might acquire a store of wisdom. That supply might stay hidden for years. Appearances may suggest that she has taken some seriously wrong turns. Winning a pre-medicine study scholarship; then, giving it up one year later to enter a convent! Leaving that convent after five years, apparently intact; then, marrying a widower with five children in tow! Moving to different states, not once but twice. Unheard of, for immigrant families whose members live no more than five miles apart! "Good God!" they whispered to one another, "can it be that the girl will turn out like her mother?"

No, not a chance. Grace and beauty were poured over her, day in and day out, providing true support; not the kind from godmothers who turn up only when salvation from some prince is in doubt. Many grand godmother-gifts came from Anne's sense of humor.

One example stands out. On one of his visits, my Dad delighted me with a Springer Spaniel puppy. He was 'springy' all right. Plans for one of Anne's treasured days off transitioned into frantic pursuit of a fleeing dog. Driving down Halsted, whistling, cooing, calling, Anne coaxed Skippy by dangling a tasty hot dog from her outstretched hand.

As the urban environment faded, and farm country appeared, Anne gave up the chase and turned the car back toward Englewood. Only much later did I realize how she must have dreaded reporting to third-grade me that my dog was gone for good.

Relief came to each of us when a neighbor stopped by several weeks later,

Crumbs in the Keyboard

informing us that one of his farmer friends was glad to have Skippy stay there and help out with wayward chickens and growing children.

It is often the memorable gestures of kind generosity, the indirect teaching, and subtle encouragements that provide us with the most powerful direction. We may easily miss the jewels passed into our possession when we are so busy managing life's many layers. Yet, the variety of those jewels slips easily, quietly into our souls. We feel a yen for creating something with flour and eggs, with cloth, by putting pen to paper-or, these days, fingers to a keyboard decorated with stray crumbs.

We find ourselves enthralled with the way e. e. cummings spread words on a page, or with Langston Hughes' images. Pen in hand, we wander through a bibliography list, searching for a reference that will take us deeper into a current journey; that of understanding our characters, ourselves and the array of gifts that continue coming to us..

Inspiration When We Weren't Looking

The Round Peg
Diana Lee Johnson

I didn't have much self-esteem growing up. What little I managed was totally destroyed by the physical abuse my daughter and I suffered at the hands of her father. *That*, I've discovered, is a very good reason to write.

Get the emotions out, and they will free you. Entertain just one person, and you garner a bit of self-esteem. Entertain two, and you nurture your own need while giving to others. So you make time, steal time, and borrow time to escape. You find reasons for housework to wait. (I've been finding them all my adult life.) One night you treat the kids to McDonald's instead of slaving over the stove; another night it's do-it-yourself sandwiches. You manage errands on your way home from work, or on your lunch hour, so you can poach a little time on Saturday.

All my life I've been a big, round peg trying to fit into a small, square hole. As a child, I didn't like to read. Now I know it's probably due to Attention Deficit Disorder. By contrast, I could tune out the world and write poetry from the age of six, then came a couple of stories. When I wasn't writing, my mind escaped into incredible tales I made up while floating around our small pool in the summer.

After my first divorce, having worked the entire thirteen years since high school, I decided to look into writing prose. I took an extension course called "Creative Writing for Fun and Profit." Well, it was no fun (the teacher didn't like anything I turned in) and I still haven't found a profit--financially, that is. I did find sanity.

Of the letters to the editor assignment, mine was the only one published. Two newspapers, a local paper and a Washington, DC " biggie," picked it up. Add a little self-esteem there.

I started writing stories. One kept getting longer, turning into a short novel. I drew from my own experiences, much embellished, of course--a divorced mother of one; abusive ex-husband; deceased, adored father. Unlike this author, the heroine found a rich, handsome, new husband. I can still hope! I began to realize the possibilities. I could write (type) a book (pre-computer days, you

Crumbs in the Keyboard

know). I'd never be able to read my own handwriting. Besides, the movies in my head ran faster than my fingers.

Write a book? What could I write about that anyone else would want to read? Hadn't I just used up all my personal experience? Well, maybe, but what about all those stories I used to dream up floating around the pool? It was exciting, and daunting.

An incurable romantic, I joined national and state romance writing groups. That's where I confirmed my suspicions. I wasn't normal. My approach was, shall we say, "unconventional?" Was I doing it all wrong? I didn't outline, plot, write descriptions of my characters, sketch out anything.

Then I saw it, heard it, breathed it and reveled in it! I understood and my heart lightened. Tasks I ignored I finally got done in record time. Movies project on the imaginary screen behind my eyes, and I try to catch them like sunbeams or butterflies. While at my "paying" job, I am forced to ignore them until I have a chance to get back to them. Even then, they sometimes go in a different direction; but no matter, they are moving about inside my head.

I'm amazed, appalled, and entertained by what my characters do and say. I rarely manipulate anything, except perhaps for historical accuracy.

Knowledgeable people speak and write of rules to move a story and maintain interest. I'm tempted to say, "I don't do that. My characters do." But I don't. I don't advertise my lack of convention, my absolute disregard for structure, my downright strangeness, if you will. I've learned that what's important is what works for me, not anyone else. I must be pleased with myself.

To compound my lack of convention, what I write doesn't fall neatly into categories. They are mainstream-romantic-mystery-comedies, with my heart and soul wrapped up in every one. Each character is a friend or foe. I know how they think and feel. They can say and do the things that I am too shy, too busy, too moral, too young, or old to pull-off. Just think about it, I can find a faithful lover, succeed in business, or kill off my boss in my own creations. It's great therapy!

How do you market yourself? It's not easy for most people. Imagine you've been on the receiving end of sales pitches for thirty-four years in public purchasing. Determination not to say or do anything that has irritated you all those years doesn't leave much.

What to do? Steal more time to research markets and send out query letters. I send out several at one time. After all, why waste a perfectly good query letter

Inspiration When We Weren't Looking

if I can re-tailor it to each prospective agent or editor I've zeroed in on? I consider myself lucky when someone asks to see a chapter or two. Then as each one comes back rejected, my heart sinks a little, and I want to throw in the towel--for a few minutes.

But that's just one, there are three more out there. Maybe one of those will be the right fit. Following that philosophy, I had seven manuscripts finished before I found a home for one.

After two divorces, three decades in purchasing, grown kids, and a grandson, I finally got my first paperback novel, but it wasn't a bed of roses. The "new" publisher didn't or couldn't keep up. Though I've received great reader's comments and encouragement from both genders, all ages, and races, the copies just aren't out there to be bought. But I haven't lost hope.

I have contracts for two other manuscripts to be turned into e-books and print-on-demand. It's not the best seller I've dreamed of yet. It's two less manuscripts to market, and I know there are plenty more where they came from.

Characters don't leave me alone. They keep knocking around in my head, waiting for me to let them out. When I do, we have a great time.

Crumbs in the Keyboard

The Call of the Novel
Cate Rowan

Four-thirty a.m. I rub my eyes and sigh under my breath.

My roommates are fast asleep in their hotel beds. I'm glad they're heavy sleepers--they'd have the right to be cranky. Even with the dim book light that shines on my laptop, the clatter of the keyboard could wake them up.

I have only three more days to write the first thirty pages of a novel--and I've never written one. Oh, I dreamed about it for years. I've longed to write since I first held a book in my hands. But I was always too scared until I learned about a contest for the first chapters of a novel. Something in me said NOW!

Maybe I need a deadline clawing at my neck to get me to do something, but at four-thirty a.m. in a hotel a thousand miles from home, I wish I didn't.

I'm at an annual academic conference to give a talk to a hundred fellow scientists in five short hours. I haven't written my talk or put the slides together. I'm here in the dark, writing my novel. I must be crazy.

I must be a writer.

With regret and a sigh, I put my novel away to work on my talk. As the morning bolts by, I collect my slides, write my speech, yelp at my watch, and hustle downstairs to look professional and collegial to an audience that wants to hear about the hand bones of animals who lived three million years ago. I answer questions, engage in debate with a feisty graduate student who doesn't like my conclusions, move off the podium and gulp a large glass of water, accept congratulations from friends and mucky-mucks alike, then scurry to my room and my novel. The world I'm creating is too enticing to be away for long.

I've only let a few of my professional colleagues know what I'm doing. My former Ph.D. advisor is supportive, though concerned--after all, why did I spend seven years getting a Ph.D. if I'm not going to use it? The words "why do you want to be a starving artist?" are never spoken, but I know they're on his mind.

When I crawl out for talks by other scientists and the obligatory meals and once-a-year get-togethers, I'm greeted with "I haven't seen you very much!" and "Well, hi there! Where've you been?"

I smile my secret smile and keep my mouth shut. I love my friends and

Inspiration When We Weren't Looking

enjoy my colleagues, but every moment with them is a moment away from the world I've made, one that could be on paper if I just had the time. Once again I regret that I couldn't escape the conference early.

At last I get up the nerve to hand one of my roommates my chapters. My heart is on pause, and the turning of each page feels like the scratch of sharp nails on my skin.

But Jennifer beams wide. She loves it! My heart resumes its vocation.

Jen, too, is a writer, though she hasn't yet found the courage to begin her own dream. She and I commiserate about wanting something very much, but being afraid to do it.

Then I turn back to my computer and type, one more barrier broken.

After a stolen nap, my eyes flare wide. My entry must be at the post office before the express mail deadline today.

I've never entered a writing contest before. So many rules! Formatting, maximum page count, five copies of the chapters, bind it *this* way and not *that* way, include a self-addressed envelope with enough return postage for all the entries with judges' comments.

I begin printing pages. It's slow. *Very* slow on my little portable printer. I glance at my watch. Again. And hyperventilate.

Is there a copier in the hotel? No, the business center is closed. Is there a copier at the post office? Maybe, but who knows if it's working.

Jennifer--an angel in disguise--offers help. If I take what's already been printed to the post office and fill out the express mail forms, she'll bring the rest to me when they're done.

I run out of the hotel, wild-eyed, the precious pages clutched to my chest. With great gulps of air I dash down the street, hoping I'm going in the right direction, but the street makes a funny turn, and I'm more nervous by the second.

An imposing gray building appears as I turn a corner, and I whisper thanks to the writing goddess. Five minutes to the deadline. Adrenaline on overdrive, I fill out the forms, make sure everything is in order, and run back outside to flag Jen down.

She sprints to me and hands me the copies, and I bind them and slip them into the envelope. Together we race up the stairs to queue at the counter.

I glance at my watch and get a shock. It's past the deadline. My blood races sharp and cold through my chest.

Finally, I reach the front of the line. The postal clerk shoots me a scathing

Crumbs in the Keyboard

look, puts the stamps on, then tosses my package in the express mail tub just as it is picked up to be taken away for delivery. I swallow my heart back down as my first pages make their way into the world.

Then I go buy Jen a big dinner, with stiff drinks for us both.

Six months later, I've just mailed my finished four hundred-page novel to the editor who judged the final round of that contest. She awarded me second place and asked to see the full manuscript, a sweet reward for pages written in the wee hours at an anonymous hotel room.

I look at the receipt for the manuscript package. It's my proof. I have joined the ranks. I am a novelist. I am exactly where I'm supposed to be.

And now, on to the sequel. "Chapter One."

Inspiration When We Weren't Looking

Writer's Block
Cheri Lee Funk

A writer friend of mine sent me some information about a book that was being published. The subject matter was obstacles women are faced with when wanting to write. I thought, okay, I sure would like to contribute, but I wasn't sure I was familiar with the requested topic. I didn't think I had overcome any obstacles. I just didn't write for years and years. It had nothing to do with marriage, childbirth, my job or any other usual obstacle that we as women face today

As a child I wrote. I wrote stories and poems and more stories. I poured out my thoughts on love, my dreams and my wishes for my life and I filled pages and pages. Then I stopped. I stopped because of an incident that happened and it has taken me until today to realize it.

I had written some of my innermost thoughts in a diary. Those words were found. My mother confronted me. Who did I think I was? What right did I have to think I was worthy of any of these things that I wanted? "Oh, I forgot, you are Queenie. Miss Queenie who thinks she is so very special."

I was struck by the utter powerlessness, shame, and just plain lack of control I felt. Someone could get inside of my head and steal my thoughts and make something evil out of them. I think this hurt worse than the beatings, for those bruises have since gone away. I never got those words back and I am not sure I would have kept them if I did.

After that day I did not write again until about four years ago when I began to deal with some past issues in my life. I was advised to journal for it would help rid me of the bad feelings. I didn't have any bad feelings. I had been beaten, molested, degraded and punished for just being alive.

What bad feelings could I be withholding? I had gotten this far without writing them down. What would happen if they were found? What would happen to me if someone read those words? How would people look at me? For thirty years I was unable to put pencil to paper.

Then one day I was lying around the pool, dozing and soaking up some sun and totally relaxed. All of a sudden I was struck by some words floating around

Crumbs in the Keyboard

in my head, words I was told as a very small child, words of such pure hatred and evil that they still made me tear up when I remembered them.

I got up, stumbled into the house and at down and wrote "My Mother's Burden." Since then, I have tried to write my thoughts about the abuse and violence. At first the words wouldn't come. It was like pulling teeth to get my thoughts out of my head, my heart, or even my soul and down on a sheet of paper.

Then three years ago, I lost Barb, my best friend. Not only was she a friend, she was one of the only people in my life that I felt actually loved me. She accepted me and made me understand that though these things happened, it wasn't what I was about and it wasn't my fault.

So I began to write. At first it was as a way to feel clean and less tarnished, then it became a way to help others that may have been through the same things. I wrote as a sort of validation to all of us that have lived through unspeakable terrors and actually come out on the other side.

Maybe a little worse for wear but actually Survivors! It has not always been easy, at times the words are still hard to find.

Recently, I was able to spend some time with Barb's mother. I told her about my desire to write and how I felt I might be able to because of Barb and her unconditional acceptance of me. She had helped me see I wasn't to blame, I wasn't evil and I deserved to be loved. Granny, Barb's mom, looked up to me and told me to write. She told me I needed to write. This opportunity was being presented to me and I needed to grab it and run with it. Barb would be with me and she would give me the strength I needed.

I was able to start writing and I am happy to say I am still writing. Though at times it is not easy digging up all of the long buried thoughts of abuse and fear and it takes lots of courage to get those words out and onto a piece of paper, I do think it is helping. Never again do I have to worry about others ridiculing me or taunting me when they read my words. I have taken away their power, for by talking about it and writing about it they are the ones that have become powerless! And they will never be able to hurt me again. I am finally safe.

Thanks Barb and Granny for helping me get through my writer's block!!

Inspiration When We Weren't Looking

After the Crumbs
Christine McClimans

"Chrissy, what are you doing?"
"Just writin,' Mama," I smiled. Little did I know I was having the first conversation that would eventually lead to my dream the dream of becoming a writer.

I wasn't quite five-years-old when I begged my Mother to teach me to read and write. I had a pad of paper and Daddy's fountain pen and was scribbling away as fast as I could. My Mother and Daddy were good critics as they complimented me on what I had just pretended to 'write.

I remember the day I asked Mom to teach me to read and write. "You are only four years old!" I remember mom saying.

"But, mom, you and daddy can read and write. Show me how!" I pleaded.

Soon after that we were in the Goodwill store and there was a huge chalkboard sitting on easel legs. It had a roller on the top with the alphabet, words and pictures to match. It soon became one of my prized possessions.

With this, some dime store chalk and a lot of patience, I was taught to write. My mother was very pleased with how determined and dedicated I became.

When I was five, I started into the first grade and already could read and print my name. I was shy and quiet but I would sit for hours and read my *Little Golden Books* and tell tall tales to my dad.

Time passed quickly and I found myself in a creative writing class my senior year. My teacher was very supportive and encouraged me by telling me that I should write a book one day. That was thirty odd years ago. I cannot remember her name but I certainly remembered her words. Life sometimes gets in the way of dreams.

I graduated high school at age seventeen and had been married for five months. No particular reason to get married except than I was in love and the year was 1968 and the Viet Nam war was raging.

Shortly out of high school, he was drafted and I followed my husband to Georgia and then to Alaska. Unlike many others, he stayed state side. He was never one to be tied down and I should have known when I was left night after

Crumbs in the Keyboard

night in that frozen wilderness that I was on the road paved to marital disaster. I spent time writing and wishing for the safety of home.

Home. Ohio was a long way away and I had plenty of time to write of my loneliness. The winters in Alaska are very long and depressing when you are left alone most of the time. I asked for a baby and felt blessed when my prayers were answered. Finally, I didn't feel so alone when he was out with his buddies because I had my child growing inside.

I started a notebook that I would put my feelings into. I was thrilled about becoming a mother and wanted to share these feelings someday with my little one.

Some things are not meant to be. Four months into the pregnancy I woke in the middle of the night scared and alone and realized that I was losing my child. The next morning, I awoke in the hospital room to find strangers at my bedside explaining what had happened and asking if I could tell them where my husband was. I was too young to realize his neglect was a form of abuse. I returned home and began to pack up the tiny apartment. It was 1971 and his tour was ending and we were heading back to Ohio, just the two of us.

We planned to drive the long trip home and to enjoy the beautiful springtime and the countryside. I planned on starting a book about the adventures that we would encounter and the sights we would see together. That was before he decided he would rather share that with a "buddy" and I should fly home, after all I did just lose a baby and the trip might not be good for me. Just like that it was settled.

Two days later, I arrived in Columbus, Ohio. It was good to finally be home. Mom and Dad were waiting and all the homesickness and loneliness seemed to melt away. It was wonderful to feel my parents' arms around me once again. It seemed that nothing could hurt me there. Driving back to the family farm I was amazed at how so much had changed in less than two years. It seemed I had been away a short lifetime until daddy's old Ford turned onto the familiar gravel driveway. I was home!

Several days later, when I hadn't heard a word from my husband, I began to worry. Later that evening I heard footsteps on the old porch and there he stood. The car had broken down somewhere in the Dakotas and he sold it for a ride to the airport and a ticket home. Everything we had owned was in that old 1956 Chevy. Part of me was sold there, too. My notebook containing all my thoughts, hopes and dreams vanished, lost to me forever.

Inspiration When We Weren't Looking

Once again my dream was put on hold. In 1971 I became pregnant again and once again I thought my loneliness would disappear. I realized that my marriage was not at all what I had hoped it would be. He spent all his free time playing with the guys. He would take the coil wire from the car so I would have to remain at home while he was off and about. We were living with my parents so I had people who cared close by.

On May 2, 1972, I gave birth to a baby boy. He was two months premature and was rushed to Children's Hospital. I barely remember hearing the news as I woke up. I do remember my husband's words, though. "You are young, you can always have another. I'm tired, I'm going home now." That was the last I heard from him for the next two days.

I went home from the hospital alone without even touching my newborn son. Michael remained in the hospital without much hope of survival. I felt so alone again. I prayed and then I prayed some more. My prayers were answered, and after thirteen days I brought my tiny son home. He was smaller than a doll baby, weighing only four pounds and eleven ounces. He grew in leaps and bounds and so did the distance between my husband and I. He was spending more and more time away and the quiet time I had planned to use to write was non-existent. He became harsh and very childlike himself and resented Michael and the time I spent with him.

Eventually, I knew the time had come that I needed to take my boy and run. He was becoming rougher and rougher and I could tell abuse was right around the corner. It didn't seem to matter much the words as I was leaving were, "Fine, you wanted him and you can take care of him."

The next six months waiting for the divorce was full of threats and demands but, secretly, after eight years of marriage, I think he was relieved. He was free to play again.

In 1974, I had another miracle on the way. I found a man who made all my nightmares disappear. He taught me to love and to trust and to redefine what family meant. He treasured Michael as his own and was only too happy to grant my wish of another child. With two small children and a full-time job I still wanted to write but once again, life put that dream on hold.

I lived through a potentially abusive relationship and am thankful I had the good sense to get away. I raised two wonderful children with the help and support of my husband of twenty-six years. I survived the anguish of being a mid-life orphan after the death of my remaining parent last year. I retired at the

Crumbs in the Keyboard

age of fifty and am now a grandmother. I have many good friends who support my goals and dreams.

I will begin another journey now, the one that I have waited to travel for so long.

For thirty-three years I have waited to live the dream. I have gathered memories and many life experiences. Through tears, laughter, and cookie crumbs I can now become a writer.

Inspiration When We Weren't Looking

Journey Through Darkness
Anna Seley

The room lay in darkness. The young girl writhed in silent emotional pain. She hated the night. Daylight could not come soon enough. However, this night something would change. Embarking on a journey out of the dark and fearful night, the youngster stepped into a new and exciting world.

I was that young girl. I hated going to bed at night. Fear of the dark haunted me each night until I turned 10 years old. I laid in my upper bunk bed with my eyes glued to the spot on the floor where the light crept under the door.

Each night I fell asleep with my head craned and pressed against my headboard. Something miraculous happened: I began to tell myself stories. I would revisit books I read and add my own dialogue or change things around in the story. This allowed me to focus on something besides the darkness.

Eventually, I created my own stories, developing characters, giving them names, devising plots, and detail descriptions. I lived in the fantasies, as sleep drifted in. The following morning I would write down my stories.

By the time I got to eighth grade, I had many short stories. Novels in my eyes, but I learned later they were not long enough to be considered novels. My ninth grade English teacher provided ten to fifteen minutes to write in a daily journal. Most of the students wrote about what they ate or what they did the weekend before. How boring. I took this exciting time to write down my stories that I created in my head the night before. My teacher encouraged me and would edit them periodically.

Throughout high school I continued to write without any mentoring or formal help. My senior English teacher allowed us to create a senior project of our choice. I wrote a full-length novel. I still have it after all these years, a keepsake of how far I've come and a reminder of where I am headed.

Because of those terrorizing dark nights, writing defines who I am. I will always write whether I am published or not. Writing is like breathing and eating to me. I need it to live a full and productive life. I see possible stories reaching in and out to me wherever I go. Every passerby has a story. I, the reflective observer, must respond, capture, and bring their story to life.

Crumbs in the Keyboard

The darkened house is quiet now. The lights have ebbed as one by one the members of the family slip into their rooms. The woman does her nightly rounds to secure the house, before drifting into the den and the waiting computer. The glowing light of the screen beckons her onward to the journey at hand. Magically and mysterious she spins her stories, creating fictional life to the characters who mentally talk to her. She no longer fears the darkness. Incredible peace permeates her soul.

Inspiration When We Weren't Looking

Belief—The Ultimate Muse
Kathleen Long

Belief. What is it? Do you have it?

I've always struggled with belief in myself. Oh, I'm confident. I always have been. You see, I'm a public relations professional. That's right. I'm one of those people. As I always say, I make a living out of putting words into the mouths of others. So what's the problem, you ask? When it comes to putting creative words out there under my own byline for the world to see, I freeze. I'm fearful. I'm scared. After all, what will others think? What will they say? Will they whisper behind my back? Fear--plain and simple.

It took a tragedy and a triumph in my life to erase the fear. It took a life-altering event to make me see there's nothing to be afraid of-if we only believe. If we believe in ourselves and in those we love, we can move mountains.

One year ago, my daughter, Emily, was diagnosed with a genetic disorder while she was in the womb. My pregnancy was spent running from specialist to specialist while praying that she'd survive to term. The doctors said she wouldn't. They said she'd be stillborn. They said she'd never survive her birth. But, she did. She was amazing. She was born alive. She cried and wiggled, she snuggled into her father's arms and in my own. She fussed when I changed her diaper and she kicked when we tickled her feet.

She was our angel.

Emily lived for five days, and in that time she taught our entire family, as well as her doctors, nurses, and everyone she touched, just what life is about. She taught us that life is not about how long we're on this earth. It's about what we do with the time we're given.

Emily taught me not to fear. She taught me not to base hope on statistics or odds, but to base it on belief. She taught me to reach for the stars. She was, and is, my ultimate inspiration. As you can imagine, her death left me empty and aching. I wanted to live. I wanted to write. I wanted to tell others about Emily. I just couldn't find my way out of the haze of grief that enveloped me. I sat and I stared. I was aimless. I was lost.

One day, I picked up a novel and lost myself between its pages. What an

Crumbs in the Keyboard

amazing gift that author gave me. For the time it took me to devour that book, I wasn't a grieving mother. I was a participant in a wonderful world of discovery, excitement and romance. What a wonderful thing! It was a gift given to me by an author who cared enough about her characters and her readers to put her heart and soul into her written words.

Slowly, the haze of grief began to lift, and creativity began to return. If it felt this good to read the words of others, imagine how wonderful it would feel to put my own words on paper. The first thing I wrote was an essay about kindness for our local paper. I wrote about the lessons Emily had taught everyone who had met her. My reward for stepping out of my fear and sharing from my heart was the smile and love on the faces of three hundred school children as they dedicated their acts of kindness to Emily's memory.

I felt empowered. I felt alive. I began to revisit my works in progress. New ideas popped into my head, and I scribbled them into my journal. Characters. Dialogues. Settings. They came rushing to the surface. They broke through the silence that had descended with Emily's death.

I wrote with a sense of freedom I had never known before. I knew, absolutely, that this was my destiny. I was no longer afraid to try.

Anytime the smallest doubt crept into my consciousness, I thought of Emily. I thought of her brave cry and the punch of her fists. I thought of how she overcame the odds against her. I thought of how she proved statistics are only numbers on a page that can't compete against the human spirit.

Today I write. I am an author. I may not be published, but you know what? I will be. I will succeed. Today my characters live in my heart and in my soul, and they come to life on my written pages. I can only hope the words I write today will someday do for someone else what so many authors' words have done for me. I hope they will provide a release, an escape, a smile, a tear or a laugh. I hope they will provide a window into the soul of another. I hope they will provide joy and inspiration. Most of all, I hope they will provide the comfort of a warm, handmade quilt on a cool autumn day when a lonely heart needs a hug.

As time passes, I continue to feel my precious Emily all around me. I sense her in the brush of a butterfly's wings as it flutters past, in the melody of a songbird at dawn, in the brilliant glow of a sunset over the bay. I feel her in the beat of my heart and in the calm of my soul. I see her influence in the words I write, and I know this. My miraculous little muse will never be far from me. She's given me a gift that I can never repay. She's given me the belief that one person - no matter how small - can make a difference in the lives of others - if we only try.

Inspiration When We Weren't Looking

Inspiration = Sugar + Spice + Dreams
Diana Rowe Martinez

Every day I wonder how I manage to juggle life and my writing into one not-so-neat package called home. Every day I struggle, maintaining a balance and sanity with two teenage daughters available to ground me into reality should I start floating away.

My writing obsessions began as a toddler. I'd scribble on a page and "read" my stories to my younger siblings before I even knew how to write. Later, when introduced to the wonderful word of letters, I couldn't get enough of this form of creative release, all the way through high school.

Then, life somehow got in the way. I married; I had two lovely daughters; I divorced. And the work really began.

As a single mother, time was an invaluable resource, and time and money were two things I never had enough. My daughters and their activities always came first, right alongside the two jobs I held to make ends (sort of) meet. Many nights after my girls' riding lessons or softball games, I would finally sit down road weary, but determined, and I'd escape into the world of writing.

At the same time, I managed to cultivate the guilt. (Guilt is courtesy of my own mother.) I should be doing the laundry, packing sack lunches, or cleaning the house. Instead, I wasted precious time writing something that would never be worth anything to anyone but myself. What was I thinking? I taught my daughters from the time they were toddlers to "always follow your dream and never give up. " I believed that, for them anyway.

Through those lean years, my daughters watched me struggle with life and finances, struggle with my dream of writing, and struggle with my frustrations. It wasn't until a few years ago that I discovered what they really thought of me.

When in the 8th grade, my oldest daughter Rachel had to write an essay about "the person she admired most." I asked her if she needed help. She adamantly refused my help. She never showed me her assignment, for the first time turning it in before I had proofed it. I promptly forgot about it, chalking her not wanting my help to her need for independence.

Once she received her grade a week later, she ran into the house, waving the

Crumbs in the Keyboard

pages in the air proudly. She handed me the crumpled papers with a smile on her face, and said, "Mom, I want you to read it, but promise me you won't cry." (Translation: "Mom, you're going to cry like a baby!" And she knew it.)

When I read the words my daughter had written so carefully and proudly, my vision blurred and my throat burned. Tears sneaked down my cheeks and my nose ran. (Not a pretty sight.) However, I remember reading the lined paper as if the neatly written words are in front of me now.

On that essay, Rachel chose me as her "person." She wrote that the reason she admired her mother was not just for all the "mother things she does, but because she has a dream and her dream is to be a writer. Because of watching my mom try so hard and write all the time, I know she's going to be a famous published author. Because of my mom trying so hard, I know I can dream and have it come true. Anything I dream is possible."

I still have that assignment tucked away in a box filled with Mother's Day Cards, wacky art assignments, and gifts that I accepted graciously, wore proudly for a day or two, and hid away as quickly as possible without hurting a little girl's feelings. Whenever I feel down, I pull those well-worn pages out, smooth the wrinkles and read the now fading pencil markings. When I read those words again, I smile a lot, cry a lot more, and remind myself that this is the same teenage daughter with the attitude that doesn't think I'm so cool anymore, but she still supports my writing.

I'll whisper, *"I'm still trying, baby girl."*

Last year that same daughter taped an index card to the bottom of my computer. She knew I was going through some tough personal times in my life. However, I still continued to write, and she knew that, too. This nearly 17-year-old printed in big letters on the card, "DREAMS: Happiness comes from taking your dreams seriously and yourself lightly."

Even though I always told my daughters that they could do anything, all they had to do was believe, without both my daughters' encouragement and support, I wouldn't believe my own words.

Thank you, Rachel and Bethany, for believing in your mother.

Inspiration When We Weren't Looking

Perfect Love
Pamela Thibodeaux

Note from the author: Burning the candle at both ends is nothing new for a woman, especially a writer. This article came at a very low time in my life. I was having trouble at my job, my writing was going nowhere and my children were growing up and moving on. Frankly, I was getting tired of the struggle and on the edge of giving up my dream of writing. God, in His infinite mercy, reminded me in one of my darkest hours that He is the way, the truth, and the light and that we should never give up our dreams. I hope it encourages you to reach for the light in your darkest moments. ~Pam Thibodeaux

She stood alone at the bottom of the falls. A chill permeated her very soul. Mist rose from the thundering water, shrouding everything in darkness. The sky was hidden by dark clouds hanging ominously above. It would be so easy to slip into the deep, swirling water that raged at her feet.

"Why not?" A voice tempted. "There's nothing left. Everything you've ever loved is gone. No light. No hope."

She shivered, pulling her sweater tighter around her slender frame as the voice assaulted the last tenuous hold she had on reality.

"Beloved." Another voice rose above the darkness. "My love is sufficient."

She knew whose voice was calling out to her. "Why?" Her heart cried. "What's the point?"

"Love bears all things, believes all things, hopes all things, endures all things. Love never fails." *His still, small voice reminded her.*

"How?" she sobbed. "I don't know how to start over. Or even why I should."

Sunlight burst through the clouds, a rainbow danced on the mist. A dove cooed as it settled, once again, on its nest. Children's laughter rang on the wind. Sights and sounds of life-of love.

Suddenly, she knew what God wanted of her.

He wanted her to live, to hope, to love. For where there is love, God is forever present. His love is perfect.

Perfect love that casts out the deepest of darkness.

Weeping soft tears of gratitude and understanding, she turned away from the darkness and headed toward the light-the light of life.

Crumbs in the Keyboard

Butterfly
Teresa T. Saldana

Once I was a caterpillar.
I wasn't ugly, but I didn't feel pretty.
I wanted to fly and be pretty like all the butterflies I would see in the sky.
It seemed that I would never fly.
All the other caterpillars seemed happy, and I tried to be happy like them. I was always doing what they did. I thought, "if they are happy doing that, then surely I will be too!"
I tried, and I tried, and I tried. I still wouldn't change, but I kept on trying.
Sometimes I would cry and wonder why I wasn't happy like all my friends. I was doing the same thing wasn't I?
Sometimes I would get scared and wonder what was going to happen to me. Would I never change into a butterfly?
The sky looked so warm and friendly, while the ground I lived on was always so cold and frightening.
One day, I was looking up into the sky when a beautiful butterfly flew down beside me. She smiled at me and shared some of the songs that butterflies sing.
I thought, "For someone so beautiful, why does she sing such a silly song?"
She asked me to try and sing some of the songs, but I said, "No, that seems so silly."
So she went away, but she told me that whenever I wanted to try and sing the song, that she would be there to teach me how to sing.
I wondered why she was so nice. Why did she smile at me? After all, I was just a caterpillar and she was a beautiful butterfly.
Everyone said that butterflies were pretty, but they were so different from us caterpillars. They said not to talk to them because butterflies sang such silly songs.
I kept trying and trying.
One day I was looking up into the sky again, dreaming about flying. The beautiful butterfly stopped again. We talked for a while and I thought,

Inspiration When We Weren't Looking

"She's not so different from me!" She asked me if I ever thought about flying. I told her, "Yes!" She told me she could help me learn to fly.
When I asked her how, she said I'd have to learn a song and that would help me learn to fly.
How silly! Learn a song, to fly?
I thought about it. I really did want to fly, didn't I? So I said okay, just a little song.
She taught me a small song, and when we finished, I thought, "What a pretty song! It's not so silly after all."
Soon I was learning longer and longer songs. I started to wonder when I would fly. I was singing the songs, wasn't I? The butterfly said that I had to learn to sing from my heart.
From my heart?
I realized that songs really had to mean something to me, otherwise they were just words to pretty music.
The next time I sang the songs, I noticed that I was starting to feel different. It scared me a little, but at the same time, I was getting excited.
I tried to tell my friends, but they thought I was silly. They told me again that butterflies are different. I said, "No, they're not, they are just like you and me, and they sing such pretty songs!" They just wouldn't listen.
I had to make a decision. Do I want to stay a caterpillar? Are my friends really having fun and being happy? I thought not.
The songs had taught me that there is real happiness and that the only way to true happiness is through the songs.
I wanted to be a butterfly!
More and more each day, I felt a change coming over me.
I started to climb a tree.
The climb was hard sometimes. It seemed so high! But I wasn't going to stop me climbing that tree!
While I was climbing, I met a butterfly who was resting on the tree. He said hello to me. I thought he was a beautiful butterfly too. We talked for a while and I rested with him.
After a while, I wondered why he never sang any songs, and why he never wanted to sing songs to me. He would never say, when I would ask him. Soon he didn't seem quite as beautiful and I realized he was turning into a moth.

Crumbs in the Keyboard

I thought, "I don't want to turn into a moth!" Moths are not very beautiful and the seem to be even more unhappy than the caterpillars.

So I started to climb the tree again.

The butterfly climbed with me. (How odd, why doesn't he fly?) I was able to see him turn into a moth more and more each day. "I'm worried," I told him, "you're losing your colors!"

He laughed and said he wasn't. Why couldn't he see the change? I tried to help him, I sang songs, but he didn't want to listen any more.

Soon, I reached a limb that I felt comfortable with and took a look around. How beautiful it is here! And Look! There were butterflies there too. They were flying everywhere and they were all singing songs. I was so happy!

It was time to change.

The moth didn't want me to change. He said I was fine the way I was. Didn't he see how much I wanted to fly? Didn't he see that I wanted to be a butterfly?

I took a good grip on the limb; all the butterflies helped me, and gave me such praise for the hard climb.

I took a deep breath and flipped over to hang from the limb.

I did it!

I held on tight so that I wouldn't fall, and not even the moth could make me let go now.

Slowly I started to change. I started slow, but soon I had a nice warm cocoon. The butterflies were still there, always helping me and giving me encouragement to hold on. Always singing songs.

The moth was still there too. He would bump his wings against my cocoon to try and get me to fall. Why did he do that?

I wouldn't let him make me fall. I held on tighter and tighter, all the while singing songs. I wanted to fly and be a beautiful butterfly.

The days would go by, the change was happening quicker and quicker. I could hardly wait!

It was getting cramped in my cocoon and I was tired of listening to the moth. I wanted to fly away with the other butterflies.

It was time to come out of my cocoon.

The moth said no, I said yes!

I started slowly. I didn't want to do something wrong to hurt my wings.

This wasn't an easy thing, to get out of my cocoon! Was I doing the right thing? Maybe I wouldn't make it out safely. I hope I don't hurt my wings.

Inspiration When We Weren't Looking

The butterflies were there for me, always singing songs. Yes it is hard, they said, but look at what happens when you're out!

I tried harder and harder. Little by little I was emerging. I was all sticky, but I knew that wouldn't last. I would dry and my wings would be beautiful.

The moth tried to tell me that I would always be sticky, that I should have stayed a caterpillar. I knew he was wrong.

I was able to get my head and shoulders and my front legs out. Whew! Was that work! I was so excited, but I knew I had to be careful or I would hurt myself. I pulled and tugged and pulled.

Soon there was only one leg sticking to my cocoon. The moth was there again. Why was he always trying to upset me? I had important work to do and I had one leg to go!

I was getting excited. I needed to calm down.

I took a few deep breaths and I sang a song. I tried not to listen to the moth.

A couple more tugs…and I was free!

I gingerly climbed on top of the limb and stretched out my legs.

I started to unfold my wings.

Slowly I stretched them out. They were so vibrant, full of color! I knew that all my patience and endurance was well worth this moment.

I thanked the songs for this beautiful gift.

For now I was a butterfly.

I had my wings, but I couldn't fly yet. The moth was in my way.

It was time to face the moth.

I sang more songs and the butterflies sang with me. I asked the moth to sing, but he said he had forgotten how. The butterflies said they would help him to remember.

The moth asked me to wait for him.

I thought about it for a moment. I'm not in a hurry to fly, I still have to dry off and strengthen my wings. I could wait for a little while.

I stretched out my wings and looked up into the sky. All my brothers and sisters were smiling down at me, giving me such praise.

I felt the breeze on my wings, and knew that soon, I too would be flying with them.

Crumbs in the Keyboard

Wisdom from the Trenches

Crumbs in the Keyboard

Uphill Climb: My Quest For Publication
Sally Painter

When I set foot on the road that lead to being published, I was naive, aspiring, optimistic and unsuspecting. Now that I've reached the top of the hill, I am battle-scarred, aspiring, optimistic, and wary.

The road that leads to publishing is different for everyone. But for most, it is truly an uphill climb. For many, it is rocky and some even give up and never venture further, while others retreat to the bottom of the hill.

It is not an undertaking for the weak-spirited. There are rites of passage along the way and every obstacle tests conviction and belief in self.

I started my climb without armor or weapon. I took refuge along the path in workshops, conferences, reading, and new friendships. Gaining skill through contests and practice, I continued climbing towards my goal. Mid-way along my path, I discovered I had gained armor and weapons against the things that stood in my way to the top of the hill. The biggest obstacle I had to face was rejection.

Rejection greeted me with a smug grin and pushed me down the hill as though I was an insignificant pest that had buzzed about its head. Each step I made towards the turn in the path away from where rejection stood, I was greeted with a swift, sometimes callous dismissal, and sent back down the path. I would take solace in the oasis of emails from friends and affirmation that I would succeed. I would nourish my failing spirit with new skills and polished armor and well-oiled weapons.

Refreshed and determined to scale the hill one more time, I would set out with query letters to agents and publishers. Rejection was always ready to emerge from hiding whenever I crossed its path. Each time, I was stronger and my enemy, rejection, was weaker. Realizing my path was barred by the ever-vigilant rejection, I retreated to my base camp and contemplated alternative ways to reach my goal.

Conventional methods had never worked for me in past careers, a lesson I had somehow forgotten in this particular battle. Perhaps I needed to implement old strategies to this new field. I would surprise the enemy and steal past his guard by entering the top of the hill through a little known, little tried path and one that few dared to brave.

I found an ally who knew about a gate that lead to the top of the hill through a smaller path, which rejection guarded, but his orders were not as harsh. He could allow certain ones to enter who might be barred from other gates. Should I try this gate? What made this gate so special? Why was I able to gain entrance through it when I had not gained entrance through the traditional gates? Perhaps the answers lie in what happened next.

Not only was I let inside and onto the hilltop, but I was greeted with cheers and celebration. The hilltop afforded a wonderful view and proved well worth the fight to get there. Soon I began to investigate the grounds and realized there were many camps on this hilltop besides the ones guarding the main entrance. I found those within my new camp to be embracing and supportive. Also, I discovered there were other hilltops beyond this one that I had not been able to see from the path. These were hilltops of reviews, readers, name recognition, and book signings.

Girded, I struck out on the climb to the review hillside and had much success with ten great reviews. Book signings is a hill I am currently climbing. This is an easier hill to scale, but takes time and money to make my way completely over.

The next difficult hill I'll face is name recognition. I am constantly climbing this hill, aided by my experiences and efforts with book signings.

Of course, the answers to the questions why and how I gained entrance are somewhat a mystery, but the answer may lie in small press having wider gates, affording those who don't fulfill the marketing mandates entry. Coloring outside the lines is often embraced within smaller presses.

Regardless which gate one uses to gain entrance onto the published hilltop, there will always be other hilltops. The view they afford drives all of us forward in our never-ending quest.

~~Good Luck~~
~~Break A Leg~~
Break a Pencil
Lori Soard

Luck—is she myth or a fickle lady? Why does the road to publication and even stardom seem to come so easily to some while others find it illusive? If you're like me, you've probably wondered if someone poisoned your fairy godmother or stole your allotted quota of easy breaks. But is success truly tied to luck or is it something more?

Luck is what we make of it. If I had given up after the first rejection, or the second, or the fifteenth…well…I would never have been published. If luck is truly being in the right place at the right time, then don't we increase our chances by being in as many places as often as possible?

If you are one of those people who can walk into a rainstorm and have a beam of sunshine shine on you, or you get unexpected phone calls telling you you've inherited millions of dollars, or someone you don't know hands you the keys to a brand new car, then this article isn't for you. If you're like the rest of us, here are some tips for courting Lady Luck and increasing your odds at getting the big break.

THE ROAD TO NOWHERE:

The first step to becoming a published or best selling or whatever your goal as an author is quite simply getting off the road to nowhere. Make a commitment to yourself and your writing. Agree that you will sit in front of your computer X number of minutes or hours each day, whether the words are flowing or not. If you don't put in the effort, you won't see the rewards. Ever hear a concert pianist who's never taken a single lesson or practiced a day in her life? Consider the computer your instrument and to improve you must practice, even if you hit the wrong key at times.

BUYING STAMPS:

Once you have completed your book or proposal (depending on where you are in your writing career) don't sit on it or edit it to death. Make sure it looks professional and polished and mail it. This can be a very difficult step, especially for new writers. I highly recommend keeping priority envelopes and the appropriate postage on hand for mailing out proposals. It makes procrastination difficult. With the new Internet services, such as Stamps. com, there is even less excuse for not mailing your proposal. Sorry, folks, but your fairy godmother will not show up and create a pumpkin pony express to ferry your manuscript to the editor-the fairy's dead remember? Someone poisoned her.

WALLOWING IN IT:

Many writers shut down after a rejection. They don't send the manuscript out again and sometimes they are frightened to send out any manuscript after a rejection. I blame this phenomenon on the opposite of Lady Luck-The Dream Thief. The best way to defeat this hateful villain is to wallow in your self-pity and anger. Eat chocolate. Cry. Write a nasty letter to the editor (do not use your stamps to mail it! Tear it up after you write it). Then pick yourself up, stick your tongue out at The Dream Thief and send that work or another work out right away (another good reason to keep stamps on hand).

COURTING LUCK:

Never miss an opportunity to tell someone about your writing and your goals. You never know when an editor, agent or Lady Luck might be eavesdropping and all your hard work and perseverance will pay off.

Now that you know the basic keys to dealing with the grief of losing your fairy godmother and Lady Luck deserting you, I have no doubt your "luck" will change. I won't say "good luck" or "break a leg", as they say in show business, or even "break a pencil. " Instead, I'll say that if you "break a pencil" you'd better pick up another one and get busy writing.

Synchronicity
Su Kopil

Synchronicity—knowing your hearts desire, not being afraid to ask for it, and accepting the opportunities that present themselves to you.

We've all heard someone say dreams can come true if you let them. Who's stopping them, you may ask? Sometimes the answer is as simple as looking in the mirror. Perhaps it is the weight of self-doubt or the fear of success holding you back. After all, having everyone from your doctor, to your mother-in-law, to your ex-lover reading the words of your heart can be a scary prospect. If you look deep enough, undoubtedly, you will find a wall you have erected, for one reason or another, blocking your path to success.

It wasn't until I tore down my own ten-foot wall, removing it brick by brick, clearing a path to my own heart's desire, that doors started opening for me. In the course of one year, I went from struggling to write with no outside support to gaining a family of supportive writers, which in turn led to the support of my own family.

I became newsletter editor of my RWA chapter, which proved pivotal in my meeting and learning from some incredibly inspirational authors. Soon I began publishing interviews and articles, which led to regular columns in two magazines.

The opportunity to join a critique group presented itself to me. Despite many fears, I joined. By the end of the year, I had published short stories, built a website, and garnered a book deal with two more in sight. It's a far cry from that struggling writer sitting alone at the keyboard and all because I had opened myself up to my heart's desire.

So go ahead and dream because dreams do come true if you let them.

Wisdom From The Trenches

How To Deal With Rejection
Elizabeth Delisi

Rejection is an unfortunate but unavoidable part of every writer's life. It goes with the territory, like pen and paper or envelopes and stamps. Each and every writer, famous or unknown, gets rejected somewhere along the way--most more than once. The trick, then, is not in avoiding rejection, but in dealing with it and learning from it.

When you receive a rejection letter, it's important to put it into perspective. Here's how I handle it:

DAY ONE:

Hour One: Leave letter out in the open where my husband can find it. Take to bed with a cup of tea and a tragic, woebegone expression.

Hour Two: Husband finds letter. Doses me with sympathy and takes me out to dinner.

Hour Three: Put on brave face and sigh, "I suppose I'll get through it" while ordering a second helping of 'Murder by Chocolate.'

DAY TWO: Catch up on all my to-be-read books. Absolutely no writing. Eat at least half a Whitman's Sampler maybe all.

DAY THREE: Sour Grapes Day. That editor wouldn't know a quality manuscript if it bit her on the nose! I'll find someone who will *really* appreciate my work.

DAY FOUR: Reread rejection letter to find out if maybe, just perhaps, that editor had one tiny little thing to say that might be useful. Maybe.

DAY FIVE: Launch into full-scale revision of work based on what the actually-very-encouraging rejection letter said. Make mental note to start exercising again to burn off all that chocolate.

When you're rejected, remember that not all editors are right on the money when it comes to picking out the next bestseller. According to *Rotten Rejections: A Literary Companion* (edited by André Bernard, Pushcart Press, Wainscott, NY, 1990), Tony Hillerman was told that *The Blessing Way* was unacceptable: "If you insist on rewriting this, get rid of all that Indian stuff." Dr. Seuss was informed that *And To Think That I Saw It On Mulberry Street* was "too different from other

Crumbs in the Keyboard

juveniles on the market to warrant its selling."

Rosalyn Alsobrook, author of *Tomorrow's Treasures* (St. Martin's Press,1997) and recently nominated for Romance Writers of America's Lifetime Achievement Award, remembers a particularly unusual rejection: "Early in my career, I sent my SASE to a publisher with a polite request for guidelines (this was before they were readily available at RWA conferences) and sat back to wait for them. A few weeks later, my SASE was returned and I opened it to find a rejection letter. "I stared at it dumbfounded. They'd just rejected my request for guidelines. What exactly were they trying to tell me? Was that a new all time low, or what?"

A cooling off period is absolutely essential before you can decide if the criticisms in the rejection letter are well founded. Set the letter aside, and return to it in a few days when your emotions have settled down. In the meantime, take time off from writing if you need to, or focus your attention on a different project.

Keep your spirits up. Remember that, while you can't be rejected if you don't submit, you also can't be published if you don't submit. That rejection letter clenched in your hand is tangible proof that you are a writer, and you're out there competing in a very tough business. Make sure that you don't confuse a rejection of your work with a rejection of yourself.

Marian Gibbons, an aspiring writer, says, "I have totally come to terms with the fact that my book is NOT ME. It's something I have made, just another product up for sale in a competitive marketplace. Although I have invested a great deal of love, attention, and effort into my writing, *I* am not being rejected if a publisher declines to buy my work. Rejections are not personal attacks and they don't even necessarily have anything to do with the quality of my work."

When you've achieved enough distance from your immediate reaction to the letter, study it again. As dispassionately as possible, try to determine if the editor's suggestions or criticisms are well founded. Remember that you're emotionally bound to your story, while the editor has a more or less objective view of the work. If you find any value, use the suggestions to rework your story and make it even better than before. Then, send it out!

Keep in mind that sometimes "no" means "maybe." If the book wasn't rejected out of hand, or the comments have a positive ring, ask the editor if she would be interested in seeing a rewrite. Many editors are willing to do so if approached by an enthusiastic writer who isn't afraid to revise.

Wisdom From The Trenches

Remember that being published isn't a "magic bullet" cure against rejection. Even multi-published authors receive rejection letters. Lori Foster, author of *Fantasy* (Harlequin Temptation Blaze, March 1998) says, "Published people, even multi-published people, still get rejections. In my case, though I'm selling very well at Temptation--a match made in Heaven for what they want and what I want to write--I'm struggling like a newbie at Desire."

According to David Thurlo, co-author with wife Aimée of over forty books including the Ella Clah mysteries; *Blackening Song, Death Walker, Bad Medicine*, and *Enemy Way*, "In addition to rejection, eventually you'll have to deal with the problems of acceptance. When you sell a project and get that final money on acceptance, you start right over again with resubmitting. Every time you finish a project, you're unemployed until the next one is accepted. Freelance writing isn't for the weak-stomached."

Finally, keep in mind the words of John Jakes: "Be persistent. Editors change; editorial tastes change; markets change. Too many beginning writers give up too easily."

Crumbs in the Keyboard

Balance and Control
Janice Stayton

Life as an author is like tightrope walking across the Grand Canyon. Did you glance down and almost lose your balance? Did you look up for guidance to allow for the Almighty's lead? Did you focus on the other side to see your daily goals? Did you trust in your creativity as the master art of placing one steady footstep in front of the other?

Nothing is impossible. There is always a way. Set your sights and go for it. There is no such thing as a problem, only answers with many solutions to choose from.

Goals are important. Spontaneity is a major factor in juggling the many chaotic events to maintain a stress-free environment. Shuffling daily responsibilities is a must. We must adjust and quickly. Doing it stress-free is possible. It's called positive choice. Choose life in this moment. We do not control what is past, nor what the future holds. We only have now, this minute. It is simply done by breathing deeply and often, living in the moment, yet keeping focused on your daily goal.

It's hard to find time to write if we allow our spouse, children, grandchildren, the upkeep of the house, or our outside professions to interfere. It can be overwhelming with a serious illness to juggle doctor appointments in the mist of everything else. No woe is me. I am who I am and I love myself. I've been given a precious gift of passionate words to share with many reading fans. Not making time to write is like not taking a cold drink of water when you are in a desert, dying.

Sure, some days it's only one page written, others more, but as you write it adds up. Does it matter how much time it takes? A few days, weeks, or months? The goal is to key in THE END. So, what's stopping you? Only yourself.

WRITE.

Wisdom From The Trenches

Chili Again
Joyce Tres

My fingers flew across the keyboard like a musician playing her favorite refrain. It was Friday afternoon and I had a thousand words to the completion of my first novel. I could hear the cork pop out of the bottle of champagne kept in the refrigerator for just an auspicious occasion. I reached for the coffee cup, which sat to the right of my keyboard, took a long sip, and felt the caffeine infuse me with a surge of determination. Setting down the cup, my fingers once again played across the keyboard. The end of the story had run repeatedly in my mind over the last six months. Elated, the story seemed to flow, the crucial end seemed to float to the tips of my fingers, and appear on the monitor screen. I could see the finish line; the end was so near.

Then a whirling sound emanated from the console that held my hard drive. The whirling turned into a grinding, metal ground metal, little square boxes and squiggly lines appeared where my last chapter had been. Then my monitor screen went black and I looked into an abyss.

"No!" I screamed. "Please, if there is a computer God, let her hear me now. I promise to back up my files more often." Nothing but blackness looked back at me. "No!" I screamed again, jumping up out of the chair, and kicking the air. "No, no, no. Don't do this."

My dog looked up from where he slept, neglected under my desk. I returned to the computer; hit the restart button, nothing. My entire novel was on that computer, my last backup a week ago. Five thousand words a day, thirty-five thousand words lost.

I looked at the computer it stared back with dead eyes. Quickly, I called my computer tech and was told the possibility of salvaging the contents on my hard drive were nil. However, he told me he would try if I brought it by the next day. Can I hope? No, he told me not to hope.

After I stared at the black monitor of my discontent for fifteen minutes, I rose to retrieve a bottle of merlot and a wineglass, and then returned to take vigil at the computer. The black screen mocked me, I poured the wine into the glass, and took a sip.

Crumbs in the Keyboard

My husband found me, an hour later, when he returned from work. My feet up on the desk, I leaned back in my chair, the bottle of merlot diminished by a glass.

"Bad day?" He leaned down, kissed me, took the glass of wine, sipped, and returned the glass to my hand.

"The computer died today and took thirty-five thousand words of my novel with it."

"I'm sorry," he said, left the room for a moment, returned with a glass, and poured some wine.

We sat there, he with his glass of wine, me with mine, and looked at the beast of a machine that ate my novel.

"Hemingway once lost a whole briefcase of work. He said it was the best thing that ever happened to him." My husband's comforting words resonated through my gloom.

"Those were the best words I'd ever written. I'm sure of it." I whispered still numb with my loss.

"You'll write the words again." He picked up the empty wine glasses, the wine bottle, and walked toward the kitchen.

I rose from the chair and followed. "You know what this means, don't you?" I wrapped my arms around him.

"Yes. It means I'll be eating chili again for at least another week." He smiled down at me.

I had to smile back. My husband eats chili every night for weeks at a time; he also shops when we need food, vacuums when the dust bunnies threaten to over take the house, walks the neglected dog twice a day, and anything else to let me write. He supports my dream when so few others have. If he can do all that, I can reconstruct the thirty-five thousand words I lost.

Who knows? Maybe losing my work will be the best thing that ever happened to me.

No, my husband is the best thing that ever happened to me. However, my finished novel will definitely come in second.

Wisdom From The Trenches

Daily Resolution: A Writer's Affirmation
Gerry Benninger

Writers seem to always have the same resolutions and, as with other groups, many repeat that resolution year after year. We promise to write more and to write more often.

It's hard to know why the same resolution seems to fit so many for so many years. Perhaps it's because some of the meanings of the word—resolution--have been lost. The primary meaning in The American Heritage Dictionary is "to make a firm decision about" and, of course, that's what we do for writing, usually with guilt and determination.

Originally, the Latin root word meant, "to loosen; to untie, release, free." In Middle English (maybe because there were so many English rebels repeatedly arrested and set free by the Norman French?) the word took on the re to become resolution and the added meaning "to relieve from obligation or debt." These meanings are still noted in the modern dictionary though rarely active in our awareness. And there are other meanings more helpful than dogged determination and firm decisions to do better. Number four, to separate something into constituent parts, to analyze; Number seven, to remove or dispel doubts; and number eight, to bring to a conclusion.

These meanings, in addition to *being set free*, are what writers need more than another firm, guilt-ridden decision to work harder. Guilt takes up a lot of time, energy, personal power and effectiveness. It destroys productivity. So here is my experimental list, my attempt at recovering the lost meanings.

RESOLVED: *to untie my inner self and free the commitment to write creatively.* It takes courage to write, to pull yourself inside out and share the resulting emotion on paper. As Katherine Dunn, author of *Geek Love*, told *Writer's Digest*, "All the talent, all the gift in the world can't put words on the page for you. What puts them down on the page is just the simple, raw guts to sit down and do it."

RESOLVED: *to analyze my purpose often enough to remember that if publishing is the purpose of writing rather than merely an end goal, it can empty my work of pleasure and of beauty.* The search for meaning, heart, personal and human discovery is the purpose for writing. Publishing is a goal aimed at sharing. Just like a touchdown in football, the goal is achieved by playing with skills developed in practice, by concentration on the play taking place right now and by commitment to be the best you can be in this moment, one play at a time.

RESOLVED: *to remove or dispel doubts*. Self-esteem, or lack of it, is at the root of all writing success or failure. Studies have shown people with higher self-esteem are more open, honest and creative. They communicate better. Self-esteem can never be given, can never come from outside but must be developed within, consciously and every day. When I decided to write for publication, my friend who had written over thirty novels showed me a little sign she taped above her typewriter. It said, "I am a published writer. " I have that same note. When I wasn't published yet, it affirmed the possibility. Now, it affirms my writing can be published again and again.

RESOLVED: *to bring to a conclusion*. Writer Ron Carlson once told a writing class at Arizona State University that beginning to write, difficult as it is, means almost nothing. What matters is to finish.

Wisdom From The Trenches

"Feeeel" Your Way To Success!
Marjorie Daniels

I used to devour self-help books by the cartload, always looking for that spark of motivation that would prod me to live a fuller, happier, more productive life. Titles such as, "*Feeling Good: the new mood therapy*" and, "*Your Erroneous Zones*" filled my bookshelves. Then one Garage Sale day I decided I didn't need all this stuff cluttering up my life. I was a big girl now; in fact I had become a tough old bird who could cope with anything life had to throw at me. So out they all went.

Then came the most colossal writer's block I'd ever stumbled on in my life. I had allowed rejection letters to get me down. In fact, I was no longer sending stuff out to editors and agents. I came close to deciding my talent was non-existent and it would be better for everyone if I stopped trying to get published and started knitting sweaters for my grandkids instead.

I dug through my overflowing bookshelves for one of my self-help books. Too late. All sold, for twenty-five cents apiece. Depression hovered like a threatening cloud.

My trusty critique group rallied round with kind words about my writing, but I just knew, deep down, that I was an impostor at this romance novel writing business. A friend lent me some motivational tapes and I walked around saying, "I feel terrific," and "I like myself," just as the speaker suggested. I felt better, but still didn't dislodge the writer's block clamped firmly on my brain.

Then another friend mentioned "*Excuse Me, Your Life Is Waiting*" a book she had just been reading, written by Lynn Grabhorn.

Impossible to say in a few paragraphs what the author needs three hundred pages to explain, but the essence of her message is bound up in the Law of Attraction. Through our feelings, which she writes as "feeeelings," we attract good happenings or bad.

She writes in a breezy, conversational style. What she has to say about the vibrations we send out, and therefore receive back, may seem laughable until you try them out. She says at the outset, "If you really think that things come to you by some stroke of good or back luck, or by accident, or coincidence, or by knocking your brains out against some very unsympathetic stone walls, then get a grip. This book could be dangerous to your discontent."

She goes on to make an excellent case for actively manipulating our feelings. Never mind that yet another rejection letter has just plopped into your mailbox. Decide to *"feeeel"* what it will be like when the call comes that the editor loves your book and wants to publish it. *"Feeeel"* your joy and pride when you hold the copies in your hand and when you autograph them for eager readers. Really immerse yourself in this scene and, besides feeling on top of the world, you'll attract the success you seek.

But how do you go about this transformation? How do you begin to dig yourself out of your morass of self-doubt? You'll have to read the whole book for a complete answer, but the seeds, for me, came in chapter six when Grabhorn talks about jump-starting a buzz of good feeling to replace the negative thoughts.

Start with a physical action, a smile, "the kind of smile you couldn't help but break into at the sight of newborn kittens tumbling all over each other, or a baby giggling just for the sake of giggling." Let the feeling grow to a soft buzz. She calls it an instant Feel Good.

I've tried it several times and it gets easier with practice. It helps you to "open your valve to the 'feel good' position." Whenever you catch yourself focusing on the *lack* of success, switch focus and feelings to the *joy* of having what you really want. Get used to what Grabhorn calls "Deliberate creating." Don't say wistfully, "I wish I could be published. Instead declare, "I INTEND to become a *multi*-published author," and start that buzz of *"feeeeling"* how it will be.

There's still a ways for me to go, but that writer's block is smashed all to pieces. I'm back into my contemporary story set in Spain and the joy of writing has returned.

When my critique group said my hero was crazy to expose the heroine to danger, and when they objected to my *dinosauric* use of the word, "limb," I decided not to feel discouraged but to glow with joy inside at the ultimate success I INTEND for my book. Sure, I'm going to listen to their good advice. My heroine will now override the hero's initial refusal to take her into danger. Great suggestion.

But I'm still going to leave that "limb" in place. I can see it right there on the printed page of my book. It *"feeeels"* just right to me.

If you need a Jump Start in your writing, or your life, read Lynn Grabhorn's book, "*Excuse Me Your Life Is Waiting*," Hampton Roads Publishing Company, Inc., 2000

Wisdom From The Trenches

The Path
Gwen Kirchner

When I was a child I imagined sitting in a snug window seat of a country house, my dress flowing around me as I scribbled away in a notebook. Once finished I would write a brief note and mail my masterpiece off to be instantly published. If you are thinking I read a lot of historical romance as a child, I did. But among those daydreams of publishing glory I never realized what sort of commitment it took to be a writer.

As the years rolled by, I toiled away on the beginnings of books, but never finished them. I would tell myself that when those five or so pages were perfect then I could move on, but they never reached my idea of what perfection should be.

I also did not write everyday, only when I thought about it or had nothing better to do with my time. *My heavens*, I would think, *I work full-time, go to school part-time, and have family obligations*, and on and on went the excuses. But no matter what happened I never abandoned my writing altogether; it was like a fever in the blood or rather in the brain. Characters and situations would fly at me in dreams and demand to be written down so I would rush to my computer and type away, but still never finish anything.

I began to wonder if I could or would really be a writer, not realizing I already was and have always been one.

Finally, someone or something bigger than me stepped in and gave me the nudge I needed. It's silly really, but I was working in a bookstore over Christmas and happened to be straightening some shelves when a book caught my eye. I purchased it and read it over one weekend. I then contacted the author, which is something I never do, to tell her how much I enjoyed her book. Lo and behold, she emailed me back. We corresponded for a number of days until I mentioned I wanted to write too. She invited me to become a part of the egroup she ran; every week we give our page goals and then had to report in the next week. Simple, right? In theory yes, but then I realized I had to actually write the pages I said I would. Big shock! That meant I had to make time for my writing. Even bigger shock!

Crumbs in the Keyboard

In the beginning it was difficult. I would whine and complain around only falling in front of my computer when I realized I had no choice. I made the commitment so I had to stick with it. Now six months later, I am nearly finished with the first draft of my book. I have gained valuable writing friends along the way and wisdom to boot. I finally understand that authors are born and we must make room in our lives for the gift that was given to us. But, and there's always one of those, we have to make the time. No one is going to force us or hold our hand. No Supreme Being is going to come down and tell us that humanity won't survive unless we finish the book, story, poem that we are working on. The path to writing opens up to us subtly every day, but we have to be aware enough to recognize it. We then have to be brave enough to start down that path.

Many published authors will say write at the same time everyday or have a set number of pages for the day and then do them. Both of these ideas are wonderful, but the most important thing to remember is this is a job, too. Just as my eight-to-five is, just as my school is, so is writing my job. I must give it the same importance in my life. Writing fulfills something in me that nothing else can and now that it is unleashed I cannot put it away again. So, I prioritize and shuffle keeping writing to the forefront.

Now, having said all of this, I can freely admit I do better on some days than others. If a friend or a member of my family is in need and calls me I drop everything and go to them. Nothing is more important than the people you love. They are the ones who support and love you no matter what. But always remember you are on the path. Sure, there will be stones or even boulders that fall in the way. But we are writers and as such have the knowledge and imagination to surmount any odds.

So, if there is any advice I can offer it's just this, once you admit the path is there and start the trip, don't stop; no matter what. We are writers and it's our gift, so put on your hiking shoes and starting walking.

Wisdom From The Trenches

You Can Make Your Dreams Come True
Joyce Lavene

How do you find your way back into an old dream?

I'd been a writer all of my life. When I was nine years old, I had a poem published about bowling. But I grew up, got married, and had three children. I didn't really have time to chase that dream. So I put it on the back burner. I wrote scraps of ideas on napkins and old phone bills.

I was working full time. I wrote a little at night. I wrote at four-thirty in the morning before work. I saved my good rejections. I saved my bad rejections. I'm not sure why. All the time, I wondered if it was really possible or if it was just a dream. A *BIG* dream--something that couldn't really happen.

Then I sent a proposal to Silhouette Books. The editor liked it and asked me to send sample chapters. I took a deep breath and sent them to her. She liked them and asked to see the rest of the manuscript. I took a deep breath, kissed the manuscript, and sent it on to her. My first book was accepted and scheduled for publication in two years. It was possible! I was on my way. I was higher than any kite!

Then my editor left Silhouette. My mother found out that she had breast cancer. I had emergency gall bladder surgery. My writing came to a screeching halt. All those dreams. All those plans.

My mother and I joked about the book coming out. I told her that I was dedicating the book to her so that she would have to survive to see it. She laughed. Her head was bald from chemotherapy. But she told me, as she always had, that I could do it.

My first book, *A Family for the Sheriff*, was scheduled for release in February of 1999. My writing slowed to a trickle while I dealt with the fear for my mother's life and my family's emotional turmoil. In March of 1998, my mother died from complications of breast cancer. My daughter's husband left her. My life was a bleak place. I kept writing and sending out proposals. I didn't look at the rejections anymore. It was the only thing that kept me going. I had another book accepted and another.

I don't know what lies ahead. No one does. But if you have a dream, do it.

Crumbs in the Keyboard

Don't wait another minute. Life is short. Don't give up because it doesn't work the first time. Or the second time. Or the third.

Don't give up because you don't know if you can hold on a minute longer because that's when something is likely to change. Anything can happen. You're as capable of being the person you dream as any movie star or author or NASA astronaut. Believe in yourself. Believe in your dream. Everything you need is inside of you. Fight for it. Don't let anyone tell you that you can't do what you dream.

I'm a full time writer now. This year, I had my 40th book contracted for publication. You CAN make your dreams come true!

Wisdom From The Trenches

Living the Dream
Joanie MacNeil

Superwoman. That's what my colleague christened me. What had I done to earn this title?

As a mature age university student, I'd juggled the birth of three babies, an assortment of assignments, lectures, tutorials, and exams with motherhood and the hard slog of life with little ones. Not to mention a good helping of life's often overwhelming problems. When I graduated, my babies were five, three and eighteen months old. There was never any doubt in my mind I would finish the course, but had to be content with the knowledge I was in for the long haul. Though I could aim for the light at the end of the tunnel, for years I could not afford to look for its glow.

But graduation day was such a proud moment. Graduation was an official acknowledgment of a very private sense of achievement. While waiting for the ceremony to start, I overheard a young woman in the row behind me comment that for her, completing her studies had been a huge effort. She'd had a baby during the course of her studies and understandably, she was very proud of herself. Her companion was impressed. "Well," I thought, "I've had three babies. Perhaps that does make me Superwoman."

Several years later, I began my writing career. Surely if I put in the effort, achieving publication would take me less than the eight years I'd spent at university. That was my benchmark. Four years later my first novel was accepted.

Even as I launched into my writing career, there were encumbrances. I worked full time, had done for a number of years, and those babies by this time were fourteen, twelve, and ten. My writing space was an old school desk nestled in the corner of the lounge room shared with television, kids and husband all vying for attention. A few months later we bought a computer and eventually, I did get my own small writing room. Unfortunately, it had doors that opened. Always there were interruptions of the two-legged variety. It was no use laying down rules that "Mum is writing and would like some peace and quiet, please." And "I will talk to you later, just let me finish this." Rules just weren't realistic. No one took any notice and the interruptions kept coming. Somehow, I learned

Crumbs in the Keyboard

to live with them, work around them, or at times, just give in.

But my daughter did take my writing seriously. At school, she attended a writing workshop given by a well-known author. I was speechless when she presented me with some words of encouragement from him, scribbled on a piece of paper. I was stunned to think she had gone to the trouble to tell him about her aspiring writer mother. And I was touched to realize how much she thought of me.

Now those babies are nineteen, seventeen, and fifteen. When I look back over those years of study and the early years of my writing career, I don't know how I managed to achieve so much. The interruptions are less, but when did things change in those intervening years? Somehow, I missed it.

I hope my story will inspire and encourage you. Anything is achievable, as long as you apply yourself, believe in yourself. Set realistic short-term goals, a base on which to build and achieve that ultimate long-term objective.

Don't treat your writing as a hobby, as something you do in your spare time. And don't allow family members to consider it a hobby, either or sway you from your aspirations. Believe in yourself. Stay focused. It's not easy, particularly in the face of opposition, rejection letters and life's other stresses, so it's important to set targets and keep them firmly in sight. Keep moving forward.

Learn to determine your priorities, especially when it comes to household chores. Procrastination is a deadly enemy. Those previously unappealing tasks like washing the kitchen floor suddenly become more attractive. It is so easy to use up precious writing time doing just one more household task instead of settling down to write. Make simple meals. If you can rope your family/partner into helping around the house, then do it.

Organizational skills are a bonus. If you don't have these to begin with, you must learn them fast if you are going to succeed. You will become an expert in time management.

Find yourself a writing group. You will need one when the combination of writing, family responsibilities and the rest are more than you can bear. And to talk writing with another writer is therapeutic, inspirational, and supportive, and it does wonders for your motivation.

Try to write something every day, even if it's just a small amount scribbled in a notebook. Establish some sort of writing pattern to keep in touch with your story. Get into the habit of writing daily.

Arrange some writing time away from the household or set some time aside

Wisdom From The Trenches

each night or early in the morning while the house is quiet.

Be positive, focus, persevere-slowly but surely is the best way to go.

What will you get for your efforts? A great sense of achievement, something for yourself, experience, organizational skills, and an ability to determine priorities. All in all, writing is a good discipline. And who knows, after all your efforts, you might be rewarded with that contract in the mail! And what a boost that will be to your confidence!

Go on. You can do it!

Crumbs in the Keyboard

The Right Answer
By Nancy Lynn

Traditional education teaches us that only one right answer exists for every problem. Lessons and exams are crafted around that belief. Students who provide the right answer for enough questions get a passing grade; the ones who don't, fail. It's normal for people to take this lesson into their lives, searching for the right answer, the magic solution, that will bring them happiness, wealth, or a two-book contract. When they don't find it, they get frustrated, and if it doesn't turn up after a little more searching, they give up. However, sometimes, all it takes to solve a problem is a new perspective.

Once there was a little book written by a fledgling author. The publishing line to which the manuscript had been targeted folded, so the author began sending queries to other publishers. Rejection followed rejection. A short time later, she heard that the publishers she originally targeted preferred stories set in North America featuring North American characters. Her story was set in Britain, and one of the primary characters was British.

The author gathered up her courage, wrote her question on a sheet of paper so she wouldn't forget it, and called The Editor. Unfortunately, the editor said readers wouldn't be interested in a British character and asked whether the character could be turned into an American. Even better, could the setting be changed, too?

Dejected and feeling foolish for not knowing about the rule before she wrote the story, the author came close to shoving the manuscript under the bed and forgetting about it. Before she did, however, she thought about possibilities:

She could change the character.
She could change the setting.
She could shelve the manuscript and move on to a new story
She could change her perspective and look for another publisher.

The author decided to try a different publisher--in a different medium. The query resulted in a request for a full manuscript, which was followed by a contract for publication.

Answers are often selected out of habit. Sometimes a solution is chosen

Wisdom From The Trenches

because it's the fastest, easiest, or least offensive. Next time you're facing a problem, try opening your mind to possibilities rather than searching for the right answer.

Try the habitual solution first, and if it doesn't work, go back and try the fastest one. If that fails, try the least offensive, or maybe the one that demands the most courage. Consider trying the one that tackles the problem in increments, so you'll have the opportunity to evaluate your progress after every step. If you run out of ideas, sit down and think of some more.

Any problem you face has many solutions. Don't give up if your initial attempts to resolve it turn out differently than you planned. Instead, change your perspective, look at your situation in new ways, and explore the possibilities. This is how dreams really come true.

Crumbs in the Keyboard

Sticks and Stones May Break My Bones, But Names Will Never Hurt Me?
Marcia Kacperski

Throughout my life, I was always chastised for daydreaming. "Quit daydreaming!" was what I had heard from family members, teachers and even friends, instead of, "What are you thinking about?" My solitary trips to imaginary places ended abruptly, and I returned to the boring present.

I loved my essay assignments in school. It didn't matter if they were personal pieces of work or book reports. All I knew was how gratifying it felt to see my thoughts materialize on paper. I believed they were all good and worthier than the mediocre grades in red across the top of the front pages.

One time in particular, in my junior year of high school, we had to write a poem. I amazed myself at the depth of the emotion I had put in the story of how a Civil War widow coped with the death of her husband who died in battle. The day they were returned to us, the teacher wanted to read one to the class. It was mine! I was so excited I could barely keep the perpetual smile off my face. She liked it! At the end of the reading, she told the class, "This student, whose name I won't mention, is guilty of plagiarism, and I will not stand for it in my class."

I went numb and never wrote again unless it was a school assignment. Even then, my heart was never in it. I was humiliated and felt my writing was worthless. I would continue to daydream, but never gave my stories words.

Thirty-two years later, I took a noncredit course in writing at our local community college. I had an idea for a story after doing some genealogy on my mysterious grandmother. The instructor read my first three-page paper to the class. Here we go again, I thought. But to my surprise, she said it was some of the best writing she had ever read. I sat in disbelief!

After that course, I repeated it again, and a third time. My self-esteem returned higher then ever before.

I recently told someone about the accusation of my poem in high school being plagiarized and how it had destroyed me. Shortly thereafter, I read that the same thing had happened to the late comedian Steve Allen in his youth and it thrilled him. He thought that if his work was good enough to be considered copied from a published author, then that was the highest compliment he could receive. Spurred on by this, he continued writing very successfully.

Wisdom From The Trenches

That changed my whole attitude toward my past event and, as you can see, I, too, am still writing. It has become my passion. Not a day goes by when I don't write something: a few pages or just one sentence. And no one accuses me of daydreaming anymore.

I don't regret those lost years of not writing due to the paralysis born from humiliation and fear. Even writing a letter was agonizing for me. What I learned through all my experiences during that time has given me much more to write about and will supply me with endless pages of adventures, rich with feelings.

Yes, words can hurt at a deeper level than the pain inflicted on the body from sticks and stones. But on that deeper level, we can choose to believe that words can never hurt us.

Let Your Imagination Fly
Sue Fineman

Sometimes I think writers have an advantage over everyone else in this life. Writing fiction opens your imagination, which can be a welcome relief in a stress-filled day.

Irritated with your boss? Give your villain some of his physical traits, and then send your villain to lunch with *his* boss. Have him accidentally spill his drink on the boss's lap, or get spinach stuck in his teeth, or make a joke about something the boss thinks is inappropriate. Or send him to the men's room before an important meeting, and then have him forget to zip his fly. Visualize a shirttail hanging through that opening, waving like a white flag.

You don't have to get violent or nasty. A little embarrassment will do it, especially in someone with an over-inflated ego. Don't hurt him. Let him do it to himself.

Do you have an insensitive co-worker who eats chocolate cake in front of you when you're dieting, and then brags about weighing the same thing she did when she married twenty years ago? Picture her breaking out in hives from the chocolate, or popping the button on her size six slacks. Take care of her in your story, in your imagination.

Does your spouse harp about how clumsy you are? Give your hero some of his traits, and then let that hero fall flat on his face or stumble into a door in front of his buddies or co-workers. Imagine him trying to explain what happened. Your heroine doesn't have to say a word. A soft smile says it all.

Whether you're a writer or not, use your imagination. Does she pride herself on her appearance? Give her a big zit on the end of her nose. Does he think he's hot stuff at work? Let him drop the pages in a big presentation and rip his pants when he bends over to pick it up. And make it a loud rip in a quiet room!

You get the idea. Have fun with it. Laugh. And let your imagination fly!

Wisdom From The Trenches

To Everything There Is A Season
Patricia Crossley

No matter how young you are, you can look back over the past years and see a rising and falling swell of activities at certain times. There are times in our lives when all our attention and energy is gobbled up by one huge, voracious need. It might be small children, it might be (sadly) the illness or death of a loved one, or it might be a demanding new job or undertaking.

When I first began to write fiction seriously (and by seriously I meant actually completing a full length book and submitting it to a publisher) I had children still at home, an extremely demanding job and a dog. My jaw dropped at the claims of some writers who wrote every day for fifteen minutes on the edge of the kitchen table, in the loo at lunchtime, at two o'clock in the morning. Don't misunderstand me, I'm lost in admiration, but I couldn't do that and stay sane.

We were fortunate enough to be able to spend every second weekend at an island retreat in the summer months. That's where I started to organize myself. On that weekend, I wrote. The rest of the family was busy and relaxed, and so was I. No distractions except to make another pot of coffee and remember to throw something on the grill for supper.

During the intervening weeks I edited what I had written, did some thinking about plot and character during my commute, read in the genre I was writing, and sat down again two weeks later to continue.

I think what worked for me was, first, the discipline of knowing when and how I would write. Second, I didn't beat myself up for not writing during the work week. I allowed myself to recognize the time and energy required by the other parts of my life.

This is how I wrote my first book, which, like most first books, will never be published. But what I learned about writing and about pacing myself stayed with me for my other books, which were published.

What drum beats in your life right now? Is it slow and steady? Frenetic? Rushing like a mighty wind? Most of us nod at the last two. If you can write at snatched moments during your busy day, more power to you. I know the ideal is

Crumbs in the Keyboard

to write every day. But, if you struggle like I did to find the time and energy to write, take a look at what's going on in your life. Can you find an hour or two on a regular basis that can be your writing time? Once a week, once every two weeks is fine, if that's all you can do at this stage of your life. I think you'll find the rhythm to catch your own productivity.

Wisdom From The Trenches

What Makes A Writer?
Lisa Craig

What makes a writer? It's the same thing that sends you searching for the perfect word. It's motivation leads you to the library for research, to the park for scenery ideas, and has you eavesdropping on the bus or at restaurants for free flowing dialog.

It drives you to the computer or a handy pad of paper every time an idea pops into your mind. The internal yearning to do it, makes you grumpy when you don't.

What is "it" you ask? It keeps you up at night jotting down ideas, scenes, or a mere particularly troubling piece of description. It sends you to critique groups to analyze and evaluate your progress.

Without it, you wouldn't have the opportunity to meet such supportive, wonderful friends. With it, you've sacrificed sleep, weekend outings, expensive shopping excursions, and a balanced diet.

Critiques, contests, insomnia, they are all part of it. You anxiously await an editor's phone call, or check your mailbox daily, hoping, praying for it.

What is "it" you ask? The answer is clear!

It is part of you!

You breathe it, think it, and live it. Best of all, you write it because YOU ARE A WRITER!

Crumbs in the Keyboard

Keeping the Faith
Helen Kay Polaski

Vanessa's eyes misted over as she returned the phone to its cradle. She drew a shaky breath and stared at her computer screen. The snow scene she'd downloaded in honor of the upcoming Christmas holiday changed several times before she was able to move again. Tears cascaded down her cheeks and her bottom lip quivered into a semi-smile. It had all been worth it.

Yes, her family had suffered through leftover dinners, and on occasion, the ultimate in housewife embarrassment--lack of clean undies--while she'd slaved away punching keys and jump-starting a career that had been less than successful in the past. But she had finished a manuscript and it had been accepted for publication.

Still shaky, Vanessa headed toward the kitchen for a celebratory fest and calming agent. If there was a reason to ruin your diet, this was it. Besides, she had plenty to be proud of this morning. Thanks to *Flylady*, her online light-a-fire-under-your-butt mentor and make-your-life-your-own-again inspiration, she'd managed to drop the kids off at school before the tardy bell. That was a small miracle in itself. And--as if that wasn't enough to put a spring in any mother's step--here it was only 8:30 a.m., and she was dressed, complete with shoes and socks! Surely that was some kind of record!

Promising herself she'd only have one, Vanessa grabbed the bag of chocolate covered peanuts and downed a handful. She still had a long way to go to be Superwoman, but right this second it was enough to know she had the stick-to-it-tiveness to not only be the best wife and mother she could be, but to also follow her heart when it came to her writing career. She'd started a romance novel and finished it! What a heady feeling!

She walked back into the dining room and patted the side of her trusty computer, then wiggled into her chair and pulled the afghan up over her knees. For long moments she watched the snowfall on the computer screen and munched contentedly.

Truly, this made her life complete.

She inched her chin up another notch, dropped in several more chocolates, and sighed. No more hanging her head, no more feeling inferior. She was now one of the elite. A mover and a shaker. There was so much more to her than that which met the eye. A stranger passing her in the mall--for that was her next step in this celebratory fest--would never know she was a novelist. Heck, her own family still didn't know!

She giggled. She was being silly. Honestly, she was an author a dozen times over if you counted all the small stories she'd managed to get published. But until ten minutes ago, she hadn't been a published novelist.

Accepted! Her jaws worked double time as the chocolate performed its magic. Wow! Who should she tell first?

Vanessa popped up from her chair, and with the chocolate in tow, began her daily routine. Despite the fact that she was a soon-to-be famous novelist, she was still a mom and household engineer. The house was a mess and it was her job to get everything squeaky clean so that when she picked up her babies from school they had a clean house to mess all over again.

As she tackled the first of four beds, she wondered what her husband would say. He'd probably plan some elaborate dinner date. She chewed on the side of her mouth. Wonder if he'd consider cleaning house for a week? Nah, what was she thinking, all she'd done was write a book not get him tickets to a Bull's game. Her mouth dropped open. Maybe he'd buy her that new computer she so desperately wanted. Oh, God, that would be wonderful. Definite bonus. Her writing buddies would be so jealous.

Vanessa snapped the sheet in the air above her daughter's bed. Her mind whirled with congratulations and pats on the back she hadn't even received yet. She giggled anew. How, who, what, where? She simply had to celebrate.

Tonight her eldest had ballet lessons right after school, her middle child had pitching practice in the evening, and the youngest had asked to bring a friend home for the night. Hmmm. She picked up the dirty laundry from the floor, then moved into the hallway and dropped the bundle outside the bathroom, and continued into the second bedroom where she repeated the process.

As she lifted her head and opened her mouth for the last morsel of chocolate, her eyes slid across the crucifix hanging on the bedroom wall. Suddenly, she knew how she could celebrate her victory while at the same time taking care of a few neglected tasks. She dropped to her knees beside her son's bed and bowed her head.

"Thank you, Lord, for my children, my husband, my life," she whispered.

Crumbs in the Keyboard

"Thank you for chocolate, and for the gift of writing."

She returned to the computer and began typing. Her husband's promotion topped the list, followed by her children's achievements. Though she ended with her own recent success, she gave herself a healthy pat on the back.

Smiling, she printed the synopsis in bold red lettering on holiday letterhead and stuffed a copy of it in with each Christmas Card.

That afternoon as chief bottle-washer and cook, Vanessa baked German chocolate cake, blueberry pie and zucchini bread. At the dinner table she morphed into her role as her family's biggest fan, and praised each of her loved ones for their accomplishments, then shared her news. The look her husband shot her way held the promise of something more enjoyable than dinner, and the children's eyes sparkled with pride.

Vanessa felt the warm glow of love surround her. She leaned over and squeezed her husband's hand. He smiled back, anticipation coloring his handsome features. Vanessa grinned. Tomorrow would be soon enough to start the sequel. She had more important things to do this evening.

Wisdom From The Trenches

Cleaning the Toilet and TV Interviews
Tammie Clarke Gibbs

Being a relative newcomer to the business of book publishing, I have to admit that I've found the whole process both an exciting and an exhausting experience. It's amazing to me how much different it is than my everyday profession.

I actually thought I had a good grip on things. After all, I do publish three magazines a month along with various other creative endeavors, but book publishing takes creativity that one step further.

As the author of a work of either fiction or non-fiction you suddenly become a commodity. Until the recent publication of my book "*Recipes for Romance from The Leading Ladies & Gentlemen of Romance: Recipes, Rendezvous & Sweet Treats for the Mind, Body and Soul*," I'd never really thought of myself as a commodity. I've written lots of things before, but somehow I've always thought of my work as the product and not me.

It came as quite a big surprise that "I" suddenly became a very important part of my "product." As writers I think we all sometimes take ourselves for granted as we pen our works of art spilling the ink that breathes life into our characters. We become so involved with our books that we seldom stop to think that "we" are the ones who will hopefully still be around long after our books go out of print. That's when we hope that someone out there remembers us and will buy yet another of our works of literary art.

Over the past several years I've had the pleasure of meeting (mostly via email) lots of aspiring and newly published authors. Some you can tell right away have that something special—an almost zeal for marketing themselves and their books. Somewhere along the line they've discovered the art of subtle self-promotion. Not only do they write dynamic books they frame them on cutting-edge web pages and never miss the opportunity to use a signature line. Some authors and prospective authors however are missing wonderful opportunities to sell themselves while promoting their books.

There are just some things that all authors should have a supply of. If you're published and don't have these items, get them and soon! If you're on your way

Crumbs in the Keyboard

to becoming published, start now building the name recognition that you will need to set your work apart from others that are scratching their way up to the status of published author.

Business Cards: plain and professional ones are best. Author Photos: publicity shots aren't just for New York Times Best-selling Authors they're for you…spend some time and money on getting some professional shots made. Publishing takes a long time, but when that call comes and you're finally on your way, time will seem to fly if you're preparing for your debut the way you should be. A bio: Don't think your bio will be of interest to anyone? Think again! You need a short version and a longer version and you will use this over and over again for all sorts of publicity things. A web site: I was very surprised by how many unpublished writers already have web sites that showcase their works in progress and contain helpful links to information in the time periods they write or to other interesting information.

These are very smart writers indeed. One of the most difficult things about publishing is identifying an audience for what you write. Authors who begin early cultivating their own unique reader base have an edge over those authors that no one has ever heard of before.

My advice to any up and coming author is to search out every opportunity they can to do what they love, WRITE. I once belonged to a writers group that questioned when I announced that I was going to publish a magazine. Somehow for some of them, it didn't ring true that I was still pursuing my writing career since I was taking a rest from my fiction manuscript. I on the other hand viewed my change in venue to finally doing what I really wanted to, WRITE. No, it wasn't as creative as my fiction, but I now have experience in marketing, ad copy writing, graphic design and publishing!

In turn, when the opportunity came along for "*Recipes for Romance*," to become my first nationally marketed title, I was much better prepared to launch what I feel like has been a successful publicity campaign. No, every author won't have the luxury or inclination to design their covers and line up television interviews, but every author does need to be aware of what needs to be done to gain the most exposure for their books both prior to and upon publication.

As prepared as I thought I was there were still other aspects of "becoming" published that I had never thought about. Take it from me, there is no time like the present to give thought to how publishing success will affect your household. So, if yours is anything like mine--you don't have the services of a maid and you no doubt have a kid or two and a hubby lingering around. They must be fed! They do have homework! They may NOT be patient ALL of the time. Oh, and

Wisdom From The Trenches

occasionally, they get tired of your never-ending affair with your computer keyboard!

If this aptly describes your household prior to publication, just imagine how it will be when you begin doing book-signings in towns you never heard of and interviews here and there with various media. Sometimes, it will get CRAZY! Then you'll realize how much fun you're having because you have reached a goal that sometime, somewhere you set for yourself. Then it will be worth all the craziness in the world.

Never forget your family and how all of this affects them. If you do they are sure to remind you! My nine-year old son, Anthony called me from his PePa's shortly after viewing my first TV interview. He was more than a little upset and asked me why I had simply referred to him as my nine-year old son. I said, "Because you are." Of course I didn't fully understand what he was really saying. He clarified, "I have a name. It's Anthony, please use it!"

Oh! I understood then. I promised I'd never not mention his name again he replied, "Good cause sons need publicity, too!" It was one of the cutest moments I can remember. I'm thinking he might grow up to be my business manager or something.

If you're thinking that all is lost and that you cannot possibly juggle one more thing much less marketing and publicity, take heart. I'll share with you a true story. It actually happened, honest! It will prove beyond the shadow of a doubt that you can mix celebrity with household cleaners!

Early into the promotion of my book, I had an opportunity to reflect on how absolutely wrecked my house was. It needed a good cleaning and that is a big understatement. I decided to take the day off and dedicate it to restoring my house to a home, a clean one.

I woke up eagerly dreading the chores that were piled up all around me. I hate cleaning the bathroom. I despise cleaning the bathroom. I had to clean the bathroom--there was no way around it, so I decided to do it first. I pulled on a pair of those rubber gloves and armed myself with Lysol (yes, it was the brand name) and my various other cleaning paraphernalia and headed for the bathroom. I grabbed that bowl scrubber, the one that looks like someone had a really bad hair day and went to town on the dreaded "toilet bowl." A few moments into my routine my phone rang. GREAT! The phone never rings until you're up to your elbows in cleaner, I thought with aggravation. However, since I do work at home, I always put on a happy voice when I answer.

"Hello, this is Lyndy Brannen with WSAV TV 3--"

Read dead silence on my side of the phone...Heartbeat--Heart skip--heart

Crumbs in the Keyboard

beat--and so on. I could have died! I almost went into shock. Was I surprised? That's an understatement! Excited? You betcha! I could not believe that he wanted to interview me. I quickly asked him if he wanted me to come to Savannah. He informed me that HE was coming here. Yes, here meant to my house. My very dirty house! Suddenly, I realized how quick an author has to think. I set up the interview at my mother's new house where she has a very large kitchen that is and was perfect for cameras.

My mother on the other hand didn't react to the news that a camera crew would be at her house at 1:30 p.m.--very gracefully.

"They can't come. My alarm people are coming at 1:30," she said.

Yep, you read it right. My mother was refusing to allow me to have an interview with the TV station that covers all of South Georgia. It took her a few moments to adjust to the shock and then she was fine and the interview was great. It was really neat watching myself on the five o'clock news. So you see, I woke up one morning thinking all that was in store was a long day of housecleaning and ended up the next day on the five o'clock news. Not bad for a day's work.

Wisdom From The Trenches

Following the Artist's Way
Robin D. Owens

The Artist's Way, A Spiritual Path to Higher Creativity, is a book written by Julia Cameron with Mark Bryan. I followed their 12 week "Course in Discovering and Recovering Your Creative Self" periodically over three years, so I didn't believe I'd been diligent until I hauled out my book.

Its corners are ratty, some pages have suspicious brown (tea/chocolate) and red (paper cut/spaghetti) stains. It's highlighted in pink, orange, yellow, green and purple with tabs for *Basic Principals, Rules Of The Road, Creative Affirmation, An Artist's Prayer*, and my favorite, *Dealing With Criticism*. Scribbled notes and terrible doodles blend with asterisks, arrows and brackets, decorate the pages.

The book's state showed that I'd worked through the course and it had made a difference.

At the beginning of the program I was writing books I enjoyed and thought I could market. In the end, I had found my true voice and was writing books of my heart.

Morning Pages. I hated the idea of 'free-writing' words, any words for three full 8 ½ x 11 pages every day. Keep the pen moving across the paper. Cameron believes that whatever is on your mind won't dribble out until after 1 ½ PAGES and it takes another 1 ½ to deal with it. True at the start, I spilled my guts from line one. Nobody reads your morning pages, not even you, until week 9.

I don't do any scheduled task (except feed cats, which is self-defense) in the morning. So the pages became evening or lunch pages for me. They worked. They cleaned out my brain of all my petty (or huge) concerns of the day so I could write. They cut down on my whining. They observed the seasons. Sometimes I filled up lines with: "Love, love, love." But that's not so bad either.

Other reasons to do the pages (paraphrases):

1.) They help us stop taking our negative Censor (Inner Critic) as the voice of reason and learn to hear it for the blocking device that it is.

2.) They get us to the other side of our fear, negativity, moods.

Crumbs in the Keyboard

3) Other writing seems to suddenly be more free, expansive and easier.

4) We identify ourselves, learn what we want and become willing to change to get it.

5) The pages loosen our hold on fixed opinions and shortsighted views. We see that our moods, views, and insights are transitory. We acquire a sense of movement, a current of change in our lives.

6) We treat ourselves more gently. Feeling less desperate, we are less harsh with ourselves and with others.

7) Morning pages end dry spells, doing the pages means we have not collapsed to the floor of our despair and refused to move on. We have doubted, but we have moved on.

Artist's Date: The artist's date can be summed up in one word: Play--Or to Pamper Yourself. Your artist is a creative child, so spend an hour once a week to fulfill it. Roll down hill, take a train, dance, draw, arrange stickers, BY YOURSELF. This was the portion of the course that I followed the least, but I still have this journal and developed a passion for stickers and I've bought four sets of metallic ink gel pens.

Tasks: Exercises. These hooked me. One in the first chapter blew my mind open. I wrote an affirmation ten times: "I am allowed to nurture my artist. " My Censor popped up: "You have so many other things to do. Your house isn't clean. Your bills aren't paid. You aren't a responsible person."

I listened and analyzed, and found out that Censor sounded like my Father. The basic thing the critic was saying, and which I truly believed, was: "You can't do what you want to do; you must do what I want you to do." And, "What you want to do is stupid and a waste of time and will never amount to anything. What others want you to do is always more important." Wow! Try it for yourself. Or try this one from chapter eight: When I was little, I learned that _____ and _____ were big sins that I particularly had to watch out for. (You fill in the blanks)

Warning: Week 4, Reading Deprivation: NO READING AT ALL, no TV, movies, radio. This is horrible, but it works, too. It was one of the most intensely creative times of my life and I was more observant of people and little dramas around me. The pressure to tell myself stories forced me to write. I still remember how incredible it felt--like a dam breaking open and writing pouring out. I was proud that I managed 5 days. I got desperate.

One evening on the bus, I looked over the shoulder of my seatmate who was

Wisdom From The Trenches

reading an article called "*Guide to Effective Deworming.*" (True story). She looked like a heroine: mid-twenties, red hair; creamy complexion; straight nose, far more interesting than the pictures of horses with strange tube-like objects in their mouths.

Ok, so I glanced at the article. I didn't read it. I just looked at the pictures.

She finished reading and flipped to the next topic. "*Mounting Blocks.*" Temptation. Really. I was writing historical romance. Words jumped out IN MY MIND: "Old tree stump, overturned bucket. " There were pictures, too, but not as interesting as horses. My heroine merely scanned the article and went to the next. "*Metabolic Disease, Test Treatments.*"

No pictures. I was saved.

After working on my fifth book, I should be writing in my journal and decorating it with stickers while listening to music. But it was fascinating to read some of the highlighted wisdom and quotes in The Artist's Way, as well as my own words. Maybe it's time to start again. One week a month and I should be done in only a year.

Crumbs in the Keyboard

Coffee In My Keyboard: Dealing With Rejection
Laurie Alice Eakes

Once upon a time, being a great letter writer, I went to my mailbox with excitement. Then I got serious about being a writer and discovered that the daily mail delivery was a time to ensure that my favorite comfort foods were on hand.

For someone who has far less self-confidence than people think I have, the decision to get serious about writing might not have been the wisest choice. But the stories were there, had always been there, and writing seemed to have chosen me. So I have learned to deal with rejection, savor the triumphs, and keep going, even when pushing one more key on the keyboard seems like getting the thumbscrews tightened. In doing so, I have found my attitude toward the rest of my life changing also.

How do I deal with rejection? Not with the standard remarks like "They're not rejecting you; they're rejecting your manuscript."

Excuse me?

When editors say, "Write from the heart," how can one say that rejecting my manuscript isn't rejecting me? I don't buy that one. Nor do I run for the cookie jar. I don't even beat up my computer. I treat it like any loss. I grieve, I rant, and I accept that the unknown editor and I didn't click. Then I return to my computer, coffee cup in hand, and reread the work with as objective an eye as possible. I find a friend willing to read the manuscript and be honest with criticism. I make changes and send again.

That all sounds pat and easy. It's not. Rejection hurts. I refuse to be philosophical about it. I let it hurt. It's like all the guys who didn't ask me out, a mother who didn't particularly want me around, a husband who found his bottle more important than I was. I survived all those rejections and became a stronger, more caring person because of them.

Rejection of a manuscript is the same thing. I live through it and get over it because I know that every pain I suffer helps me create a stronger character in myself. Through that learning process, I become a stronger writer. Even my rejection letters started commenting on my wonderful characters. When the publishing contract finally came, reviewers commented on my great characters.

Wisdom From The Trenches

These observations make me smile because one of my first writing teachers told me my characters were two-dimensional. Years and many rejections later, I read how much people like my characters, and, even though I suffer through the rejection or smile through a good review, I take the balm of knowing I have grown, that I took criticism and turned it to good, and spread it over the wound of my baby not being wanted. It and many cups of coffee, get me through long nights meeting deadlines.

To say that one isn't being rejected, only one's work is being rejected is not cold comfort; it's useless comfort. I put a piece of myself in everything I write, so of course I am being rejected. Yet, as I keep going, working through the pain as I would any grief in my life, I find myself stronger as both a person and a writer.

Crumbs in the Keyboard

James Said
Christine McClimans

I used to doubt myself. I used to write poetry but I was not satisfied. I wrote the poems from my heart with all the passion I could muster, but I desired more. I have had a hidden dream of writing since I was a little girl and had no one to share this type of passion with.

Writers are like mothers. They seem to have a different kind of heart.

"Chrissy, why don't you write? You have the imagination and the heart," my mother suggested. She always was the first to recognize my potential.

September 7,1998 Mom was very impressed as my poetry began appearing on the "Web Page for Writers."

December 8,1998. My personal life took an emotional turn. That day I had experienced the death of my mother and I was overwrought with grief. As the days passed I had to accept the reality of my loss and I was slowly realizing the fact that I just wasn't able to write any more. All the time in the back of my mind I could hear her saying, "Chrissy, why don't you write?"

Mom always believed that people emerge into our lives to deliver a message of hope and encouragement. Mothers are seldom wrong.

Enter my friend, James.

Christmas had been an extremely hard day. I wanted to escape to happier times. I turned to my trusty computer and off I traveled to my own little world.

I had re-visited the "Web Page For Writers," but instead of reading my words, I read a piece titles, "*Far Away Places*."

I decided to write a note to the author to tell him how much the story brightened one of my saddest days.

The next day I received this reply: "Take your time about your writing. Right now, you are full of feeling as a result of the holidays and the circumstances surrounding your mother's death. Sit back and just *be* for a while; feel your feelings. After you have lived through this period of your life, you will be able to reflect on this time and write again with a new richness."

He further encouraged me as he wrote, "Peace be unto you my friend." As I read his words tears of sadness and tears of joy mixed. Mother was correct. I

Wisdom From The Trenches

should write and magically I had just been sent the message I needed to continue with that dream.

Without his kind words I might have never written another poem that would touch another's heart or a story that would inspire.

I am thrilled with the words I create with my writing.

Yes, once I used to doubt myself, but that was before James said, "Keep Writing!"

Crumbs in the Keyboard

Stranded with a Few of My Best Friends
Lisa Craig

If I were on a deserted mountaintop or beach or stuck on Survivor Island with only a pad of paper and pen, what would be the five most important books I would need for reference? My preferences here are not listed in the order of importance, because they are all equally valuable. I believe each of these books is critical to a well-rounded writer's library and no matter where you're going, you always have room to pack a few extra books.

Techniques of the Selling Writer, by Dwight Swain. This book has been around the block a few times, but the information is tried and true and covers everything about writing a book from start to finish. This book isn't genre specific, which really allows your imagination to be your guide. The author walks you through the fundamentals in writing and even once a writer has mastered those processes, this reference can be used to identify problems.

The Writer's Journey, Mythic Structure for Storytellers and Screenwriters, by Christopher Vogler. This reference provides great insight on how to structure plot and is helpful for troubleshooting. Vogler's insights are especially applicable to the writer's life, which also has as many twists and turns, if not more than your plot itself.

Story: Substance, Structure, Style, and The Principles of Screenwriting, by Robert McKee. Whether you're writing a screenplay, a children's story, or a literary work of art, the teaching in this book help to challenge you as a writer to go beyond cliché and really push the limits. This book has been invaluable to me, because it identifies the more elusive components that distinguish quality stories from ho-hum. I've only had this book a little less than one year and already, have a few frayed pages from continual use. For me, this book makes me think bigger, and helps me to reach for extraordinary ideas that work! I won't leave home without this baby.

Making a Good Writer Great. A Creativity Workbook for Screenwriters, by Linda Seger. Yes, this says it's a book for Screenwriters, but in my opinion, it speaks to all writers. This book combines craft and creativity and provides writers with the knowledge necessary to write at the highest artistic

Wisdom From The Trenches

level. The exercises within can be reused time and again and push a writer to think outside the box. Not a paint-by-numbers approach, instead this author guides you into unlocking and strengthening your own, original voice.

The Complete Writer's Guide to Heroes and Heroines by Tami Cowden, Caro LaFever, Sue Viders. This book is new to arrive on my writer's reference shelf, as it just came out in June. All I have to say, is what too you so long! I classify this book as an owner's manual for all the people in your life, as well as the characters running through a writer's imagination. Because of the organized way the information is presented, this reference can be used on the fly when a character might be giving a writer trouble or can be devoured as a whole. Without solid, 3-dimensional characters, a writer doesn't have a story and this resource is invaluable for helping a writer create story people that jump off the page and into a reader's life. Through the authors' masterful use of abundant examples, the mystery of characterization was demystified for me. This resource puts a name to sixteen archetypes (eight female and eight male) that have existed throughout literature and film. I can't imagine having to do characterization without this book!

These are certainly my top picks. I am confident that if I am ever stranded, each and everyone of my "best friends" will see me through.

If your writer's library is missing any of these references, I highly recommend that you run (don't walk) to your nearest neighborhood bookstore to snatch up a copy of whatever you're missing.

By His Grace
Terri Hartley

I need not wonder "why" I'm here,
His purpose for me is quite clear.
To grow, to learn, to live and strive,
It's by His Grace that I'm alive.

I smile each day as I awaken,
My feet set on a path yet taken.
Another day to get it right,
To walk by faith and not by sight.

He's given me all that I need,
Through knowledge I will plant the seed.
He gave us all free will and choice,
And through our prayers, He hears our voice.

I do not question "where" today,
He guides my steps along the way.
"As you walk slowly down the street,
Show loving kindness to all you meet."

I cannot change the world you see,
For there is just but one of me.
And in His time, He'll make things right.
So walk by faith and not by sight.

Recommended Resource

It's My Life Now:
Starting Over After An Abusive Relationship or Domestic Violence
(Routledge; ISBN: 0415923581)

Why do I still feel so sad? How should I deal with other people's reactions? How can I feel safer? How can I still love him? How can I trust men, or myself, again?

These are just a few of the questions and challenges facing women who have left abusive relationships. While many books offer women advice on how to get out of abusive relationships, no book, until now, has addressed the emotional, psychological, and practical needs of women who have already left an abusive partner.

It's My Life Now offers survivors of relationship abuse and domestic violence the practical guidance, emotional reassurance, and psychological awareness they need to heal and reclaim their lives after leaving their abusers. Worksheets and self-exploration exercises throughout the book help survivors monitor their progress as they navigate the crucial process of rebuilding self-esteem, trust, confidence, and emotional strength.

Sensitive and compassionate discussions on all relevant issues from dealing with the needs of children to handling chance encounters with a former abuser to enhancing the ability to assess potential future mates, all combine to make this book a working manual for women who are, in so many ways, starting their lives over after an abusive relationship or domestic violence.

Written in reassuring, supportive, and accessible language by two authors, a renowned therapist and an eminent professor of psychology, *It's My Life Now* is an indispensable road map along the path of healing for survivors of domestic abuse and for the family and friends who love them.

Notes From the Authors of It's My Life Now: Starting Over After An Abusive Relationship or Domestic Violence:

Those who have never experienced an abusive or violent relationship often believe that upon finding her way out, a victim's difficulties are solved: her life is good, she is safe, and her recovery will be swift. But survivors know all too well that leaving is not always the end of the nightmare; it is the beginning of a difficult journey toward healing and happiness. Most survivors of these relationships find that once they are free of the relationship, their problems do not diminish or stop, but rather, they continue to experience emotional and psychological difficulty. This is because abusive relationships have the power to destroy victims' self-identity, self-esteem, self-confidence, ability to trust others, and belief in their own abilities to rebuild a violence-free, rewarding life.

We have written *It's My Life Now* to offer support and assistance for survivors after they finally manage to leave their abusers. Issues we cover include the practical (such as, personal safety, legal problems, financial matters), the emotional (such as, overwhelming post-relationship feelings, the horror of sexual abuse, dealing with loss, regaining self-esteem, learning to love again), and the psychological (such as, how this could have happened, strategies for preventing it in the future, lingering feelings of love for the abuser, managing stress, dealing with the children, the temptation to go back). *It's My Life Now* is designed to benefit any woman who is struggling with the aftermath of abuse or violence no matter how much time has passed since she left her abuser. Survivors find themselves grappling with this rebuilding process months, years, and even decades after leaving the violent relationship.

We hope and believe our book offers the understanding and support they need to start, continue, or complete their healing process. Our book is also extremely helpful for survivors' caring friends and family who wish to assist them along the path of recovery.

Our message to you, the survivors:
This time of transition from an abusive or violent relationship to your new abuse-free life is an exciting, yet difficult journey. We truly believe, in our hearts and our minds, that you have the ability to transform your life; to love and respect yourself; to establish healthy, caring relationships; and to be happy. We wish you an inspiring, wondrous, and successful journey.

~~Meg Dugan & Roger Hock

Meg Kennedy Dugan is Program Director of the AmeriCorps Victim Assistance Program in New Hampshire. Ms. Dugan has been a therapist for over 15 years, counseling many survivors of relationship abuse and domestic violence.

Roger R. Hock is Professor of Psychology at Mendocino College in California and the author of Forty Studies that Changed Psychology: Explorations Into the History of Psychological Research

Afterword

This book is about hope. Hope survives even in the face of adversity. There is hope out there and it is only a phone call away.

The National Domestic Violence Hotline is a nationwide database providing toll-free access to immediate help from anywhere in the US, Puerto Rico, and US Virgin Islands. With 24 hour/7-day-a-week availability, and over 139 translators in addition English and Spanish, the organization can connect any individual to aid, including directions to local domestic and other emergency shelters, legal advocacy and assistance and social service programs.

It only takes one call. There is hope. Be courageous, it's your life.

1-800-799-SAFE (7233)

1-800-787-3224 (TTY)

Contributors

Laura M. Alcott
Laura Mills-Alcott is a writer of historical romance fiction set in England during the Regency and Elizabethan eras. She is also the owner of The Romance Club (www.theromanceclub.com). Beyond her writing, Laura spends her time being mother to her three beautiful children (Jared, Jordan and Jacob) and remodeling a very large Cape Cod. That is a book in itself.

Pamela Arden
Pam Payne (aka Pam Arden) married her love-at-first-sight hero 29 years ago and they now have four children and 2 grandchildren. Pam juggles her writing in between writing romance reviews, selling magazine ads, volunteer work for several writer's organizations, home schooling her youngest son, gardening, mowing, and caring for a five-acre mini-farm full of goats, ducks, chickens. www.pamelaarden.com

Barbara Baldwin
Barbara Baldwin writes everything from poetry to grants, novels to short stories, getting her inspiration from everything around her. That is, when she's not working at being a wife, mother, teacher and student. Writer0926@yahoo.com

Robin Bayne
Robin Bayne lives in Maryland with her husband/hero, where she works as a mortgage underwriter by day and fiction writer by night. With her son at college, she finds more time and less crumbs! Her fifth book, "Charity's Prisoner," was just released by Treble Heart Books. Visit her at www.robinbayne.com

Gerry Benninger
Gerry Benninger shares a home with her single mom daughter and grandchildren while working as an editor, teaching Creative Writing at Phoenix College, and writing for Romantic Times Magazine, local and national newspapers, and several little literary publications, including Story Magazine.

Jessica Bimberg
Jesica Bimberg has a wonderful husband, three wonderful children, and a full

Contributors

load of course at the local community college. Writing has always been her escape and helps to keep her sanity intact

Barbara Donlon Bradley
Barbara Donlon Bradley works full time, is a mom and a published author. If that isn't enough she also is her local Romance Writers of America chapter newsletter editor, a RWA Chaplink Advisor, and managing editor of Spin - World Romance Writers Journal. Plus she's taking Taekwondo. When asked when she sleeps she giggles and asks "What's that?" Barbara's first full length Time Travel romance novel "A Portrait in Time" is now available at HardShell Word Factory.

Leslie Burbank
In addition to penning a series of children's books and an action adventure screenplay, Leslie Burbank's passion is writing historical romance set in medieval Ireland, Scotland and Wales. Her first published novel, "To Tame A Viking" was released in December 2001 by Echelon Press. She and her husband, Leland Burbank, are covers models, gracing the covers of such authors as Elizabeth Rose and Shannon Drake.

Cherie Claire
Cherie Claire is the author of "The Acadians Ballad" historical trilogy by Zebra (July and November, 2000, and March, 2001) and the mother of two boys, both who still have trouble sleeping.

Tammie Clark Gibbs
Tammie Clarke Gibbs is the author of "Recipes for Romance from the Leading Ladies & Gentlemen of Romance: Recipes, Rendezvous & Sweet Treats for the Mind, Body & Soul." November 2001 Primmrose Press. www.recipesforromance.com

Kim Cox
Kim Cox, author of "Suspicious Minds," married 16 years, has two grown sons and one grandson, works an outside job full-time, contest coordinator for FTH Online RWA chapter, editor for The Pen is Mightier, and WRW's Spin journal and also treasurer for WRW. /www.kimcox.org

Lisa Craig
Colorado native Lisa Craig has been writing award winning contemporary romance and women's fiction novels for ten years. An accomplished Internet Consultant and web designer, specializing in author web sites, she spends her time immersed in technology or writing, now that her son is grown. She shares

her life with her husband and the two family dogs. www.lisacraig.com

Amy Crawshaw
Amy B. Crawshaw is a wife, mother, and writer. She lives with four kids, three dogs, two cats, one part-time job, and a white linoleum floor in western Pennsylvania. Reading and writing are a perfect escape from her busy schedule.

Patricia Crossley
Patricia Crossley leads a busy life after retiring from educational administration. Three grown kids and a husband with a passion for sailing keep life interesting. Apart from her writing, Pat loves to travel and at the moment is based in East Africa, volunteering for an educational organization that sends poor, bright girls to High School. Home is now in Victoria, B. C. Canada. Pat has more information about Canada's West Coast (oh! and her books, of course!) at www.patriciacrossley.com

Kathleen Crouch
Kathleen Crouch is the author of "The Game of Chance; A Self-Instructional Textbook," 1976; "Educational Media and Materials," 1976; and "The Art of Listening , 1978. She is currently working on her first fantasy romance.

Marjorie Daniels
Marjorie Daniels lives in Sidney, a small seaside town on Vancouver Island. Besides her addiction to writing she also likes to dance, to paddle dragon boats and run sprints in Seniors' Games. She has two grown kids, two grandsons and a lifelong lover who happens to be her husband, Danny. http://members.shaw.ca/marjedan

Elizabeth Delisi
Elizabeth Delisi is a fiction author, an editor for several electronic publishers, a staff writer and class instructor for the website NovelAdvice, and a newspaper columnist. She lives in Kansas with her husband, three teenagers, dog and cat, and loves to have visitors to her web page: www.elizabethdelisi.com

Trudy Doolittle
Trudy works as a Management Consultant for a global consulting firm and can be found jetting around the country, guiding companies in their Human Resource software implementations. At night, while in her hotel room, she sits on her bed with her laptop, crafting romances. Her latest is a short story, "A Gift of Time," is published in an anthology of short stories, "Romancing the Holidays." www.trudydoolittle.com

Contributors

Laurie Alice Eakes
Laurie Alice Eakes is the author of four published novels and several short stories. She is also an editor, teacher, and grad student working on her Master of Arts degree in creative writing. She lives outside Chicago with a cat, two dogs, and the man who makes her believe in romance. www.Lauriealiceeakes.com

Jacqueline Elliott
Jacqueline Elliott is a wife and mother of two. She fits writing in between a part time job and raising her family. She must be doing something right because her first novel, Shadows In The Fire, is being released in December 2001. You can visit her at www.geocities.com/jacquelle2000/

Sue Fineman
Sue Fineman, wife and proud mother of three adult children spends hours at the keyboard every day. She uses real life situations spiced with imagination in her novels. "What's funnier or more bizarre than true life?" You can email her at: sue.fineman@worldnet.att.net

Cheri Lee Funk
Cheri Lee Funk lives in Southport, NC where she is still trying to figure out what she wants to be when she grows up. She loves the ocean and producing a group of online e-zines called HeartTalk. Visit her at www.angelfire.com/nc3/HeartTalk/

Holly Fuhrman aka Holly Jacobs
Holly Jacobs Fuhrmann writes as Holly Jacobs for Harlequin Duets and Silhouette Romance. She writes as Holly Fuhrmann for ImaJinn Books. You can visit her online at www.HollysBooks.com for more information about her upcoming books.

Marilynn Griffith
Marilynn Griffith shares her writing space with six amazing children and her husband of ten years. She divides her time between the "babies" in her head and mothering and home schooling her "real-life" children. Her motto is: "Blessed are the flexible, they will not be broken."

Terri Hartley
Terri Hartley is an eleven-year veteran homeschooling mom of two. To her credit are two published poems, "The Angels Tears" and, "By His Grace." Her children love writing stories and plays. Presently, she's researching a true love story that spanned continents and hopes to have it completed in the coming year.

Crumbs in the Keyboard

Elaine Hopper
Elaine Hopper always dreamed of being a published author before the milestone year of 2000, and her 40th birthday. She got her wish when New Concepts Publishing released her first contemporary romance, "Tigers Play Too Rough" with 6 months to spare. At home in South Florida with her husband of 22 years, 5 lovely children, one grandson, several cats, and a demanding full time job, Ms. Hopper still finds time to write. www.elainehopper.com

Diana Lee Johnson
A Purchasing Professional for 35 years, Diana is also a survivor of domestic abuse. She says writing since the age of 6 keeps her sanity, and has lead to publication of 3 novels with 2 more contracted, and, she hopes, many more to follow. Proud of her seventeenth century American roots, she indulges her passions for history and story-weaving by escaping into her writing. www.dianaleejohnson.com

Pamela Johnson
Not wanting it any other way, Pamela Johnson claims her life is like "that guy on Ed Sullivan twirling a dozen plates at once on tall poles! It's easy," she says, "I just use Rubbermaid dishes!" Three full novels, several anthologies, a newspaper column, shorts stories, poetry, articles, and writer's groups keep her juggling her career with four kids, and a "true knight-in-shining-armor" husband. Visit her life at www.pjohnson.homestead.com/homepage.html

Marcia Kacperski
Marcia Kacperski is writing an historical novel about her grandparents' immigration experience to the U.S. Europe. She has written an article for the group Earthwatch and also writes reviews for the bookstore where she works. Her husband helps in the care and feeding of their two dogs, two cats and parakeet.

Shirley Kawa-Jump
Shirley Kawa-Jump is a wife, mother of two and full-time writer who spends more time carpooling than sleeping. Her latest book, "How to Publish Your Articles," is in bookstores nationwide and on her website, www.shirleykawa-jump.com

Stacey L. King, aka Dana Elian
Stacey L. King, aka Dana Elian, is a work-at-home cover artist, web designer, and author. Her first book, "Music of my Heart," is available now from Echelon Press. She lives near Fort Worth, Texas, with her soul mate husband of ten years, two rambunctious children, and two adoring dogs. You can visit her on

Contributors

the web at www.danaelian.com or www.staceylking.com

Gwen Kirchner
Gwen Kirchner writes full-time in her dreams, but unfortunately the reality of a job, classes, and other sundry duties usually causes her to be rudely awakened.

Su Kopil
Su Kopil believes if you have the courage to dream you have the potential to turn that dream into reality. Determination, perseverance and heart will see you through! Her novella, "A Home For the Holiday" is included in Awe-Struck Publishing's "Season of Romance" released November 2001. www.earthlycharms.com

Janet Lane
Janet Lane, married and mom to two teen daughters, runs her home-based business, racks up the miles traveling around metro Denver to gymnastics meets and piano lessons, dusts when cornered--er, rather, dusts in the corners--and burns the midnight oil, writing the novels of her heart.

Joyce Lavene
Joyce Lavene has written and sold 40 novels with her husband/partner, Jim. They welcome readers to their websites: www.joyceandjimlavene.com and www.sharynhowardmysteries.com

Nancy Lepri
Nancy C. Lepri spent her mid-life crisis earning an AA and BA degree. A freelance writer/artist for more than nine years, she teaches on-line courses for writing and illustration, as well as edits an on-line magazine. Presently rewriting a children's chapter book for about the 100th time, she's also illustrating picture books. When not working, she and her husband of 30 years, Art, enjoy the beach and traveling

Kathleen Long
Kathleen Long is blessed with her 11-year marriage, her own business, local volunteer work and her writing and knows that in real life, as in fiction, the next great adventure may lie just around the corner . www.kathleenlong.com

Lisa Marie Long
In between loads of laundry, trips to the vet, and home schooling a busy preschooler, Lisa Marie Long occasionally finds time to write award-winning historical romance. Lisa thinks there's nothing more magical than bringing two lost souls together and making them fall in love. Visit her web site for writing

articles and to read her monthly column on home horticulture for the Oregon State University Extension Service at www.columbia-center.org/lisamarie

Nancy Lynn

Nancy Lynn juggles writing with a career in local government and the care and feeding of a husband and two critters. Her romantic comedy, "Whatever It Takes," is scheduled for release in June 2002 from Novel Books Inc. and her articles on writing have appeared in ByLine Magazine. www.authorsden.com/nancylynn

Joanie MacNeil

Joanie MacNei is an Australian romance novelist and writer of short stories. www.atrax.net.au/userdir/Joan/indexpage.html

Margaret Marr

Margaret Marr lives in the mountains of western North Carolina with her two sons, eight cats and one dog. When she's not working on a novel she loves to be outdoors doing everything from fishing in the dark to hiking. Visit her at: www.Margaretmarr.com

Diana Rowe Martinez

Diana Rowe Martinez somehow balances marriage and mothering of two teenage daughters with her full-time freelance writing career and college while still managing to squeeze time in to write romantic comedy and suspense novels. www.dianarowe.com

Christine McClimans

Christine McClimans, a freelance writer/ photographer, combines her magic eye of photography with her heartfelt words of writing to create Dream Escapes. Her belief being: "Everyone needs a place to Dream and Escape" She is currently residing in North Carolina where she is writing her first novel. fictionwriter.tripod.com/McClimans.html

Cathy McDavid

Cathy McDavid has been juggling life and writing for the past seven years, sometimes successfully and sometimes not, but always with great fun. Fortunately, this wife, mother, office manager, RWA Chapter President, and caretaker of several dozen animals--has three arms. How else could she manage everything? Visit her at www.cathymcdavid.com

Lori McDonald

Lori McDonald is a full-time mom, writer and Indiana Pacers fan. She has had

Contributors

articles published in Girls' Life and Brio magazines. Lori shares two children with her dear hubby of 13 years and she's got to have her daily dose of chocolate.

Maureen McMahon

Maureen McMahon was born and raised in Michigan, but now lives in Victoria, Australia. Likened in style to Mary Stewart and/or Barbara Michaels, she has published two mystery suspense novels, and an anthology of short stories. She writes and teaches creative writing with the support and inspiration of her husband, her two teenaged children and a menagerie of pets, including a cantankerous cockatoo named Willy. Visit her personal website, www.maureenmcmahon.com

Janet Miller

Janet Miller writes computer software when she isn't working on her first novel. She manages to freak out her children with her "dirty books", but her husband of twenty-five years has lived too long with Janet to be surprised by anything she does.

Ariana Overton

Ariana Overton--multi-published author, cover artist, editor and investigative reporter--delves deeply into the minds and motives of serial killers with her graphic murder mysteries. Combined with the talents of her British husband Max, a PhD and a published author of historical novels, the term 'Histories & Mysteries' takes on new meaning. www.angelfire.com/ri2/theovertons

Robin D. Owens

Robin D. Owens has been writing seriously longer than she cares to recall and made her first sale last year. HeartMate, December 2001, was the first futuristic/fantasy purchased for Jove's Magical Love line. Explore your creativity at: www.robindowens.com

Sally Painter

A native North Carolinian, historical romance novelist, Sally Painter lives with her husband, daughter and cat, Bow, in the Blue Ridge Mountains. In December 1999, she and Lori Soard joined their talents to form World Romance Writers. Visit Sally at www.sallypainter.com

Julie Pitzel

Julie Pitzel is a single mother who's gone back to school for a computer networking degree. Balancing school, writing, and her home life, she's decided if something has to suffer it should be the housework.

Crumbs in the Keyboard

Helen Kay Polaski
Helen Kay Polaski, number seven in a family of 16, has three children with her husband of 25 years. Family, the essence from which she draws her strength, always comes first. Helen, a 15-year journalist, freelances for several Michigan newspapers and has recently finished her first novel

Sharon Porpiglia
Western New York based, freelance writer/mentor, Sharzi Avins, aka Sharon Porpiglia, divides her time between mothering her two human children and her three furry children, and her duties as Chief Publisher/Editor of The Pen Is Mightier Ezine, *and chat co-host on AOL's Daytime Writer's Group and Literary Magic.. She has written for several online services, including Business Week, iVillage, AOL's Workplace Channel (now Work & Careers), and others. She is a former staff writer for MyMagazine. members.aol.com/RitrsPulse/Pen.html*

Cate Rowan
Cate Rowan is writing her second fantasy romance while maintaining her day job as a college professor. She hopes that someday the IRS will receive lots of money from her royalties and nothing at all from a university's withholdings.

Teresa Saldana
Teresa Saldana, mother of two and grandmother of one, divides her time between her family and her craft stand. She is continuing her education for a degree in History Education. She uses her writing as a form of emotional release, and loves to find escape from rigors of a hectic life in the words of fellow writers.

Candace Sams
Candace Sam and her exceedingly patient husband make their home in Grand Bay, Alabama. Her love of the paranormal she writes and for things that "go bump in the night" came from her years of work as a police officer and ambulance crew chief. Her writing talents aren't the only thing she's known for, as she holds several titles and medals in martial arts and serves as the senior woman on the US Kung Fu Team who exhibited in China at the request of the Chinese government in November 2000. "I like the kicky, throw-you-down down stuff!" www.candacesams.com

Laurie Schnebly Campbell
Laurie Schnebly Campbell spends weekdays writing commercials for a Phoenix advertising agency, and weekends writing Silhouette Special Editions--like the one Romantic Times ranked among "the best 200 books ever." www.writersplace.com/campbell

Contributors

Joni Seabolt
Joni Hames Seabolt makes her home in Northeast Georgia with her husband of fifteen years, their two teen sons and preschool daughter, their mother-to-be Spaniel, Wendy, two birds and a rabbit. The youngest of six, Joni started writing at an early age, and still pens her poetry and lyrics the old fashioned way...in a giant notebook.

Anna Seley
Anna Seley, married 28 years, has 3 children and 2 grandchildren. She teaches 7th grade, tends a rose garden, loves to do crafts and spend time on the Oregon coast. Her motto is: "The Journey is as important as the Destination." She can be contacted through her egroup. groups.yahoo.com/group/CreateCritiqueMotivate/settings

Rae Shapiro
Rae Shapiro lives in Van Nuys, California with her husband of forty-five years. Upon retiring from thirty years of teaching preschool in 1990, she purchased a computer and took friends' advice and started writing. After many non-fiction pieces and earning her Masters' Thesis in Early Childhood Education, Rae turned to fiction, and finaled at the 2000 Houston Writers' League Conference Competition. She was a proud participant in Barbara Delinsky's "Uplift," an anthology referring to, and in financial aid of, breast cancer research in September. 2001.

Kathryn Smith
Born and raised in Cincinnati, Ohio, Kathi Smith lived for short periods in Indiana, Florida and Nebraska before settling permanently in Colorado. She describes herself as "a nerd with the soul of an artist." She changed careers from computers to writing and now proclaims herself "broke but fulfilled" She is published in both print and online mediums.

Pamela Gayle Smith
Pamela Gayle Smith describes herself as married 32 years, the mother of three and grandmother of eight. She loves writing poetry about everyday life, "nothing fancy, just plain homespun story poems, as my Grandson calls them."

Pat Snellgrove aka Ann Patrick
Pat Snellgrove (Ann Patrick) lives in small town rural New Zealand. She has been writing for many years, but success only came three years ago when New Concepts Publishing accepted her first book. Her motto is "If at first you don't succeed, try, try again."

Crumbs in the Keyboard

Lori Soard
Lori Soard has a Ph.D. in creative writing and teaches writing courses. If you ask her about her life, she'll tell you it's filled with make-believe and magic, and she couldn't be happier. You can visit her at www.lorisoard.com or contact her at PO BOX 452, Greenfield, IN 46140

Janice Stayton
Janice Stayton balances a twenty-seven year marriage, the full-time mothering of four children, enjoying her grand children, writing fiction and articles, while moderating the Founders Maintenance at yahoogroups.com

Karen L. Syed
Karen L. Syed calls Grand Prairie, Texas home. With a full schedule of events, she divides her time between The Bookshelf (her small independent bookstore), her job as an Editor/Marketing Executive at Echelon Press, and her writing career. Other than trying to give Nora Roberts a run for her money, Karen is working hard to get overachieving entered into the Olympics as a winter event. She currently has seven books available and is the proud survivor of spousal abuse!

Pamela Thibodeaux
Pamela S. Thibodeaux is the author of "Inspirational with an Edge!" romance, Contemporary romances that are sensual but stay within Biblical principles. Check out Pam's website: www.pamelathibodeaux.com

Vurlee Toomey
*In the four years since Vurlee Toomey started writing seriously, she has learned to juggle life and writing. After three years and five wedding dates, she recently married her knight in shining armor. Between work and family, she has managed to find the time to write with the help of her menagerie of three cats and a female Doberman, all of whom think they're her muse.
us.geocities.com/vurleeb/index.html*

Sheryl Hames Torres
Sheryl Hames Torres balances a 19 year marriage, the full-time mothering of two kids, custom needlework, restoration of antique needlework, writing, co-hosting a weekly online writing chat, articles, and the secretarial duties of WRW with one motto: "The more chaos the better!" Her Halloween tale, The Masquerade, *is included in the anthology,* Seasons of Romance, *released in November of 2001, from Awe-Stuck Publishing.
www.hometown.aol.com/babynerd/ index.html*

Contributors

Joyce Tres
Joyce Tres also writes under the pseudonym Patricia DiMiere, she is working on two novels and recently completed collaboration on a book of short stories for women with author Sara Russell scheduled for publication March 2002.

Jennifer Turner
Born blonde and Polish, Jennifer Turner has utilized her unique perspective to write historical and contemporary romances. She resides with her husband, a red-headed Texan, and her three children in Wisconsin. Between her commitments to family and writing, she actively pursues three things--chocolate, chocolate, and more chocolate.

Rebecca Vineyard
Rebecca Vinyard, a former journalism major and e-zine editor, has two novels in current release: "Diva," a historical romance, and "Deadly Light," romantic suspense. Look for her article, Synopsis Basics, in Moira Allen's book, "The Writer's Guide to Queries, Pitches and Proposals, and in the October 2001 issue of The Writer magazine. She's a member of the Dallas chapter of the Romance Writers of America and the webmaster of Romance Central.

Linda Voss
Writing about science and technology by day for over 20 years (minus grad school and Peace Corps service), Linda Voss' (Kaitlynn Merlot) nights belong to creative fiction, her husband, and two German shepherds.

Kate Walsh
Kate Walsh is a writer who wandered through raising children, teaching, nursing, professional dance to the present endeavors including poetry, short stories and a novel in progress. Kate and her husband share the joys and challenges of combined families with children and grandchildren. They reside in Michigan City, Indiana

Carrie Weaver
Carrie Weaver was born and raised in Arizona, where she lives with her husband and two sons. Her first romance novel was published in 2000, and a short story, "Sweet April," is featured in "Romancing the Holidays, Vol.1." This heartwarming anthology is now available at online and neighborhood bookstores, or directly from Elan Press.

Denise Weeks, aka Shalanna Collins
Denise Weeks writes mysteries under her own name and fantasy/YA fantasy as her alter ego, Shalanna Collins. A graduate of Southern Methodist University,

she is also an accomplished pianist and avid trivia player. Her novel, "Dulcinea: or Wizardry A-Flute," written as Shalanna Collins, was the first runner-up in the 1996 Warner Aspect First Novel Contest. Watch for the sequel, "Dulcinea's Dragon." members.home.net/shalanna/

Laurie White
Laurie White began writing in 1991, but didn't start pursuing it as a career until 1996. Since then, she has completed three manuscripts and begun work on a fourth. Laurie writes contemporary romantic suspense, and is a board member of several RWA chapters.

Tabatha Yeatts
Tabatha Yeatts admits to writing while surrounded by other karate parents, all listening to forty children shouting "HI-YA!" but says an hour of uninterrupted stillness sends her into paroxysms of glee.

Carol Zachary
Mika Boblitz, aka Carol Zachary, lives in Maryland with her husband, Chip, and their son, Zachary. She is a full-time mother and a writer as time allows. Her first completed novel, "Red Shoes & A Diary," won the 2000 Harlequin Blaze contest and the 2001 TARA First Impressions contest. Mika is currently working toward the dream of seeing her name on the shelf at Waldenbooks. You can follow her journey to publication on the website: www.CarolZachary.homestead.com/home.html

Lori Zecca
Lori Zecca has come full circle-from NY-based production editor to sales/marketing director, to published author. Oh-did I mention, full-time wife and mother, writer, RWA and MORWA member, and my own publicist? Check out my new novel at: www.authorsden.com/lorizecca

Permissions

Permissions continued from page 4

What Did I Do--So I Can Do It Again. Reprinted with permission. ©2001 Robin D. Owens.

Top 10 Things Not to Say To An Editor. Reprinted with permission. ©1995 Lisa Craig.

Mama's Five Myths About Writing. ©2002 Denise Weeks.

Writing As An Explorer. Reprinted with permission ©1993 Gerry Benninger.

When the Writing Gets Tough. Reprinted with permission. ©2000 Barbara Baldwin.

Walk With Me in the Rain. Reprinted with permission. ©2000 Barbara Baldwin.

We're All In This Together. Reprinted with permission. ©1999 Cheré Coen.

Lynne's Book. ©2002 Diana Lee Johnson.

Pinwheels and Hats. Reprinted with permission. ©2000 Holly Fuhrman.

Sushi Break. ©2002 Elaine Hopper.

There Are No Shortcuts. ©2002 Sheryl Hames Torres.

Out of the Mouths of Babes. ©2002 Julie Pitzel.

My Mom Writes Books! ©2002 Elizabeth Delisi

Peace Between The Lines. ©2002 Marilynn Griffith.

Everything Has Its Season. ©2002 Lisa Marie Long.

Grand Theft Manuscript. ©2002 Carrie Weaver.

Day-to-Day Determination. ©2002 Jennifer Turner.

Spaces of Time. ©2002 Jacqueline Elliot.

Steps to Writing Time. ©2002 Robin Bayne.

Steps (poem). ©1995 Robin Bayne.

To My Children. ©2002 Tabatha Yeatts.

The Mom Story. ©2002 Rebecca Vineyard.

Crumbs in the Keyboard

I Owe My Career To Burger King. ©2002 Laurie Schnebly Campbell.

Oh The Noise! ©2002 Margaret Marr.

Hot Sex and Cold Dinners. Reprinted with permission. ©2001 Mika Boblitz.

My Mother Writes What? ©2002 Janet Miller.

A Day in the Life of a Writing Mom. ©2002 Lori Zecca.

When and How. ©2002 Jessica Ann Bimberg.

Creative Moms Have No Down Time. Reprinted with permission. ©2000 Cheré Coen.

Shadow Stretches. ©2002 Amy B. Crawshaw.

The Juggling Act. Reprinted with permission. ©2001 Shirley Kawa-Jump.

Stealing Minutes. ©2002 Cathy McDavid.

A Two-Page Day. ©2002 Maureen McMahon.

There Resides In Me. Reprinted with permission. © 2000 Stacey L. King.

The Napkin. ©2002 Pamela G. Smith.

No! I'm NOT Just Housewife! Reprinted with permission. ©2000 Lisa Marie Long.

Life is Good. Reprinted with permission. ©2001 Sharon Porpiglia.

You Don't "Work". ©2002 Nancy Lepri.

Still Learning After All These Years. ©2002 Kimberly Cox.

Rise & Shine. ©2002 Laurie White.

So You Think You Want to Be a Romance Writer? ©2002 Pamela Payne.

Broken Promises. ©2002 Pamela G. Smith.

Road Warrior. ©2002 Trudy Doolittle.

Writing With Pain, Fatigue, and a Fuzzy Brain. ©2002 M. Kathleen Crouch.

What Goes Around Comes Around. ©2002 Barbara Donlon Bradley.

A New Perspective on Rejection. Reprinted with permission. ©1997 Lisa Craig.

Permissions

Write to Survive, Survive to Write. Reprinted with permission. ©2000 Robin D. Owens

A Career Based on Two Words. ©2002 Pamela Johnson.

The Other Woman. ©2002 Leslie Burbank.

The Muse. ©2002 Joni Seabolt.

Never Plan a Day of Writing. ©2002 Pat Snellgrove.

A Writer's Moon. Reprinted with permission. ©2001 Barbara Baldwin.

The Muse As a Puppy. ©2002 Linda Voss.

The Blair Writing Project. ©2002 Lori A. McDonald.

Soap Bubble Rhetoric. ©2002 Barbara Baldwin.

Dreams. ©2002 Janet Lane Penaligon.

Caller ID and the Neurotic Writer. ©2002 Laurie Schnebly Campbell.

Where Do You Get All Those Crazy Ideas? ©2002 Denise Weeks.

Another Point of View. ©2002 Candace Sams

The "Muse"-ings of an Author's Cat. ©2002 Vurlee Toomey.

It Never Occurred To Me. ©2002 Ariana Overton.

Dreams vs. Reality. Reprinted with permission. ©2001 Su Kopil.

Spun Yarn. ©2002 Bridget Terri Hartley.

One Moment In Time. ©2002 Laurie Alice Eakes.

The Value of Human Life. ©2002 Karen Syed.

I Found My Lights. ©2002 Rae Shapiro.

The Nature of the Beast. ©2002 Kathryn Smith.

Subtle Delights. ©2002 Kate Walsh.

The Round Peg. ©2002 Diana Lee Johnson.

The Call of the Novel. ©2002 Cate Rowan.

Crumbs in the Keyboard

Writer's Block. Reprinted with permission. ©2000 Cheri Lee Funk.

After the Crumbs. Reprinted with permission. ©2001 Christine McClimans.

Journey Through Darkness. ©2002 Anna Seley.

Belief—The Ultimate Muse. ©2002 Kathleen Long.

Inspiration = Sugar + Spice +Dreams. ©2002 Diana Rowe Martinez.

Perfect Love. Reprinted with permission. ©2001 Pamela Thibodeaux.

Butterfly. ©2002 Teresa T. Saldana.

Uphill Climb: My Quest for Publication. ©2002 Sally Painter Kale.

Break a Pencil. Reprinted with permission. ©2001 Lori Soard.

Synchronicity. ©2002 Su Kopil.

How to Deal With Rejection. Reprinted with permission. ©1998 Elizabeth Delisi

Balance and Control. ©2002 Janice Stayton.

Chili Again. ©2002 Joyce Tres

Daily Resolution: A Writer's Affirmation. Reprinted with permission. ©1993 Gerry Benninger.

"Feeeel" Your Way To Success! Reprinted with permission. ©2001 Marjorie Daniels.

The Path. ©2002 Gwen Kirchner.

You Can Make Your Dreams Come True. ©2002 Joyce Lavene.

Living the Dream. ©2002 Joanie MacNeil Gillham .

The Right Answer. ©2002 Nancy McLane.

Sticks and Stones. ©2002 Marcia Peterson

Let Your Imagination Fly. ©2002 Sue Fineman.

To Everything There Is A Season. Reprinted with permission. ©2001 Patricia Crossley.

What Makes a Writer? Reprinted with permission. ©1997 Lisa Craig.

Permissions

Keeping the Faith. ©2002 Helen Polaski.

Cleaning The Toilet and TV Interviews. ©2002 Tammie Clark Gibbs.

Following The Artist's Way. Reprinted with permission. ©1999 Robin D. Owens.

Coffee In My Keyboard: Dealing With Rejection. ©2002 Laurie Alice Eakes.

James Said. Reprinted with permission. ©2001 Christine McClimans.

Stranded With A Few Of My Best Friends. Reprinted with permission. ©2000 Lisa Craig

By His Grace. Reprinted with permission. ©2001 Bridget Terri Hartley.

To order additional copies of Crumbs in the Keyboard

Send check or money order for the amount below, along with your name and address, to:

Crumbs in the Keyboard
Echelon Press
P.O. Box 1084
Crowley, TX 76036

$13.99 for each book
plus
$3.00 shipping for one book,
$.75 for each additional book

Or visit our website to order online with your credit card.
www.echelonpress.com

Please fax or email for quantity discount.

Fax: 702.447.5489
Email: crumbs@echelonpress.com

Printed in the United States
1465200004B/307-318